Enemy in the Mirror

Enemy in the Mirror

ISLAMIC FUNDAMENTALISM AND THE LIMITS OF MODERN RATIONALISM

A WORK OF COMPARATIVE POLITICAL THEORY

Roxanne L. Euben

PRINCETON UNIVERSITY PRESS

PRINCETON, NEW JERSEY

Library of Congress Cataloging-in-Publication Data

Euben, Roxanne Leslie, 1966–
Enemy in the mirror : Islamic fundamentalism and the limits of modern
rationalism / Roxanne L. Euben.
   p. cm.
Includes bibliographical references and index.

ISBN 0-691-05843-1 (cl : alk. paper) — ISBN 0-691-05844-X (pb : alk. paper)

1. Islamic fundamentalism. 2. Islamic countries—Politics and government.
3. Rationalism. I. Title.
BP166.14.F85E93   1999   320.5′5′0917671—dc21   99-10153

This book has been composed in Caledonia

The paper used in this publication meets the minimum requirements of
ANSI/NISO Z39.48-1992 (R 1997) (*Permanence of Paper*)

http://pup.princeton.edu

Printed in the United States of America

10 9 8 7 6 5 4 3 2 1

10 9 8 7 6 5 4 3 2 1
(Pbk.)

FOR MY PARENTS

My First and Finest Teachers

Let us consider abstract man stripped of myth, abstract education, abstract mores, abstract law, abstract government; the random vagaries of the artistic imagination unchanneled by any native myth; a culture without any fixed and consecrated place of origin, condemned to exhaust all possibilities and feed miserably and parasitically on every culture under the sun. Here we have our present age, the result of a Socratism bent on the extermination of myth. Man today, stripped of myth, stands famished among all his pasts and must dig frantically for roots, be it among the most remote antiquities. What does our great historical hunger signify, our clutching about us of countless other cultures, our consuming desire for knowledge, if not the loss of myth, of a mythic home, the mythic womb? Let us ask ourselves whether our feverish and frightening agitation is anything but the greedy grasping for food of a hungry man.

—Friedrich Nietzche, *The Birth of Tragedy*

Contents

Preface

THIS BOOK reflects the nexus of two political and intellectual interests or, perhaps I should say, preoccupations. The first interest really presented itself to me as a question, sparked by a paradox in contemporary politics: why is it that secular liberal democracies such as the United States are witnessing sharply declining rates of voter turnout and increasing alienation from politics at the very moment that religio-political movements are galvanizing peoples into extraordinary attempts to remake the political world?[1] For observers who see in the fall of the Berlin Wall the triumph of democracy or, at the very least, the triumph of the liberal capitalist state, this might seem an inappropriate question. Yet it is by now well recognized that the end of the Cold War has not revealed such a tidy landscape; those who wish it did, it seems, must attend to precisely these political paradoxes. This is especially so because in the late twentieth century it has become almost commonplace to unmask science, secularism, and rational accounts of nature and human nature as but several narratives among many that may or may not capture partial truths about the world in which human beings live. Such claims suggest that the search for knowledge must include forays into experiences and phenomena heretofore forced into the shadows by the discourse of rationality. Religious experiences and answers to questions about what makes life worth living, how humans ought to live, and what institutions are best for living with each other—experiences once relegated by reason to the periphery of politics or consigned to a period of historical immaturity—now press upon the consciousness of a remarkable variety of political actors, commentators, and intellectuals across cultures, demanding and receiving new consideration.

The second interest arises from a tension within Western political theory. This is a tension between, on the one hand, political theorists' aspirations to engage questions about the nature and value of politics that, if not universal, are at least pressing to a broad range of peoples and cultures and, on the other, a political theory canon almost exclusively devoted to Western texts. Such an observation has been the occasion for a myriad of debates about multiculturalism and the canon in countless academic fields. This tension at no time suggested to me that political theory must fail to illuminate the broader world in which human beings live; on the contrary, my central argument is that this tension can recall students of politics to the promise contained in an older, yet never quite lost, understanding of theory as inherently comparative, one defined by certain questions about living together rather than particular answers.

These preoccupations at first blush bear an uneasy relation to each other; perhaps at second and third blush as well. Yet they have occasioned for me an extraordinarily rewarding journey across disciplines. This book is the result of that journey, and it is thus interdisciplinary in several senses of the word. It is interdisciplinary because I define fundamentalism in a way that leaves open the possibility that dogmatic disputes about "foundations," "fundamentals," are not solely the purview of religious activists but also capture an aspect of ostensibly secular debates where the sacred text in question is, say, a constitution. It is also interdisciplinary in the sense of engaging literature from a variety of fields and subfields: in the course of this work I draw on political, social, and critical theory, poststructuralism, Islamic thought, anthropology, comparative politics, and Near Eastern studies. I draw on such literature not only to make a substantive argument regarding an interpretation of Islamic fundamentalism, but also to demonstrate how and why an adequate understanding of concrete phenomena such as Islamic fundamentalism, on the one hand, and the study of political theory, on the other, demands an integration of theoretical and comparative approaches to the study of politics.

In the end, then, this work blurs the academic boundaries commonly demarcated by the terms "comparative politics" and "political theory." Indeed, my own view is that such boundaries often obstruct our ability to see the ways in which comparativists must, and at their best often do, incorporate the study of political thought into explanation, and how comparative questions militate against the danger of Western political theorists theorizing in a historical and cultural vacuum. It is nevertheless the case that some chapters here are more concerned with what are commonly understood as questions of comparative politics, and others will be identified as chapters of political theory. Chapter 2 and to some degree chapter 3 are concerned with both the substance and methodology of social scientific explanations of Islamic fundamentalism and an interpretive approach to understanding. Chapters 3, 4, and 5 are primarily concerned with political theory and comparative political theory: in them, I analyze Islamic fundamentalist political thought, Islamic modernist political thought, and Western critiques of modernity in contemporary political theory. The project is intended, however, as an integrated whole: if the chapters do not neatly fall into groupings by discipline, I have achieved some measure of success in this.

Any broadly interdisciplinary work takes certain risks by traversing several academic terrains into which other scholars have burrowed specifically and deeply. There is always the lurking danger of becoming the Lenny Bruce of scholars: "Is there anyone in the room whom I *haven't* offended?" It is in this connection that I must express my profound gratitude to the various colleagues and mentors who have greatly assisted me in my effort to do justice to the disciplines and arguments I engage in the course of this work. Foremost among them are Abdellah Hammoudi, Alan Ryan, and John Waterbury, all of whom struck a remarkable balance between the roles of intellectual partisan and serious critic. Their guidance, breadth of knowledge, and intellectual engagement made this interdisciplinary project not only possible but enjoyable. My discussions with George Kateb and my father, J. Peter Euben, have been extraordinary: always attentive to the political and moral stakes in even the most academic of arguments, they have both, on several occasions, not only recalled me to the reasons I undertook this project in the first place but helped me recognize them.

I have also benefited enormously from the close and critical readings of portions of this manuscript at various stages provided by Shahrough Akhavi, Shlomo Avineri, James W. Bailey, Lawrie Balfour, Judith Barish, Seyla Benhabib, L. Carl Brown, Edmund Burke, III, Fred Dallmayr, Amy Gutmann, Jeffrey Isaac, Ann and Warren Lane, Daniel Sabia, William Shepard, Emmanuel Sivan, and Keith Topper. I am particularly indebted to Hilary Persky, and not only for her friendship; her encouragement and intellectual engagement have contributed immeasurably to this project over the years. Of special note is Jonathan Perry, to whom I owe a debt of gratitude far surpassing words. His intensity of imagination, creativity, and moral compassion never cease to inspire me; he has taught me to listen in novel ways, and to hear in new registers. Without his patience, love, and sheer human kindness, this book would not have been possible.

Finally, I am grateful to the University Center for Human Values, the Woodrow Wilson Society of Fellows, the Center of International Studies, and the Program for Near Eastern Studies, all at Princeton University. They have not only provided generous financial support, but also furnished me an invaluable opportunity to confer with students and faculty from a variety of disciplines in and beyond the Princeton University community. I am also beholden to Donald Puchala and the Walker Institute of International Studies and the Office of Sponsored Programs and Research at the University of South Carolina, Columbia, for their support, financial and intellectual. For their efficient assistance in checking citations and reviewing transliterations in preparation for publication, I thank Sherry Marousek and Aisha Musa. Last but most certainly not least, I would like to thank the members of the Department of Political Science and the Committee on Academic Research at Wellesley College for their immediate and extraordinary support as this project drew to a close.

A final note is perhaps in order about the image on the cover of this book. The image is referred to as "Raising a Ghost by Magic Lantern" in an 1870 book entitled *The Magic Lantern: How to Buy and How to Use It*, also *How to Raise a Ghost*.[2] It depicts a later incarnation of the *phantasmagoria*, the precinematic effect originally popular in France in the late eighteenth century. As Barnouw describes it, the phantasmagoric effect involved the projection of lantern light through a slide onto layers of gauze, which appeared translucent to the audience. The area around the image was blacked out so that the projected figure floated as if without context and spectators could not tell its distance from them. By moving the lantern around, the projectionist could make the image appear to grow or diminish or suddenly black out. Used primarily by magicians and mediums, by the mid-nineteenth century the phantasmagoric effect was achieved more precisely by the use of a sheet of glass tilted at an angle, the use of limelight, and the involvement of a living person rather than a slide. The effect was that the stage seemed to be occupied by both actors and ghosts, interacting with each other, while the sheet of glass, the lantern, and the lantern operator were invisible to the audience.[3]

Theodor Adorno, Walter Benjamin, and others have used the word "phantasmagoria" to refer not only to these precinematic forms of representation, but also to the "occultation of production by means of the outward appearance of the product. . . . [T]his outer appearance can lay claim to the status of being. Its perfection is at the same time the perfection of the illusion that the work of art is a reality *sui generis* that constitutes itself in the realm of the absolute without having to renounce its claim to image the world."[4] In other words, it comes to indicate the concealment or mystification of the mechanisms by which an image is produced, so that the image appears as reality.[5] This phantasmagoric effect captures a central argument of this book, that is, that the post-Enlightenment rationalist methods scholars use to study politics actually produce an image of Islamic fundamentalism while concealing such "mechanisms of production" within claims of rationalist objectivity. The fact that the "ghost" in this particular depiction of the phantasmagoric effect is shrouded evokes perhaps the most common visual image of Islamic fundamentalism in Western scholarship and media: the Muslim woman covered head to foot in the Iranian *chador*. The image thus says less about what Islamic fundamentalism "really is" than about the ways in which rationalist assumptions derived from Western history and experiences—and the fears they express and repress—produce our understandings of fundamentalism.

A Note on Spelling

There are complex transliteration systems by which scholars have rendered Arabic terms into English. This book is intended for readers with a variety of backgrounds and interests; for the sake of uniformity and accessibility, then, I have opted to use the common spellings of proper names and terms available to a nonspecialist. For the sake of consistency, with less familiar terms, titles, and names I have striven to follow the spelling conventions that guide common transliterations of Arabic into English. To accomplish this, I have used minimal diacritics: in particular, ' is used to represent *'ayn* and ' is used to represent *hamza*.

Enemy in the Mirror

CHAPTER ONE

Re-Marking Territories

DESPITE a diversity of political sensibilities and theoretical concerns, political theory in the late twentieth century can in many ways be characterized as postfoundational. Rawlsian and other liberal theorists are concerned to show that the basis of the well-ordered society need not presume a metaphysical conception of the good.[1] This need to rebut charges of metaphysics is driven by political imperatives, in particular plural and conflicting theories of the good and the understanding that any defense—rational or otherwise—of metaphysical foundations has become an anachronism in post-Enlightenment theoretical discourse. Theorists grouped roughly under the umbrellas of postmodernism and hermeneutics share this understanding despite radical differences with liberal premises. For Michel Foucault as for Hans-Georg Gadamer, the very possibility of political knowledge requires debunking notions such as science and epistemology that refer to and therefore presume the existence of truths outside of language, history, and human interests. Even someone like Jürgen Habermas, who is simultaneously critical of the postmodern repudiation of the Enlightenment and aspects of liberal discourse, shares this unease with the very concept of transcendent foundations. Contemporary political theory is thus embedded in what could be called an antifoundationalist discourse; within the parameters of this discourse, the particular problematic of political theory is how to construct a just society without the transcendent foundations thought to have previously sustained it.

The paradox, however, is that these attempts to theorize community without recourse to metaphysical truths take place in a world where political practice is increasingly dominated by those who take such truths as a given. That is, at the very moment political theory is coming to terms with the end of foundations, political practice is spinning off into a world driven by foundationalist certainties and the attempt to remake political, cultural, and economic power in accordance with them.[2] From abortion-clinic terrorism in Pensacola, Florida, to settler violence in the Occupied Territories, to the Islamic governments of Iran and the Sudan, to the American embassy bombings in Africa, to the establishment of a shadow system of medical clinics and banks by the Islamic groups in Egypt, religio-political fundamentalists in particular have made their influence felt in local, national, and international arenas. Importantly, the surge in fundamentalist activism transcends any one geographic area or particular religious tradition. Fundamentalist power is certainly nowhere more evident nor more threatening to advocates of democracy and/or a Western-driven post–Cold War order than in the Middle East. Yet in January 1994 former Vice President Dan Quayle met with religious-right activists in Florida and pledged allegiance to "the Christian flag, and to the Saviour, for whose Kingdom it stands, one Saviour, crucified, risen, and coming again, with life and liberty for all who believe."[3]

How do we,[4] as Western students of politics, make sense of the increasingly foundationalist turn of political practice within a theoretical discourse that no longer sees any place for metaphysics in political life? While framed in terms of the more explicitly theoretical approaches to the study of politics, this question captures a dilemma facing political science generally. For while debates about epistemology and foundations may be associated with the more explicitly normative disciplines, self-styled descriptive disciplines are always wedded to an epistemology. In particular, "nonnormative" descriptions are wedded to a post-Enlightenment epistemology defined by the commitment to reading the political world as understandable, explicable, and knowable by way of human reason and methods. Such an epistemology at once determines how we come to know the world and constitutes the range of what is knowable. This suggests that the more our stories about politics—whether explicitly normative or apparently descriptive—are committed to a rationalist epistemology, the more difficulty we may have in compassing the significance of practices guided by and defined in terms of belief in divine truths unknowable by purely human means.

We can see examples of these difficulties in two recent theses about the demise of the Cold War and the trajectory of future international conflict. There is, for example, Francis Fukuyama's celebration of "the total exhaustion of viable systematic alternatives to Western liberalism," and the "end point of mankind's ideological evolution and the universalization of Western liberal democracy as the final form of human government."[5] Echoing the Enlightenment's faith in the march of progress through history, Fukuyama suggests that all conflicts will be resolved within a universalizing narrative of liberalization and modernization. Nationalist, ethnic, and religio-political conflicts and ideologies appear in this light to be the virulent but ultimately doomed expression of peoples and states still "in history" in what is inexorably becoming a "posthistorical" world. Such conflict and violence will continue as "impulses incompletely played out,"[6] but the implication remains that, in Didier Bigo's words, "as they are devoid of sense, they will exhaust themselves with the actors."[7] While Fukuyama concedes that Islam does in fact constitute a "systematic and coherent ideology, just like liberalism and communism, with its own code of morality and doctrine of political and social justice," he concludes that Islamic cultures "cannot challenge liberal democracy on its own territory on the level of ideas"; on the contrary, the Islamic world has revealed itself to be manifestly "vulnerable" to the conquest of universal liberalism.[8] The martial metaphor for the tensions among ideas and principles is familiar but nevertheless revealing: Fukuyama's language here reifies complex phenomena in the service of Western triumphalism and elides important distinctions among Islam, Islamic fundamentalist ideas, and Islamic fundamentalist militarism.

Contrary to Fukuyama's optimism, it is of course now abundantly clear that the end of the Cold War has presaged not a world in which the challenges to Western liberalism have been exhausted, but one apparently quite hospitable to the survival and increasing stridency of movements and people who reject it. The demise of Cold War politics and categories has laid bare loyalties, identities, affiliations, and commitments supposedly rendered obsolete by the ascendancy of ideological conflict. Those of us living in the West do not have to go as far afield as the Middle East to see this point; we have only to look around us to see it is so. Thus at the other extreme from Fukuyama's Hegelian reading of the post–Cold War trajectory are theories that draw more on a Hobbesian paradigm of international politics to underscore the inevitability of international conflict.[9] As represented by scholars such as William Lind and Samuel Huntington, the Cold War is interpreted as the last in a series of "Western civil wars" (the phrase is Lind's) that began in the conflict of seventeenth-century Europe.[10] In this narrative, the passing of this stage in history, and of the Cold War in particular, has laid bare a "Hobbesian as revised by Morgenthau"[11] world, one dominated by curiously immutable and constitutively antagonistic cultural entities.[12] On Huntington's post–Cold War map, old ideological dichotomies of West versus East are reinscribed along the lines of culture: "the Velvet Curtain of culture has replaced the Iron Curtain of ideology as the most significant dividing line in Europe."[13]

In Huntington's schema, Islamic militancy is cast as one significant dimension of the final evolutionary stage of international conflict, the clash between "the West and the rest."[14] Here the West is defined in terms of a commitment to "individualism, liberalism, constitutionalism, human rights, equality, liberty, the rule of law, democracy, free markets, the separation of church and state," and arrayed against it are often opposing identities and movements implicitly understood to be united as "agents of disorder" in the post–Cold War interstate system, an expression of particularisms and differences over universality and equality.[15] "We are facing a mood and a movement far transcending the level of issues and policies and the governments that pursue them. This is no less than a clash of civilizations—the perhaps irrational but surely historic reaction of an ancient rival against our Judeo-Christian heritage, our secular present, and the world-wide expansion of both."[16]

Huntington's thesis captures, I think, a popular mood: to many in the West, Islamic fundamentalism seems a particularly foul emanation from that netherworld of fanaticism, where disciples of the violent and the irrational abound, a prejudice catalyzed by the bombings of the World Trade Center in 1993 and the American embassies in Kenya and Tanzania in August 1998. Thus it is perhaps not surprising that Huntington's clash of civilizations has found expression in an even darker vision whereby the rise of fundamentalism is portrayed as *the* threat to the New World Order. Here the confrontation between religio-political insurgency and secularism is understood as part of a New Cold War, "global in its scope, binary in its opposition, occasionally violent and essentially a difference of ideologies."[17] Indeed, Islamic fundamentalists have been described as "religious Stalinists," language that replicates the very Manichaeanism for which fundamentalists are rightly criticized.[18] In its most extreme formulation, this vision has devolved into a caricature of Islam as the "Green Peril" (green is the color of Islam) advancing across the world stage, an image that echoes both the "Red Menace" of Cold War discourse and anti-Asian polemics about the "Yellow Peril." This, in turn, has been expressed in and reinforced by the selective application of the highly mechanistic determinism of "domino theory" to Islamic fundamentalism by American policy analysts—just as it was applied to communism in the Cold War.[19] "Broadly speaking, green has replaced red as the rising force, but we concentrate our attention and our decisiveness on a secondary front facing a defensive opponent; and we spare our means on more sensitive fronts with potentially offensive opponents. Tense in a calm zone, relaxed in a tense zone, we can, as usual, be attacked from the rear. The nuclear and rational North deters the nuclear and rational North, not the conventional and mystical South."[20]

While characterizations of Islamic fundamentalism as the "Green Peril" and part of the "New Cold War" are by no means universal,[21] it is nevertheless striking that this sense of inevitable danger from the South (or East, depending upon one's vantage point) closely resembles the former menace from the Communist East and that, furthermore, these fears should find such strong expression at the very moment many argue the West has reached a pinnacle of international power.[22] I suspect that this sense of danger is only partially related to a genuine sense of Western military, political, or cultural vulnerability; it also reflects a growing sense of alarm and surprise that phenomena such as Islamic fundamentalism have survived into the modern era at all—the flip side of Fukuyama's insistence that such fundamentally archaic impulses are destined to extinguish themselves in a flash of predictable but nonsensical violence. Indeed, the repeated invocation of terms such as "*re*surgence," "*re*vival," and "*re*emergence" to describe religio-political militancy suggests a will to believe that the disenchantment of the world has truly reduced the purchase of such "irrational" commitments, rather than having just pushed them underground or out of sight. We are taken off guard, alarmed and frightened as if confronted by a ghost that

should not be. Old specters haunt modern politics in new guises: if the Soviet Union disintegrates into warring republics, Lind prophesied in 1991,
"the twenty-first century could once again find Islam at the Gates of Vienna,
as immigrants or terrorists if not as armies."[23]

Neither of these two apparently contradictory theses, the "end of history"
and the "clash of civilizations," occasions discussions about the status of
truth or the tension between politics and metaphysical conceptions of the
good on the part of their authors; they are intended as persuasive, realistic
reflections of the world as it is and will be. And as descriptive accounts of
contemporary international politics, both narratives acknowledge and find a
place for the persistence of political practices such as fundamentalism, if
only in passing. Yet they too seem finally unable to encounter the content or
import of such political practices in any meaningful way. By this I mean that
both pessimistic and optimistic prognoses of the post–Cold War world are
content implicitly to assume and thus reinforce the idea that religio-political
movements (among others) stand in relation to Western, secular power and
international order as the chaos of the particularistic, irrational, and archaic
stand in relation to the universalistic, rational, and modern. My point is not,
of course, that such a subtext in some sense *originates* in these accounts. On
the contrary, they are only the most recent expression of it. Similar assumptions pervaded coverage of the Iranian Revolution in 1979: images of figures
clad in black, faces distorted by fury, fists thrust out in defiance of the "great
Satan" fulfilled many Western fears about the lethal chemistry of religious
militancy and Islam. My point is rather that in such narratives political Islam
is registered primarily if not exclusively as a threat to modern, legitimate
politics, a phenomenon to be contained or overcome. It is not so much that
these theories are wrong, but that the very definition of legitimate politics
presupposed by them overdetermines the equation of political Islam and
menace.

Post postmodernism, it is perhaps obvious to point out the ways in which
our scholarly categories and narratives at once express and reproduce particular historical and cultural assumptions about the world (although that is not
all that they do); yet these post–Cold War theses reveal the anxieties and
presuppositions at work in the intersection of Western social scientific
scholarship and Islamic fundamentalism in particular. Such anxieties in part
originate in and are exacerbated by the cultural distance and historical antagonism between "East" and "West," between what is understood to be
"us" and "Islam." But they are also written into the paradox with which I
began this chapter: the disjuncture between a world that is more, rather than
less, marked by what I have called foundationalist political practices, and a
profoundly this-worldly scholarly discourse that sees no place for such foundationalist certainties in modern political life or, by extension, regards such
political practices as a threat to modern politics. This paradox suggests, of

course, that along with others who study the "non-Western"world,[24] students of Islamic fundamentalism must worry that the tried and true tools
with which we in the West study political life may distort our understanding
of practices cross-culturally. But it also suggests that many of our descriptive
and theoretical tools for understanding are inadequate to the task of studying foundationalist political practice in particular, whether we seek to explain practices of Islamic fundamentalists in Algeria or Christian fundamentalists in America.

COMPARATIVE POLITICAL THEORY AND FOUNDATIONALIST
POLITICAL PRACTICE

To rephrase the question I posed earlier: given the way our intellectual
categories reflect and reproduce ambivalences and preconceptions about
the relationship between metaphysical truths and politics, East and West,
legitimate and illegitimate politics—in short, "prejudices" (to use Gadamer's
meaning) that are part of our Western tradition—how do we make sense of
the increasing power of Islamic fundamentalism in the modern world?[25]
This book is intended, in part, as an answer to this question. The answer, like
the question, works on two levels, substantive and methodological.

I offer an interpretation of Islamic fundamentalist political thought in an
attempt to provide a window into fundamentalists' own understandings of
the movement's meaning and purpose. In chapter 3 I analyze the ethico-
political worldview of one particularly influential Islamic fundamentalist
thinker, Sayyid Qutb. I concentrate on Qutb as the thinker whose systematic
analysis of Islam, modernity, and political action has shaped the commitments of a generation of Sunni fundamentalists. I argue that Qutb's political
thought is an indictment not just of Western imperialism and colonialism,
the corruption of Middle Eastern regimes, Arab secularist power, or modernity per se, but also of modern forms of sovereignty and the Western rationalist epistemology that justifies them. The remarkable impact of Qutb's
ideas on the contemporary movement narrows but does not bridge the gap
between Qutb's intent and how his arguments are disseminated, received,
and reinterpreted. My reading is not a substitute for such a genealogy, nor
is it intended as an analysis of Qutb's complete oeuvre.[26] I approach Qutb's
final stage of thought with a particular set of purposes. As a highly influential
theorist of fundamentalism who was himself a part of the early fundamentalist movement in Egypt, Qutb's work is an opportunity to bridge the theory
and practice divide: it is instructive on its own terms as a text of fundamentalist theory and symptomatically, as a guide to understanding the appeal of
fundamentalist ideas in the modern world.

Indeed, although Qutb was an Egyptian Sunni Muslim, his critique of
modernity arises out of a widely shared experience of colonialism and cul-

tural imperialism whereby modernization and modern political thought were intimately intertwined with the experience of foreign domination.[27] The breadth of this experience provides the context for my argument in chapters 3 and 4 that Qutb's critique is neither unique nor idiosyncratic: despite crucial differences, Qutb shares with other Islamic fundamentalist thinkers a rejection of modern forms of sovereignty and of human claims to knowledge that justify them, and an insistence that, by contrast, God's knowledge of the deepest meanings of human existence justifies divine rule over both moral and political life. Thus, although Aziz al-Azmeh is in some ways right to point out that "there are as many Islams as there are situations that sustain it," I want to claim that there are unifying patterns at least to Islamic fundamentalists' constructions of "tradition" out of the Qur'an and the life of the Prophet and that, moreover, Qutb's worldview lends crucial insight into them.[28]

My argument here must be distinguished from the contention that there is a monolithic Islamic tradition, a "single place or uniform culture called Islam" that reacts uniformly to a unilinear process of modernization throughout the Islamic world.[29] On the contrary, any religious tradition is inevitably a site of contestation informed by the cultural, historical, geographical, and political context in which it is located.[30] Moreover, as Nicholas Dirks argues in regard to India, in a postcolonial world, such a simple opposition between tradition and modernity makes little sense because "much of what has been taken to be timeless tradition is, in fact, the paradoxical effect of colonial rule, where culture was carefully depoliticized and reified into a specifically colonial version of civil society."[31] Thus, in invoking an Islamic fundamentalist "worldview," I refer not to the revival of an essential Islamic tradition, but rather to the ways in which the global ascendance of Western cultural, political, and economic norms has presented a common set of dilemmas and problems to prevailing understandings of "Islamic tradition,"[32] an interaction that has produced a particular "remake of things traditional, one among other possible remakes of things traditional, themselves impossible to apprehend as substances and in an unmediated way."[33]

My analysis of Qutb's political thought is also an occasion to elaborate, by argument and example, what I call comparative political theory. Generally speaking, the project of comparative political theory introduces non-Western perspectives into familiar debates about the problems of living together, thus ensuring that "political theory" is about human and not merely Western dilemmas. It is perhaps best understood as a hybrid of the contemporary disciplines of political theory and comparative politics, for it entails the attempt to ask questions about the nature and value of politics in a variety of cultural and historical contexts. This presumes an understanding of political theory as defined by certain questions rather than particular answers: What is the good life? What is the nature of legitimate authority? Of justice? What is the right relationship of individual to society? This approach builds on the possibility that disparate cultures are not worlds apart, morally and cognitively incommensurable, but exist in conversation with one another, even if they have serious moral and political disagreements.[34] Importantly, this possibility is not premised upon the existence of universal and perennial questions that arise by virtue of being human. Indeed, the universality of such questions cannot be assumed; the extent to which we do or do not share certain dilemmas with others by virtue of being human is a debate central to the project of comparative political theory itself. Rather, the possibility of such conversations is tied to the syncretism that is a hallmark of a world marked by extensive Western cultural influence: in a postcolonial world increasingly marked by neocolonial globalization, questions we take to be ours have ceased to be so exclusively (if in fact they ever were) because they have come to frame the sensibilities of non-Westerners as well.[35] This is not, however, because Europe and the Americas are "the only true subjects of history," while all others are condemned to be only "perpetual consumers of modernity" or mere elaborations of Western hegemony.[36] Rather, it is the case because those in the postcolonial world must choose their "site of autonomy" as Chattergee puts it, from a "position of subordination to a colonial regime that had on its side the most universalist justificatory resources produced by post–Enlightenment social thought."[37]

Against, then, the assumption that " 'only the West has produced political theory,' " and therefore that political theorists need not "ask the question whether non-Western styles of thinking about society do more adequately reflect the social experiences of the West as well," I want to argue that political theory is an enterprise perhaps produced by, but not coterminous with, "Western civilization."[38] Broadening the parameters of political theory in this way makes room for the possibility that there is humanly significant knowledge outside the confines of the Western canon, but, as Salkever and Nylan argue, emphasizing shared dilemmas and questions rather than universal truths enables the project of comparative political theory to avoid the conclusion that cultures are morally and cognitively incommensurable without imposing supposedly universal categories and moral rules.[39] This, in turn, establishes the possibility of and conditions for conversations across cultures. Such recognition is transformative, opening theoretical discourse to admit of parallels and comparisons that narrower conceptions of political theory occlude.

Understood in this way, it is my contention that comparative political theory does not signify an erosion of the integrity of political theory as a field but rather entails a reclamation of its foundations: in one of the earliest known uses of the word theory, Herodotus describes the journey of Solon from Athens for the sake of theory.[40] Theory at that time connoted the act of observing, seeing, witnessing; more particularly a theorist (*theoros*) was, as

Sheldon Wolin describes it, "a public emissary dispatched by his city to attend the religious festivals of other Greek cities."[41] Over time, "theory" was linked to observation of different and often alien lands, institutions, and practices, a journey that not only produced knowledge of other political worlds, but also "could eventually issue in a critical sense toward the particularity, even arbitrariness of [one's] own culture and stimulate a drive to find a higher unity or reality beneath the particularity of appearances, whether in nature, Being or human nature."[42] This suggests that theory was and still is an inherently comparative enterprise at least in part because it is through comparisons that we are led to question the "naturalness" of our own perspective. Such questioning both presupposes and makes possible a critical distance toward everyday practices, a distance crucial to self-knowledge, learning about others, and making sense of the world in general.[43]

That theorizing is an inherently comparative enterprise is evident, for example, in the periodization of Western intellectual thought—the very notion of "the Dark Ages" presupposes a comparison across time and history. Indeed, we are always comparing our present to our past, and our present to the present of others to define what we are and have become. In chapter 4, I undertake just such a comparison across time. In contrast to Qutb's insistence that modern rationalism is inimical to the substance of and authority behind absolute Islamic truths, I examine two significant nineteenth-century Islamic "modernists" who argue that Islam properly understood is the religion of reason. In chapter 5, I explore a particular comparison across cultures: I analyze the ways in which Qutb's anxieties about the costs of modern rationalism are mirrored in Western critiques of modernity, and what Richard Bernstein has called the "rage against reason," that define modernity as crisis, and specifically as a decay in meaning that is the legacy of the Enlightenment.[44] Ultimately, I argue that in such cross-cultural critiques of modernity we are witnessing not "antimodernism" but rather "modernities," that is, multiple perspectives on and attempts to redefine what it must mean to live in the modern world.

A virtue of comparative political theory is that it makes possible many such unimagined connections and conversations. Indeed, while this work takes up a specific analysis of Islamic and Western political thought, it is also an occasion to argue for the possibility and necessity of conversations about the nature and value of politics among political theorists from a variety of traditions. This raises the distinct possibility that non-Western perspectives may provide new (that is, new to the West) answers to our old questions. Yet it is not my contention that, for example, Qutb provides a novel or viable way of configuring modern sovereignty or political action, or resources for a reconstitution of moral and existential meaning compatible with democratic principles and practices. I do argue that in introducing Qutb's non-Western perspective into our study of modernity, we may see previously unimagined connections to the Western canon of political theory, and, moreover, it may be that Qutb's answers actually transform the nature and focus of the questions themselves. Examination of his perspective thus illuminates the extent to which modern ideas we value are experienced and redefined in other cultures and so broadens our very understanding of the "modern condition." At the same time, the comparison with Western voices illuminates our own ambivalences regarding modernity and rationalism, thereby revealing the fissures *within* the category of "the West."

This "view from both sides" thus lends insight into the world of Islamic fundamentalism and Western anxieties about modernity expressed by a remarkable variety of voices, from Christian fundamentalists to American politicians to political philosophers. These arguments indicate, of course, that Qutb is not as pathological or even as culturally idiosyncratic as he initially appears to a Western audience, but they also challenge the often implicit equation of the "modern condition" with the "Western condition." This suggests that political theory can be enriched by hearing Qutb's voice not only because of the ways it speaks to our concerns but also because of the ways it mirrors, challenges, enlarges, and transforms them. Indeed, given these arguments, I want to suggest that this cross-cultural comparison may ultimately undermine the very opposition between "Islam" and "the West." Such oppositions can be useful heuristic devices with which to grasp and order unwieldy terrain, yet in a postcolonial world grown smaller and more interdependent through globalization, the lines between "us" and "them" have dramatically shifted and become more permeable. Moreover, such oppositions makes less sense in light of the mutual debt between Europe and Islam dating back centuries: as Francis Robinson points out, both Christian and Islamic civilizations are embedded in Semitic traditions of prophecy, Muslims reintroduced many lost classical texts to Europe, and medieval Islamic philosophy is itself an amalgamation of Islam and Greek philosophy. "Is it really feasible," Robinson concludes, "for Muslims and Westerners to represent each other as so profoundly different and separate when so much has been shared over so long?"[45] And while it is now commonplace to note the ways in which colonialism constituted the world of its "subjects," as Dirks notes, colonialism in fact "remade the world": "colonialism was not some historical process that simply took place in colonial locales, but rather was fundamental to the construction of modern selves and societies in the metropole as well as the colony," shaping the meaning of "Europeanness" for example, as well as Other.[46]

Underlying this discussion of comparative political theory in general, and the comparisons opened up through an analysis of Qutb's political thought in particular, is a methodological argument for an approach to studying political phenomena that engages the participants' ideas on their own terms, or at least on as close to their own terms as is possible for an interpreter whose position is exterior to the worldview of the subject. It may be helpful to understand this approach in relation to the notion of a "thick" description, in this case of the participants' ideas.[47] This notion of a "thick" description derives from a semiotic approach to culture, an approach that, as Clifford Geertz describes it, takes culture as a context, an "interworked system of construable signs" in terms of which social events may be rendered intelligible.[48] Of course, there is a difference between a social action rendered from the actor's point of view and a written text, the import of which depends not only on the view of the author but also on the putative influence of such a view on participants' action more generally. Nevertheless, the concept of a "thick" description and the semiotic approach to culture on which it is based is useful here because it presumes not only the possibility of intelligibly rendering the world of the "Other," but also that interpretive accounts are central to the endeavor: as Geertz states, "[t]he whole point of a semiotic approach to culture is . . . to aid us in gaining access to the conceptual world in which our subjects live so that we can, in some extended sense of the term, converse with them."[49]

This approach views understanding as a reciprocal, transformative, and, perhaps above all, ongoing process. However, the pleasant trope of "conversation" must be invoked in the study of Islamic fundamentalism with caution, for in a postcolonial world such "dialogues" across cultures often take place under conditions of radical inequality among and between regions, economies, and cultures. This is not the same as saying that all cross-cultural understandings are inevitably and merely rearticulations of colonialist and imperialist power, doomed to express a new Orientalism: I do not subscribe to the claim that there is no reality "out there," independent of language, power, and human interests. Yet it is nevertheless the case that the truths pursued under these circumstances—to varying degrees, it seems, the circumstances of much interpretation—are necessarily incomplete, for what is possible is not final Truth but "the new partial truths and the near images of power" that facilitate a better grasp of the world in which human beings live.[50] Thus it is my contention that as human beings are inescapably situated, the dialogic model recommends itself not because it is invulnerable to distortions of power but because it is less susceptible to them than explanatory models that insist upon explaining "the politics of all society in terms of such functions, for instance, as 'interest articulation' and 'interest aggregation' whose definition is strongly influenced by the bargaining culture of our civilization, but which is far from being guaranteed elsewhere."[51] In attending to socially mediated understandings the interpretive approach to studying the "human sciences" remains permanently open to the ways in which systemic inequalities in a postcolonial world are implicated in cross-cultural dialogue, and so to the finitude of our capacity to understand.

Importantly for my argument—and for the attempt to understand the growth of Islamic fundamentalism—such an interpretive approach is not just about making otherwise alien ideas intelligible by paying attention to fundamentalists' self-understandings but is also and crucially about constructing adequate causal explanations. Although this may seem quite obvious, it is often the case in debates about social scientific methodology, and about rival interpretations of Islamic fundamentalism in particular, that this emphasis on ideas, or the explication of meanings, is taken to exclude the substance of and methodology behind causal explanations that focus on the impact of social and economic conditions, and vice-versa.[52] Indeed, "interpretation" and "explanation" are in this context often taken to signal fundamentally antithetical approaches to knowledge about the political world. However, my interpretation of fundamentalist political thought and the methodology underlying it is intended not to replace but to complete current social scientific explanations of Islamic fundamentalism. For in insisting that fundamentalism is merely epiphenomenal, such explanations preclude the possibility that fundamentalists are drawn to religio-political ideas in much the same way that activists have been drawn throughout history to democratic, liberal, or Marxist ideals.

Indeed, it often seems as if ideas and beliefs we regard as reasonable— ones we often hold— frequently do not require social scientific explanation at all. The events following the fall of the Berlin Wall bring this point into sharp relief: few observers seem to have the same difficulties understanding "democracy" as a value capable of inspiring mass action as they do entertaining the possibility that Islamic fundamentalists may also seek an intrinsically compelling ideal. This suggests that interpretive accounts are particularly critical when the object of study is as contentious and resistant to analyses of rational self-interest as fundamentalism, whether it is Islamic, Jewish, or Christian fundamentalism in America.[53] For the reflex to dismiss fundamentalism as irrational or pathological is not merely a product of the almost habitualized prejudices and fears operative in the relationship between "the West" and "Islam" but, as I have argued, also a function of the way a post-Enlightenment, predominantly rationalist tradition of scholarship countenances foundationalist political practices in the modern world. Of course, explication of fundamentalists' vision cannot by itself explain the increasing strength of fundamentalism. As meaning and function are mutually determinative, the historical, economic, cultural, and political context is necessary to explanation. But by the same token, this strength cannot be taken only as an index of socioeconomic discontent; it is also a testament to the moral power of fundamentalist ideas themselves.

Insisting on the centrality of participants' self-understandings to explanation does not require abandoning a perspective impartial enough to allow critique and evaluation of such understandings. Indeed, it is my contention that an interpretive understanding does not preclude critique but in fact makes critique possible by deferring the intrusion of our own assumptions about divine truths in political life, the "essential nature" of Islam, or the "universals" of human psychology. Yet in this work I am less interested in the contradictions of Qutb's arguments or the dangers of his political thought than in the perspective expressed in it, for it seems to me that all too often the study of Islamic fundamentalism suffers not from a dearth of critique but from a paucity of insight. My purpose here derives from my sense that fundamentalism is becoming more rather than less powerful, and that those who are worried about the challenge fundamentalism poses to liberal or democratic theories of politics are ill-served by the suggestion that fundamentalism signifies the resurgence of the irrational, the stubborn persistence of the archaic and particularistic, or the veil that masks what are essentially structural tensions. Such stories function ultimately to discredit adherents as fanatical lunatics or agents of regressive chaos, or to reduce fundamentalist ideas to mere conduits; they all miss the opportunity to understand the appeals of fundamentalism.[54]

Thus, although advanced in the context of an argument about Islamic fundamentalism, it is my hope that these substantive and methodological arguments may shed light on the mounting political and theoretical challenge to liberalism, democracy, and rationalism both at home and abroad, and concomitantly, on the expanding world of what I have called foundationalist political practice. Indeed, as I will suggest in the concluding chapter, despite crucial differences, Christian as well as Islamic fundamentalists share a preoccupation with the erosion of values, traditions, and meaning seen as constitutive of post-Enlightenment modernity.[55] Such commonalities suggest that fundamentalism in its many varieties may be the radical conclusion of a more widespread conviction that contemporary life is plagued by a multifaceted alienation requiring redress. Put slightly differently, fundamentalism can be understood as part of the larger attempt among various groups and theories to "re-enchant" a world characterized by the experience of disenchantment, one expression of what Nietzsche describes as the "metaphysical urge" to construct myths that give meaning to life and its struggles.[56] Given the strength and political and cultural diversity of voices intent on "re-enchanting" a disenchanted world, then, we need to understand to what extent they are capturing and exploiting real or perceived failures of post-Enlightenment, rationalist ways of understanding and thus organizing political life.

In taking seriously fundamentalists' own account of the movement's meaning and purpose, I am not attempting to render fundamentalism more reasonable, "rational," or palatable than it is, but rather to provide a window into a world often distorted by our own cultural experiences and anxieties. Importantly, such an endeavor requires that we resist the tendency to dig in our heels, to assert the essential rightness of democratic, liberal, and secular values, and to rail against the irrationality of antidemocratic, religious intolerance. This openness need not lend strength to either a desire to recreate archaic forms of thought and social organization, or signify a nostalgia for some idyllic and nonexistent past. Nor need it be in the service of sympathy. Indeed, my solicitude toward radical religious perspectives on modernity in this book derives not from reverence, but from a double-edged skepticism: a skepticism of universalizing truths in any form—including those rationalist truths that deny their own universalizing tendencies—and of easy dismissal of other points of view as wrong and dangerous. To be honest, skepticism must be skeptical of itself; in this instance, then, it requires entertaining religious truths without affirming, defending, or advocating them. Indeed, as Derrida argues, the "virtue of critique" entails submitting the critical tradition to a

> deconstructive genealogy that exceeds it without yet compromising it. . . . The *same duty* demands tolerating and respecting all that is not placed under the authority of reason. It may have to do with faith, with different forms of faith. It may also have to do with certain thoughts, whether questioning or not, thoughts that, while attempting to think reason and the history of reason, necessarily exceed its order, without becoming, simply because of this, irrational, much less irrationalist. For these thoughts may in fact also try to remain faithful to the ideal of the Enlightenment . . . while yet acknowledging its limits, in order to work on the Enlightenment of this time, this time that is ours—*today*.[57]

This means that for the sake of understanding what fundamentalism is about, we must strive, in this case against our own moral impulses and intellectual reflexes, to hear voices critical of our own deeply held convictions about the way the world does, or should, work. The challenge is to seek to understand such voices in spite of the danger they may present, and also *because of* that danger. Hearing such voices makes it possible not only to learn about other perspectives in the world but also to refine our own perspectives about the world. This serves many of us in our commitment to strengthening democratic principles and practices by enabling us to acknowledge the ways in which modern, rationalist ways of organizing and defining political life have, for many, already failed to provide compelling answers to questions of meaningful coexistence.

THE POLITICS OF NAMING: DEFINING FUNDAMENTALISM

Given the diversity of movements "fundamentalism" encompasses, any definition of fundamentalism is, not surprisingly, highly contested. The very use of the word gives rise to debate. "Fundamentalism" literally refers to an early twentieth century American Protestant movement that called for religion based on a literal interpretation of the Bible. In the context of a history of Western colonialism and imperialism, the application of a specifically Western and Christian term to the Islamic world is rightly suspect.[58] Indeed, there is no word for fundamentalism in Arabic: the closest word in Arabic, *usuli*, was coined specifically to approximate the English "fundamentalism" (*usul* can be translated to mean fundamentals, or roots). Many have argued that the specifically Western origin of the word, coupled with the pejorative connotations attached to it by journalists and academics who condemn the phenomenon, make it a term that "almost guarantee[s] misunderstanding."[59] Esposito argues that "it tells us everything and yet, at the same time, nothing."[60] For how can one concept derived from a specific moment in Christian history simultaneously gather together the assassins of Egyptian President Anwar Sadat, the Branch Davidians in Texas, the Hindus who attacked the mosque at Ayodhya, Pat Robertson, and Israel's Gush Emunim? It is no accident that several preeminent books on the subject avoid the word altogether. In his book on Islamic, Christian, and Judaic religio-political movements, Gilles Kepel uses terms such as "movements of re-Judaising," "re-Christianization," and "re-Islamisation." In his 1985 book on Islamic activism, Kepel prefers "Muslim extremism" to Islamic fundamentalism. Emmanuel Sivan opts for "radical Islam," and others have offered alternatives that range from "*integrisme*" to "revivalism" to "Islamism."[61]

Of course, the cultural origins of such terms as "nationalism," "conservatism," and "socialism" have not prevented their application elsewhere. More importantly, however, I want to suggest that "fundamentalism" is a useful heuristic device that, if not pushed too far, illuminates theoretical rather than specific structural continuities among religio-political movements of the twentieth century.[62] John O. Voll describes it in relation to Sunni fundamentalism as "the reaffirmation of foundational principles and the effort to reshape society in terms of those reaffirmed fundamentals."[63] Similarly, I use "fundamentalism" to evoke the literal meanings of the word: fundamentals, origins, foundations. "Fundamentalism" thus refers to contemporary religio-political movements that attempt to return to the scriptural foundations of the community, excavating and reinterpreting these foundations for application to the contemporary social and political world.

This definition emphasizes three aspects of fundamentalism. First, it emphasizes fundamentalism's political nature to the exclusion of phenomena such as mysticism, for example, Sufism in Islam. Fundamentalism is not defined by, in Weber's terms, an "other-worldly" orientation in which salvation requires withdrawal from mundane affairs. It is a movement in which salvation is possible only through participation in the world, or more precisely "within the institutions of the world, but in opposition to them."[64] Second, this definition limits the discussion of fundamentalist movements to those that are part of scriptural religious traditions where the "fundamentals" in dispute are located in sacred foundational texts, whether it be the Torah, the New Testament, or the Qur'an.[65] While origins have always been a contested source of legitimacy for many communities, the radicalism of fundamentalists lies in their conviction not only that textual authority is guaranteed by its divine author—for on that Muslims, for example, generally agree[66]—but also that the essential core of the sacred text is clear and not subject to contestation; on the contrary, it is human interpretation that introduces the fallible into the words of the divine. Fundamentalists tend to reject the authority of past religious commentaries and textual interpretations in favor of what the text "really says," thereby denying that determining what the text "really says" is itself an act of interpretation. Such an antihermeneutical stance places fundamentalists in an epistemologically privileged position from which to determine, once and for all, the one and only authentic way to live in a collectivity as a Muslim, a Christian, a Jew. Such claims can and have justified the excesses of totalitarianism; if we take politics to entail public contestation about the very nature and purpose of collective life, such claims are essentially antipolitical as well.

Voll's definition captures the dynamics of revivalist movements throughout time; yet the third aspect I would like to emphasize here is the extent to which fundamentalism is a response to a particular set of dilemmas associated with the "modern" world. In this sense, one might be tempted to use the word "reactive," as does Sivan, for example, when he argues that fundamentalists are distinguished by the fact that they are "reacting to modernity," and as Martin E. Marty assumes when he writes that fundamentalists' "essential feature is not that they are reactionary but that they are reactive: They 'fight back' . . . in the name of God or the sacred against modernity, relativism and pluralism."[67] Yet I am inclined to agree with Ira Lapidus, who argues that Islamic fundamentalists "may be understood as a reaction against modernity, but more profoundly they are also an expression of modernity."[68] Indeed, my reading of Qutb's fundamentalist political thought suggests that to even claim that fundamentalism is "reacting against modernity" is to beg the very terms and questions fundamentalists seek to contest. It is thus perhaps more accurate to say that fundamentalism is profoundly critical of as well as constituted by assumptions regarding the requirements of modernity and modern politics.

This definition of fundamentalism accentuates some aspects at the expense of others. I have emphasized continuities in methods of interpretation rather than, for example, organizational continuities such as patterns of recruitment or socioeconomic similarities; for while a hierarchical organizational structure is indeed a feature of fundamentalist organizations, it is not distinctive to fundamentalists. Of course, one might object that there is nothing inherently religious in the process of excavating, reinterpreting, and reapplying sacred foundations to contemporary dilemmas, and this is precisely the point I want to raise. Defining fundamentalism in terms of the way it contests and reformulates not only the interpretation of original foundations but also the criteria by which such interpretations are authorized suggests that the term "fundamentalism" may also capture aspects of, for example, the way some American conservatives claim a monopoly of interpretation on such ostensibly secular yet foundational and "sacred" texts as the American Constitution. It can be argued that this understanding runs so counter to the conventional religious connotations of "fundamentalism" as to empty it of meaning. On the other hand, it allows for the distinct possibility that there are secular as well as religious fundamentalists, and that the distinction between them is not as obvious as it intially seems.[69] In this way, "fundamentalism" may usefully capture certain dogmatic strategies of interpretation and authorization in disputes about sacred foundations, religious and secular alike.

Projections and Refractions: Islamic Fundamentalism and Modern Rationalist Discourse

> It is not so much the ideological mobilization in the name of Islam
> to fight against those who deny our personality, our authenticity,
> to fight our historical adversary. . . . It is not so much that as it is our
> attachment to God. . . . But for you, this spiritual region remains
> voluntarily opaque. You do not want to see it. You do not want to
> look at it. . . . People do not come to Islam as an alternative for
> their social misfortunes. People come to Islam in response to a call,
> a call which goes very far and deep in the human soul. I do not
> know by which accident of history or by what misfortune "Homo
> Occidentalus," as you say, has lost this organ which permits the
> perception of things that are spiritual. . . . All that he has left are
> elements of economic, political and social analysis . . . things that
> are earthbound in some way.
>
> —Abdessalam Yassine

WHAT IS the meaning of Islamic fundamentalism? How can and should we, as Western students of politics, make sense of its growing appeal in the modern world? From modernization theory to structural-functionalism, from class analysis to rational actor theory, there are a variety of models that can be used to answer these questions. Yet such methodological diversity belies the agreement among current social scientific explanations that fundamentalism is reactive, defensive, and nativistic, its appeal a function of its efficacy as a conduit for the fury, fear, insecurity, and alienation that are the concomitants of trying socioeconomic conditions and political circumstance in the modern world.[1] Fundamentalism, so it is claimed, is epiphenomenal, and its causes are said to lie in the disenfranchisement and unfulfilled expectations that are endemic to modernization in a late-developing region, in the growth of anti-Western sentiment, in psychological insecurity and intolerance of ambiguity, in the emergence of a particular class with particularly reactionary, conservative ideological tendencies, in the failure of the leftist regimes and alien ideologies in the Middle East, and in the lack of alternative channels for political expression in the context of state repression.

Such convergence in the social scientific study of Islamic fundamentalism is not necessarily the product of considered agreement but rather the result of a historically and culturally contingent intellectual inheritance: the discourse of modern rationalism. Despite the language of science, objectivity, and universality, this discourse interprets and structures political life through the opposition of a notion of rationality to irrationality derived from distinctively Western moments in modern political and social thought. Of particular relevance here are the specific moments in which reason is celebrated as the means by which to know and thus master the world; as the opposite of the authority of religion, tradition, habit, and faith; as a category reflective of the emerging commitment to a division between the science of fact and questions of value; and moments in which the increasing scope of instrumental rationality in all aspects of human life is seen as constitutive of "modernity."[2] There are, of course, many and varied "rationalisms" in the history of Western thought, but it is through such culturally specific intellectual moments as the "progress of reason" articulated in the European Enlightenment and nineteenth-century theories of rationalization that the expansion of rationality was linked first to the advance of Western culture, then to the advance of all civilization. Importantly, in this modernization narrative,[3] the rise of rationality was itself made possible by—and subsequently reinforced—the retreat of an authoritative transcendental order from the public realm and, concomitantly, the eclipse of the epistemological, historical, and political certainties such an order was thought to have sustained. In other words, only when the divine order of things no longer held sway could rationality become a dominant force in public life. Thus rationalization became the measure and substance of modernity itself.

That said, it is worth noting that the nature and boundaries of "the modern condition" are contested even within Western culture. For example, while Reinhard Bendix calls late eighteenth-century Europe a "historical turning point," he takes great pains to point out that the modernization process during this period must be seen as the continuation of a process that began in the late fifteenth century, that is, that so-called modern elements were in evidence long before the advent of "modernity."[4] In his history of social theory, Geoffrey Hawthorn acknowledges the "distinctiveness of the European Enlightenment" in the challenge to religious faith and in the "triumph of reason" but cautions that it must be seen within the context of a gradual evolution from the medieval period to the Renaissance to the Enlightenment.[5] In political theory, the beginning of modern political thought tends to be dated from the seventeenth century, but even that is contested. Hegel thought that Hobbes marked the beginning of modern thought; Leo Strauss argues in his later works that Hobbes's political theory is notably continuous with medieval theology whereas Machiavelli's realism marks the starting point of "modernity." Yet while such historical boundaries are contested, as both an epoch and sensibility the category "modernity" apparently retains its hold upon scholars because of common features. As Falk describes it, both modernism and modernity (in Bruce Lawrence's sense)[6] are

> associated with the ascendency of reason, science, and statist forms of political organization as they emerged in Europe during the 13th to 17th centuries, culminating in the triumph of industrial capitalism in the 19th century, and, finally, complemented by the October Revolution in Russia that brought state socialism into the world. Implicit in the dynamic of modernism was its globalization by way of colonialist extension and capitalist expansion. A strong feature of modernism was its basic secularism, finding meaning in the combination of materialist and scientific developments that made knowledge the equivalent of what an earlier age had regarded as salvation.[7]

Having said this, in this chapter, I argue that explanatory models derived from modern rationalist discourse and the worldview in which it is embedded not only reflect but help constitute the meaning of the resurgence of Islamic fundamentalism. The current image of the fundamentalist phenomenon is thus in part a function of the paradox I explicated in the introductory chapter, that is, the way rationalist discursive assumptions apprehend and organize a movement grounded in the imperative of divine sovereignty and absolute truths of revelation. Ultimately, rationalist interpretations must be understood to express Western conceptions of truth, political fears, and cultural unease as much as they describe what fundamentalism "really is." As is perhaps obvious, this argument is indebted to both Edward Said's and Michel Foucault's researches into the relationship between knowledge and power.[8] Particularly germane here is Foucault's discussion of the way discourses considered to be scientific are constituted by and expressed in rules and institutions that control, produce, commandeer, and centralize knowledge, disqualifying all other sets of knowledge as "inadequate to their task or insufficiently elaborated: naive knowledges located low down on the hierarchy, beneath the required level of cognition or scientificity."[9] Thus for Said, Orientalism connotes not only a field of investigation but an exercise of power: Orientalism is part of the story of cultural hegemony, and the Orient is one of the Others against whom European culture formulated and asserted, and continues to assert, its superiority.[10] Orientalism is premised upon, in Said's words, "exteriority," for the Orientalist makes the Orient speak to a Western audience, indicating that the Orientalist is outside the Orient. In the context of radical inequalities of power, Said argues that Orientalism is in this way more revealing of the formation and presence of European-Atlantic power than as a valuable or truthful discourse about the Orient itself.[11] Understanding Orientalism as a discourse, as opposed to a field of study or an academic body of literature, captures the extent to which European culture not only managed but produced the Orient. This is so because the object of study is manufactured by, as well as reflected in, the scholarly endeavor.

Emphasizing the Western origins of rationalist discourse supports Said's point about the connection between exteriority and power: analyses embedded within Western constructs not only reflect the "facts" about the world but also produce, constitute, and control a series of images of the world. A rationalist analysis is not simply the application of nonnormative, ahistorical constructs to political phenomena but involves the translation of all culture through the filter of Western categories of knowledge. Thus, in the tradition of both Foucault and Said, my concern in this chapter is as much with the assumptions and categories that constitute the rationalist discourse as with the putative accuracy of modern rationalist theories about the world. I want to explore how such categories continue to shape and define contemporary social science scholarship about the political world, Islamic fundamentalism in particular.

More specifically, my argument is that rationalist discourse has a disciplinary effect on the study of fundamentalism: in treating it as instrumentally rational, rationalist analyses implicitly bracket the substance of fundamentalist political thought as irrelevant to properly scientific explanations. As primarily materialist accounts, such analyses both assume and reinforce an understanding of fundamentalism as epiphenomenal: they *assume* fundamentalism is a reflex reaction to certain political or socioeconomic circumstances, and in so doing they *reinforce* the neglect of a fundamentalist system of ideas as a substantive vision for the world. Put slightly differently, since Islamic fundamentalism is a convulsive reflex of the body politic, to understand it requires, not submersion in the way action is expressive of a "system of meanings," but a scientific study of correlations among urbanization, expanding education, commercialization, industrialization, and alienation that "produce" Islamic revival.[12]

> [Such approaches] go directly from source analysis to consequence analysis without ever seriously examining ideologies as systems of interacting symbols, as patterns of interworking meanings. Themes are outlined, of course. . . . But they are referred for elucidation . . . either backward to the effect they presumably mirror or forward to the social reality they presumably distort. The problem of how, after all, ideologies transform sentiment into significance and so make it socially available is short-circuited by the crude device of placing particular symbols and particular strains (or interests) side by side in such a way that the fact that the first are derivatives of the second seems mere common sense.[13]

Such accounts identify ideology and fundamentalism as "functionally equivalent" and, in so doing, express "the fundamental assumption of the social sciences that they do not have to concern themselves with the *substance* of a historical and political phenomenon, such as religion . . . but only with the *function* it plays in society."[14] The rationale of fundamentalism can be deciphered only when the meaning of fundamentalist action is abstracted from the religious faith that sustains and inspires it. The study of modern Islamic fundamentalism is thus often reduced to an examination of fundamentalist political behavior divorced from fundamentalists' own understandings of action: ideology is understood as the set of beliefs that at once obscures and expresses what are essentially structural tensions. Indeed, the very translation of religious ideas into the terminology of "ideology" points to, in its Marxist understanding, a reality behind action that must be uncovered.[15] In recasting religio-political practice as epiphenomenal, this analytic tradition thus repeatedly fails, as Lawrence puts it, "to take account of the autonomous nature of the religious impulse."[16]

I want to argue that this rationalist "functionalization" of fundamentalism paradoxically produces a more subterranean image of fundamentalism as irrational. In these explanations, fundamentalism is at one and the same time a by-product of and an atavistic reaction against modernity, and, more specifically, against the rationalization of society, economy, and politics that is the defining feature of the modernizing state. Islamic fundamentalism is caused by social change, but inasmuch as it virulently opposes that social change, it is implicitly regressive. The refuge of the antidemocratic, the frustrated, the antirational, irrational or at the very least archaic, fundamentalism thus represents the regrettable but ultimately transient birth pangs of a culture entering the modern world. In this way, social scientific explanations portray the Islamic fundamentalist as the paradigmatic irrational rational actor, that is, the actor apparently rational enough to gravitate toward an ideology that is an effective and therefore appealing vehicle for essentially pathological reactionary sentiment.[17] The subtext of this reading is that the growing appeal of fundamentalism owes little to its own inherent power as a moral ideal.[18] As Foucault has pointed out, to be irrelevant is to be shut out of the realm of what is normal and acceptable; it is to be silenced as if mad. This suggests that the categories and methods employed in these social scientific explanations do more than neglect the import of fundamentalist ideas; they actually distort them.[19] Such distortion thus sustains the impression that the content of fundamentalist ideas is "beyond the pale," outside the realm of rational discourse. As Taylor argues in the context of a very different kind of social upheaval:

> The strains in contemporary society, the breakdown of civility, the rise of deep alienation, which is translated into even more destructive action, tend to shake the basic categories of our social science. It is not just that such a development was quite unpredicted by this science, which saw in the rise of affluence the cause rather of a further entrenching of the bargaining culture, a reduction of irrational cleavage, and increase of tolerance, in short "the end of ideology." . . . It is rather that this mainstream science hasn't the categories to explain this breakdown. . . .

These can only be interpreted within the accepted framework of our social science as a return to ideology, and hence as irrational. . . . within the accepted categories this irrationality can only be understood in terms of individual psychology; it is the public eruption of private pathology: it cannot be understood as a malady of society itself, a malaise which afflicts its constitutive meanings.[20]

In the following discussion, I want to illustrate as well as argue that a number of social scientific models of explanation converge around a particular image of Islamic fundamentalism as a reactionary reflex against modernity, and the Islamic fundamentalist as an "irrational rational actor." I do not attempt to evaluate these explanations in the conventional sense of judging their accuracy or predictive capacity; here I am less interested in questions of "facticity" than in the explanatory frameworks employed.[21] This is not an attempt to discredit or discard such explanations, but rather to insist that we can begin to evaluate how and when such understandings make sense only after we have examined the contours of, and limitations inherent in, the discourse constitutive of them. Of course, one of the implications of this analysis is that judging the usefulness of such explanations is a matter not just of assessing the accuracy of supporting data but of attending to how and why the data are gathered, assembled, and interpreted to produce a particular image of fundamentalism.

In arguing that the substantive convergence in social science is a product of common methodological assumptions that, among other things, tend to emphasize the function as opposed to content of fundamentalist commitments, I conclude that "better" understandings of Islamic fundamentalism are ones that begin by attending to the inherent power of the ideas themselves and hence, the relevance of political actors' normative commitments to explanation. Such understandings do not replace the functionalization of ideas with an exclusive emphasis on the explication of meaning; indeed, such a dichotomy is itself problematic because meaning and function are dialectically and mutually determinative. Rather, I suggest that given the particular distortions at work in current explanations of Islamic fundamentalism, a dialogic model of interpretation is especially useful because it places fundamentalist ideas at the center of understanding yet insists that there is a perspective sufficiently distant from that of the participants to, first, recognize material conditions that constrain and enframe their actions, and, second, critique and evaluate their experience of the world.

THE IRRATIONAL RATIONAL ACTOR: THEORIES OF ISLAMIC FUNDAMENTALISM

First political modernization involves the rationalization of authority, [and] the replacement of a large number of traditional, religious, familial, and ethnic political authorities by a single, secular, national political authority . . . Secondly, political modernization involves the differentiation of new political functions and the development of specialized structures to perform those functions. . . . Office and power are distributed more by achievement and less by ascription. Thirdly, political modernization involves increased participation in politics by social groups throughout society. Rationalized authority, differentiated structure, and mass participation thus distinguish modern polities from antecedent polities.[22]

[Modernization is] the process by which historically evolved institutions are adapted to the rapidly changing functions that reflect the unprecedented increase in man's knowledge, permitting control over his environment, that accompanied the scientific revolution.[23]

An early interpretation of the rise of twentieth-century Islamic fundamentalism appears in *The Passing of Traditional Society*, Daniel Lerner's analysis of modernization in the Middle East. Lerner describes modernization as the "infusion of 'a rationalist and positivist spirit'" without which Middle Eastern societies are locked in an increasingly unstable paralysis born of tensions endemic to late-developing traditional societies.[24] As part of the larger attempt to explain why modernization is not proceeding properly in the Middle East, *The Passing of Traditional Society* provides an account of early fundamentalist movements as a reaction against and obstacle to the process of modernization: the problem is analyzed in terms of a Huntingtonian tension between the entrenched power of traditional patterns of governance—hierarchical, patriarchal, and patrimonial—with limited institutional capacities and the rising expectations of a "transitional" populace increasingly desirous of greater opportunities for advancement.[25] Frustrated and depressed, the overeducated, underemployed class who might have led the modernization process under more fruitful economic circumstances gravitate toward "the extremes of political action, attracted toward the instruments of propaganda, agitation and violence, by which they hope to disrupt the settled order and to speed their way toward a more satisfying way of life."[26]

The Egyptian Muslim Brotherhood, then, is just one example of the "extremist factions" that arise to capitalize on and express socioeconomic disaffection.[27] As fundamentalism is epiphenomenal, fundamentalist ideas are reduced to "ideology," which, in turn, simultaneously expresses and obscures the real source of the problem—the combined processes of modernization and disenfranchisement, and in particular rapid urbanization amidst limited resources, the spread of education amidst increasing unemployment, increased literacy within an exclusionary regime, rising expectations in a context of grim socioeconomic prospects. The appeal of Islamic fundamentalism in particular is thus understood in functionalist terms, that is, by reference to its efficacy as a channel for this material discontent; [28] yet it at the same time represents the last flare-up of archaic impulses at the very moment the culture lurches into modernity.

> The tradition of all the dead generations weighs like a nightmare on the brain of the living. And just when they seem engaged in revolutionizing themselves and things, in creating something that has never yet existed, precisely in such periods of revolutionary crisis they anxiously conjure up the spirits of the past to their service and borrow from them names, battle cries and costumes in order to present the new scene of world history in this time-honoured disguise and this borrowed language.[29]

> [Religions are] nothing more than *stages in the development of the human mind*— snake skins which have been cast off by *history*, and *man* [is] the snake who clothed himself in them.[30]

In "Islam and the Revolt of the Petit Bourgeoisie," Michael Fischer offers a class analysis of contemporary Islamic fundamentalism—or what Barrington Moore, Jr., refers to generically as the nativist response to the erosion of tradition—that echoes the image of fundamentalism in Lerner.[31] Exhorting the scholar to look below the ideological rhetoric of fundamentalism, Fischer argues that the explanation of Islamic revival can be found in the "structural problems of mass society": the combined impact of urbanization, expanded education, and the world economy on Middle Eastern politics.[32] More particularly, it is an expression of the frustrations and political inclinations of a class whose nature and identity has been crucially shaped in the cauldron of structural problems generated by the combined processes of modernization.

Unlike Lerner, Fischer is careful to acknowledge that the rise of fundamentalism is not in some sense the *necessary* by-product of certain structural conditions. "The point is not that unemployment and rising expectations necessarily feed neo-traditionalist political responses; rather these demographic and social class shifts need to be evaluated in estimating the power of interests and ideologies in Middle Eastern societies."[33] Yet despite this caution, Fischer's class analysis here suggests that the search for understanding involves penetrating the mystifications of ideology and alienated sentiment to the structural realm: "we have arrived in a complex world of ademocratic mass politics where one needs to look below the 'borrowed language and time-honoured disguises' to the structural problems of mass society."[34] Such penetration presumes that the realm of meaning and the realm of action and its causes can be disentangled for the purposes of explanation and further implies that the material world is where we will find the actual socioeconomic developments that are the key to interpreting political action.

More particularly, Fischer draws upon Ernest Gellner's description of traditional Islam as a dynamic between an urban style that tended to be scripturalist, individualist, unitarian, and puritanical, and a rural style characterized by mediation, ritual hierarchy, and devotional excess.[35] Importantly, Gellner argues, the defining feature of modernity is the ascendence of the urban style and the increase in the authority and numbers of the petite bourgeoisie, the class that embodies that style. Building upon Gellner's analysis and Pierre Bourdieu's description of the petite bourgeoisie as an insecure group of shopkeepers, clerks, teachers, and craftsmen, Fischer argues that the petite bourgeoisie is a "reservoir for conservative puritanical class status concerns," of which fundamentalism is an expression.[36] "Their aspirations are not toward European life-styles, but toward traditional Arab town-styles. The appeal of fundamentalist reformism to this class thus is both against the excesses of ecstatic and mediated rural religion, seen as internal corruption of Islam by superstition, but also against external corruption by Westernization."[37]

Already given to reactionary politics, the children of the petite bourgeoisie form a "pool of educated discontents," the product of the expansion of education within the context of limited social mobility. Moreover, the Islamic form of the activism is not only a reflection of the petite bourgeoisie's puritanical tendencies, but also of the fact that leftist opposition (Communist parties, liberal parties, any parties but the government party) is most often the first channel shut down by insecure authoritarian regimes. Hence, Islamic fundamentalism is portrayed as the ideology of a schizophrenic petite bourgeoisie that is activist by nature—that is, given to employing whatever modes of political action are available, efficacious, and appealing— and drawn toward "cultlike movements focused around charismatic leaders who provide compelling descriptions of evil."[38] Philip Khoury puts this argument even more bluntly: "For the classes sponsoring revivalism, Islam must be seen as the vehicle for political and economic demands, rather than as being itself the 'impulse' behind these demands. . . . Islam is their most convenient, readily available ideological instrument."[39]

> The significance of an action or class of them is to be understood not directly and primarily in terms of its motivation but of its actual or probable consequences for the system.[40]

The image of Islamic fundamentalism derived from both Lerner's *Passing of Traditional Society* and Fischer's "Revolt of the Petit Bourgeoisie" is echoed in a collection of explanations I group under the heading structural-functionalist, that is, explanations that find the meaning of fundamentalism by identifying its function within a particular social order.[41] Much like Lerner's modernization explanation and Fischer's class analysis, these texts offer functionalist accounts of the rise of fundamentalism, with a particular emphasis on the particularities of the Middle Eastern experience. Here, fundamentalism is understood as the instrumentally rational response to historically and culturally specific failures within the context of modernization. Fundamentalism's appeal is again interpreted through its function, but its function is embedded in the details of Middle Eastern politics: it is the most efficient vehicle to register the reactionary frustration and fury generated by the failure of leftist regimes to confront and solve the socioeconomic problems of the modern(izing) Middle East.

For example, in Emmanuel Sivan's *Radical Islam*, Islamic fundamentalism is understood as a reaction against modernity, a backlash fueled by the failures of a series of regimes—liberal, socialist, nationalist—to cope with the social and economic difficulties facing a number of Middle Eastern nations in the contemporary world. *Radical Islam* is primarily a history of ideas, but Sivan also advances a causal explanation that frames his analysis of ideas: the strength of Islamic fundamentalism is interpreted, at least in part, as a reflection of the failure of leftist intellectuals and progressive regimes to offer a successful and timely alternative to the fundamentalists' particularly powerful recipe. As Sivan puts it, the combination of political and cultural protest—where the agenda for structural change is couched in the terms and concepts of Islam—enables fundamentalists to tap into the deep familiarity of traditional Islamic beliefs.[42] Given that leftists were steeped in the foreign languages of Marxism, socialism, and liberalism, the contrast between their discourse and that of the fundamentalists became increasingly stark to postcolonial Middle Eastern Islamic societies, still embittered by the 1967 Arab defeat by Israel. Since then, the language of Islamic politics has set the terms of the debate, and the ranks of the fundamentalist groups have swelled in numbers.

This interpretation also appears in a series of influential articles published in the *International Journal of Middle Eastern Studies* in the 1980s. Nazih Ayubi, for example, argues that Islamic movements are an indigenous reaction to a succession of failures by regimes embracing such "alien" theories of community as nationalism, liberalism, socialism, and Marxism. Islamic fundamentalism's appeal, then, is partially a function of its status as an indigenous ideology and partially a product of the fact that there are no alternatives available to register political demands.[43] Likewise, Hamied Ansari argues that fundamentalism "is an angry statement directed mainly against the ruling authority for its apparent failure to ameliorate the social and economic conditions under which they live." It is the refuge of those (primarily the lower middle class) who feel deprived; "the resort to Islam [is] more a sign of protest than a way of life."[44] To these three factors—failures of leftist regimes, unavailability of alternative political channels, Islam as an "indigenous ideology"— Saad Eddin Ibrahim adds a fourth: "the Islamic group fulfills a de-alienating function for its members in ways that are not matched by other rival political movements."[45] Much scholarship on Islamic fundamentalism since these analyses echoes or develops these basic arguments, as does a substantial amount of media coverage.[46]

Once again, Islamic fundamentalism is explained by reference to causes external to the intrinsic appeal of the ideas themselves: fundamentalism is still regarded as a by-product of social change. Furthermore, despite the language of and emphasis on "local" circumstances, these explanations remain parasitic on the paradigm of modernization where the combined processes of urbanization, expanded education, and industrialization challenge regimes unable to adapt and cope. Ibrahim rightly notes the reductionism in modernization theories that implicitly regard Islam as the opposite of secularism, science, and technology. But in these explanations, the causes of Islamic resurgence remain located in the combination of modernization processes and state failures. In part, it is with this paradigm in mind that Sivan repeatedly calls Islamic revival "antimodernist,"[47] and Ansari suggests that the rise of Islamic militancy is the "product of circumstances closely associated with rapid urbanization and rural migration into the cities."[48] Thus, this is less a departure from modernization per se than an attempt to refine and particularize it with data regarding the impact of socioeconomic processes within a specific cultural and political context. As Ibrahim states: "Nothing can guard against such overreactions more than careful in-depth observation of the indigenous scenes. Specificities and local particularities have to be identified and correlated with the alleged Islamic revival. No matter how great the temptation to generalize, such scientific quests must be checked until sufficient numbers of case particulars have been documented and analyzed. Only then will inductively based generalizations make sense."[49]

> I have come to the position that the economic approach is a comprehensive one that is applicable to all human behavior, be it behavior involving money prices or imputed shadow prices, repeated or infrequent decisions, large or minor decisions, emotional or mechanical ends, rich or poor persons, men or women, adults or children, brilliant or stupid persons, patients or therapists, businessmen or politicians, teachers or students . . . all human behavior can be viewed as involving participants who maximize their utility from a stable set of preferences and accumulate an optimal amount of information and other inputs in a variety of markets.[50]

Although rational actor theory has only recently begun to focus on religious action, and fundamentalist action in particular, its ambition to explain all political action, regardless of cultural specificity, makes it a model worth inclusion here.[51] There are now several different accounts of the key assumptions that define "pure" rational actor theory, but for the purposes of argument let me begin with Becker.[52] Becker's assumption is that people engage in maximizing behavior, and that there are "markets that with varying degrees of efficiency coordinate the actions of different participants . . . so that their behavior becomes mutually consistent," and that preferences are stable.[53] Kristen Monroe usefully breaks these down into seven assumptions: (1) actors pursue goals; (2) these goals reflect the actor's perceived self-interest; (3) behavior results from conscious choice; (4) the individual is the basic unit of analysis; (5) actors have preference orderings that are consistent and stable; (6) if given options, actors choose the alternative with the highest expected utility; (7) actors possess extensive information on both the available alternatives and the likely consequences of their choices.[54] Once these universal psychological assumptions are established, the rational actor analysis of Islamic fundamentalism is a matter of filling in the blanks. Fundamentalists' goals can be understood in terms of a need for belonging, or for security, for example, and hence membership itself can be conceived of as a self-interested goal.[55] Unlike the materialist and functionalist explanations previously discussed, rational actor theory explains the growth of fundamentalism by reference to its intrinsic appeal, but once again such appeal is understood not in terms of the moral power of fundamentalist worldviews but because of the "advantages they seem to bestow on people regardless of their moral outlook, or even whether they have a moral outlook."[56] Thus, for example, if fundamentalists conceive of martyrdom as the price of salvation, even self-sacrifice can be construed as an expression of rational, self-interested behavior.

Amartya Sen notes that this model makes it possible to "define a person's interests in such a way that no matter what he does he can be seen to be furthering his own interests in every isolated act of choice."[57] Thus as rational behavior is construed in terms of acting to achieve a desired end, the model insists that if fundamentalist action results in efficient fulfillment of the actor's intended goals, it is rational. As Wilcox argues in his study of support for the Christian Right in America, "citizens who are motivated to support Christian Right groups are those who find the religious and political values and positions expressed by the groups congruent with their own . . . citizens are supporting groups that espouse their values and beliefs."[58] Outside the purview of the rational actor model are crucial features of fundamentalism—for example, the role of divine authority in all aspects of human life, the importance of emotion and intuition for religious devotion, the ways in which divine omnipotence is understood *in terms of* the limits of human comprehension. What is thus perhaps most peculiar about the rational actor model is the insistence that all behavior can be explained simply by recasting each action as an instance of rational behavior "properly understood," that is, intelligible to market logic. For as Diesing rightly notes,

"Salvation is a definite end, so it can have means and a technique of achievement; but it is not alternative to any other end. It is priceless. The technical question, 'What must I do to be saved?' makes sense and can be answered; but the economic question 'How much is salvation worth to you?' does not."[59]

Much of the rational actor literature pertaining to religion is concerned with such issues as time allocation in religious participation, the calculus by which consumers choose one religion over another, and fundamentalists' economic positions. Those who do take up the question of religious participation in general, however, tend to bypass any interpretive accounts of participants' behavior in favor of ascribed needs and benefits that render such behavior intelligible to market logic. For example, Azzi and Ehrenberg argue that religious participation is related to an "afterlife consumption" motive. Iannaconne briefly suggests that religious commodities include assurance and security. Michael Hechter argues that intentional communities (groups such as communes or religious sects that are bound by shared commitments rather than kinship or marriage) seek a strictly enforced solidarity as "insurance against the vagaries of nature and human relations."[60] These examples seem to substantiate Monroe's suggestion that the logic of rational actor theory tends to portray fundamentalists as "risk-averse" and too immature and unintelligent to cope with the stresses and strains of modernization and secularization.[61] Taken together, such analyses suggest that religious participation in general, and fundamentalism by extension, fulfills a need to belong, a need to escape the press of difficult lives, or a need to relieve the stress and uncertainty of modern life.[62] Such references to religion as provider of consolation and escape amid conditions of insecurity and misery hearken back to Adam Smith's account of that "melancholy and gloomy humour which is almost always the nurse of popular superstition and enthusiasm":

> as soon as [the villager] comes into a great city, he is sunk in obscurity and darkness. His conduct is observed and attended to by nobody, and he is therefore very likely to neglect it himself, and to abandon himself to every sort of low profligacy and vice. He never emerges so effectually from this obscurity, his conduct never excites so much the attention of any respectable society, as by his becoming the member of a small religious sect. He from that moment acquires a degree of consideration which he never had before.[63]

It is important to note that these particular explanations inject a certain substantive content into the utility that agents are maximizing and thus exceed the austere formalism of what could be called pure revealed preference theory.[64] However, the revealed preference argument that "fundamentalists must get something out of fundamentalism or else they would not be fundamentalists" is a tautology.[65] How do we know that fundamentalists have a preference for fundamentalism? They have revealed it by becoming fundamentalists. As Steve Bruce points out, if utility is a matter of social construction, it is "construed in very different ways by different people. . . . We have no way of identifying costs or reward except through the responses of those who make the choices, which is circular, because it is precisely those choices we wish to explain."[66] Thus even the most austere version of rational actor theory has very little to say about fundamentalism because, given its basic assumptions, it concludes only that fundamentalists have a revealed preference for fundamentalism. The more substantive rational actor interpretations surveyed here, however, entail the analytic marginalization of fundamentalist ideas: the only relevant information is those aspects of the fundamentalist's so-called character—such as insecurity, immaturity, or intolerance of risk—that render fundamentalist membership and behavior intelligible to market logic. In these instances, rational actor theory begins and ends with an image of Islamic fundamentalism as the refuge of the disenfranchised, those unable to cope with the challenges and insecurity of modern life. While fundamentalist action may be understood as instrumentally rational, its appeal is nevertheless rendered as a function of psychological insecurity, strain, or perceived deprivation.

For many, the convergence of these social scientific models around a common explanation of Islamic fundamentalism is itself confirmation of its accuracy and objectivity. But I have suggested that the image of Islamic fundamentalism as a conduit for an antimodern backlash is parasitic upon a paradigm of rationalization where modernity is defined both by the ascension of rational forms of organization in politics, economy, and society, and in opposition to what Huntington called "antecedent polities," that is, those polities in which tradition, faith, kin, and clan hold sway. Such a paradigm is not merely reflective of fact but also the product of a culturally constructed discourse about the nature and function of rationality in modern Western thought. Many Enlightenment philosophers, Marx, and Weber are crucial, abeit paradoxical figures in the development of this paradigm, for it is from their formulations of reason and theories of rationalization that the crucial features of the modern rationalist discourse have been carved.[67]

The scholarship on just the period of the Enlightenment is voluminous, full of complex and detailed debates, yet it is clear that rationalist philosophers of the Enlightenment were crucial to the development of the epistemological and methodological claim that reason is both the means by which we come to know and master the world, and that facts about and actions in the world are legitimate because they are rational. Here, then, are the outlines of a worldview in which the scientific, political, economic, and philosophical advances associated with the ascension of reason in Western thought come to constitute the very meaning of modernity. Moreover, since "reason is . . . only a phenomenon whose very existence requires its opposite to define itself against," it is also built upon a particular construction of the "irrational" against which it defines its own hegemonic significance.[68] Thus embedded in the Enlightenment's (re-)definition and elevation of reason is the creation and subjection of an irrational counterpart: along with the emergence of reason as both the instrument and essence of human achievement, the irrational came to be defined primarily in opposition to what such thinkers saw as the truths of their own distinctive historical epoch. If they were the voices of modernity, freedom, liberation, happiness, reason, nobility, and even natural passion,[69] the irrational was all that came before: tyranny, servility to dogma, self-abnegation, superstition, and false religion.[70] Thus the irrational came to mean the domination of religion in the historical period that preceded it. No longer merely descriptive, through these Enlightenment thinkers' conscious construction of their own endeavor, historical epochs became linked to the evaluative categories of rationalism; the development of reason was grafted onto the course of history. Put another way, the course of history was reinterpreted as the development of reason. The Western evolution from feudal and ecclesiastical domination to rational modernity was no longer a matter of mere historical interest: here Western history has become the paradigmatic case of modernization, the beacon that "shows to the less developed the image of its own future."[71]

In Marx and Weber the linkage of modernization and rationalization finds even fuller expression, for although both Marx and Weber attend to the costs and contradictions of rationalization, aspects of their work and interpretations thereof[72] have functioned within Western thought to sustain the assumptions that "modern rationality" is defined in terms of the erosion of religious and traditional models of meaning, identity, and authority, and that the movement from the "traditional" to the "rational" defines not just the advancement of Western history, but the entry of all cultures into the modern world.[73]

For example, while Marx's work is in many ways a critique of the Enlightenment,[74] Marx took the Enlightenment's philosophy of history to its logical conclusion by reading Western history through progressive stages in the relations of production, and thereby locating capitalist countries in an advanced position on a teleological spectrum of development, a spectrum that placed—by virtue of more primitive relations of production—the rest of the world behind.[75] In this way, Condorcet's intuition that "savage nations" presented no permanent barrier to progress could be empirically grounded through a firm grasp of the history of the relations of production.[76] Moreover, as Arendt argues, Marx's conviction that "political action was primarily violence and that violence was the midwife of history" meant that scientists would do best to study productive activity and set aside "what each period says about itself and imagines it is."[77] In the work of Marx, "the father of the social science methods," aspects of culture such as religion are thus transformed into just so many ideologies whose mystifications obscure the real motor of history.[78]

Similarly, although Weber regarded the process of rationalization with a pessimism that suggests modernity may be as much a curse as a blessing, his theory of rationalization has sustained a picture of modernization as "disenchantment," the progression from a world dominated by tradition and "magic" to one characterized by the ever increasing dominance of instrumental reason.[79] Here the demise of a transcendent order of things from which to derive the standards and criteria for establishing truth and judging value transforms reason from a means to uncover unassailable truths about the world to a technique in the service of mastery. For Weberian "disenchantment" at once entails the disappearance of magic and the sacramental forces that had previously given much of the world its meaning and the rise of a capitalist cosmology where all questions of meaning can find their answer only in the purposive, organized, and logical force of efficiency, elevated to a cultural value.

This is not to suggest that these rationalist assumptions are in some sense "caused" by these theorists. Nor do I wish to imply, for example, that since Marx and Weber theorized extensively about rationalization in history, they are "rationalists." My purpose here is delimited by the arguments of this chapter: to underscore the precedents that betray the historically contingent and accidental origins of modern rationalist assumptions and, in so doing, to problematize the image of Islamic fundamentalism produced by social science models parasitic upon them. For as Foucault argues in his discussion of genealogy, the secret of history is not an uncovering of timeless, transcendental origins, but rather the discovery that "they have not essence or that their essence was fabricated in a piecemeal fashion from alien forms." As truth is historically constructed rather than metaphysically grounded, it entails an excavation not of (traditionally) historical "facts" but of discursive assumptions.[80] Just so, the discursive assumptions of modern rationalism coalesce in and through the particular moments in European thought I have so briefly sketched: "Western" becomes firmly linked to "modern" and "rational"; such linkages come to be constructed upon the subterranean but no less powerful definition of the "irrational" in terms of nonrational sources of knowledge such as habit, tradition, faith, unexamined thought, and religious authority; rationalism emerges as a technique of means and mastery rather than arbiter of values and ends; and the association of history and rationality is abstracted from its Western cultural context such that rationalization is no longer merely an account of Western history, but a scientific standard by which to measure and evaluate the past, present, and future of developing countries.

MEANING AND POWER: A DIALOGIC MODEL OF INTERPRETATION

Given the limits of rationalist explanations analyzed above, a dialogic model of interpretation may be usefully employed to generate a "better" understanding of fundamentalism. In referring to a dialogic model of interpretation, I invoke a tradition that traverses a vast amount of literature and many debates that are beyond the scope of this work; here I draw on debates within and about hermeneutics, a tradition that, in its modern formulation, has been influenced largely by the work of Martin Heidegger and Hans-Georg Gadamer but has been elaborated in a variety of disciplines by a variety of scholars.[81] As set out by Gadamer in *Truth and Method*, the dialogic model of understanding starts with the premise that language—or "linguisticality"—is the basic mode of human existence. Thus an interpreter sees all objects of interpretation from within the horizon of her own worldview, her own beliefs, norms, and practices.[82] As a result, Gadamer argues, it is illusory to posit a neutral observer over against a set of linguistically unmediated things-in-themselves: "We cannot see a linguistic world from above in this way, for there is no point of view outside the experience of the world in language from which it could become an object."[83] Abandoning the notion of the neutral observer is simultaneously an abandonment of a positivist epistemology that sustains a conception of understanding as discovering the objective and final truth. Instead, understanding comes to be seen as a dialogue between two horizons of meaning, neither of which can claim a monopoly on truth. And "[i]f interpretation is always a hermeneutic mediation between different-life worlds and if the hermeneutic 'initial situation' is itself caught up in the movement of history, the notion of a final valid interpretation makes no sense."[84]

Importantly, if understanding emerges in the context of certain transforming and transformative discursive practices, the substance of the conversation cannot be evaluated independently of the dialogic structure. The conditions of dialogue—the participants, the traditions of which they are a part, the prejudices they bring to the conversation—are actually constitutive of the range of claims that are advanced and mediated. Understanding is thus not a matter of seeing things-in-themselves from a neutral vantage point, but a "fusion of horizons": "All understanding is interpretation, and all interpretation takes place in the medium of a language that allows the object to come into words and yet is at the same time the interpreter's own language."[85] For Gadamer, the hermeneutic orientation is that of a partner in dialogue with others in the past and present, a stance that assumes that we have no monopoly on truth and concomitantly enjoins an openness to other meanings.

> [A] person trying to understand a text is prepared for it to tell him something. That is why a hermeneutically trained consciousness must be, from the start, sensitive to the text's alterity [otherness]. But this kind of sensitivity involves neither "neutrality" with respect to content nor the extinction of one's self, but the foregrounding and appropriation of one's own fore-meanings and prejudices. The important thing is to be aware of one's own bias, so that the text can present itself in all its otherness and thus assert its own truth against one's own fore-meanings.[86]

Thus understanding emerges from a dialogue in which participants attempt to cross divides of meaning by acknowledging and appropriating their own prejudices within a language that evolves to accommodate and ultimately transform disparate understandings into mutually intelligible meanings. As Fred Dallmayr aptly puts it, such dialogue "does not mean the enactment of a ready-made consensus (the subsumption of particulars under a universalist umbrella) nor the conduct of random chatter. . . . [D]ialogical exchange has an 'agonal' or tensional quality which cannot be fully stabilized; as a corollary to self-exposure, it requires a willingness to 'risk oneself,' that is, to plunge headlong into a transformative process in which the status of self and other are continuously renegotiated."[87] Such a reciprocal and transformative enterprise is meant to displace the notion of cultural practices as irretrievably locked away into hermetically sealed boxes of meaning, while at the same time challenging the possibility that there is a transcendent position from which to see the one-to-one correspondence of truth to "linguistically naked" facts in the world. Learning from others means learning not only from the past and present, but being open to future interpretations that may benefit from experiences and observations not yet available to present understandings. This underlies the notion of the "inexhaustibility" of the meaning of texts, and the challenge to the possibility of an objectively valid interpretation.

However, debunking the monopoly of truth implicit in positivist epistemology is not the same as saying that all meaning is subjective and relative: "Being bound by a situation does not mean that the claim to correctness that every interpretation must make is dissolved into the subjective or the occasional. . . . Thanks to the verbal nature of all interpretation, every interpretation includes the possibility of a relationship with others."[88] The very structure of language itself contains the possibility of understanding what is foreign. As Habermas puts it, "we are never locked within a single grammar. . . . Rather, the first grammar that we learn to master already puts us in a position to step out of it and to interpret what is foreign, to make comprehensive what initially is incomprehensible, to assimilate in our own words what at first escapes them."[89] In this way Gadamer's insistence that language contains the possibility of mutual understanding challenges relativism in its strong form, that is, the insistence on the closedness of linguistic worldviews such that the intersubjective meaning that potentially grounds judgment across cultures is a contradiction in terms.

However, as Jürgen Habermas points out in his debate with Gadamer, a purely dialogic model of understanding is limited. For while Habermas is critical of positivism, he also suggests that Gadamer's model of understanding reduces social inquiry to a dialogic explication of meaning, a process inattentive to the ways in which language can distort and conceal as well as express the social, political, and economic conditions of life. Habermas argues that there are social processes such as labor and power that, while linguistically structured, are not exhausted by their symbolically transmitted meaning. That this is so is clear from the way that a change in the mode of production is, for example, not only the result of a new interpretation or a different way of seeing things but also entails a "restructuring of the linguistic worldview" itself.[90] Language is the medium of all social interaction, but Habermas argues that it is also a medium of domination and social power. As such, language can be seen in relation to—as well as constitutive of—social processes "not reducible to normative relationships."[91] Thus the linguisticality of social interaction is not incompatible with the notion of actual and real social processes that, while linguistically structured and symbolically transmitted, nevertheless act upon social life.[92] The empirical sciences, for example, "simply do not represent an arbitrary language game. . . . Through them the factual constraints of the natural conditions of life impinge on society."[93]

Along with Gadamer, then, Habermas's emphasis on language serves to critique positivist models of social science inattentive to language as the medium of all social interaction. But Habermas's discussion of labor and domination as well as linguisticality serves as a corrective to Gadamer's almost exclusive emphasis on social inquiry as explication of meaning. That is, Gadamer advances a weak form of relativism, not by insisting that cultures cannot speak to one another, but by describing understanding as a process entirely constituted by linguistic accommodation and mediation such that there is no space for critique. Habermas's corrective to Gadamer's hermeneutical project, however, shows how a dialogic model of interpretation can attend to actors' self-understandings without requiring that the interpreter abandon a perspective that makes both evaluation and critique possible. Against the objection that Gadamer's model of interpretation endangers the possibility of objectivity, Habermas's critique thus shows that the dialogic model does not endanger objectivity per se. Rather it challenges a particular standard of objectivity, a positivist conception derived from a model of the natural sciences whereby truth is a matter of one-to-one correspondence to facts.

It is beyond the purview of this work to delve into the intricacies of these epistemological debates about objectivity in the philosophy of social science. For my purposes it is perhaps sufficient to point out that this redefinition of objectivity is necessary because objects of the social sciences differ in methodologically significant ways from those in the natural sciences. A positivist philosophy of science takes the natural sciences as its "methodological ideal or standard"[94] and thus presupposes an essentially Hobbesian ontology of self and society, one where human beings are fixed objects in nature and society is constituted by them.[95] But since man is a "self-interpreting animal"[96] capable of both intentional action and transformation, such a positivist understanding misses the essentially social nature of human beings, and the ways in which society is in part constituted by shared meanings. This is not to say, as some have argued Gadamer implies, that objects are reducible to socially constituted meanings. It is to say that social inquiry modeled on the natural sciences is inadequate because it is insufficiently attentive to the fact that human beings, while objects in nature, are not only objects in nature.

According to the dialogic model of understanding as corrected by Habermas, adequate explanations thus require an interpretive approach because "the elements constitutive of an individual's self-understandings are *identified and understood* in terms of a socially shared language and therefore in terms of intersubjective (not simply subjective) meanings."[97] Such hermeneutically informed explanations do not therefore abandon a standard of objectivity but rather take on an additional criterion for adequacy. This additional criterion is the imagined reconstruction of what the subjects of the interpretation would themselves say in response.[98] The standard employed is not one-to-one correspondence between postulated knowledges and objects as facts, the positivist idea of a correspondence between interpretation and "linguistically naked" things-in-themselves.[99] Rather it is a standard of compatibility between the explanation of the interpreter and the understandings of participants. It is what Alfred Schutz refers to as the "postulate of adequacy":

> Each term used in a scientific system referring to human action must be so constructed that a human act performed within the life-world by an individual actor in the way indicated by the typical construction would be reasonable and understandable for the actor himself, as well as for his fellow-men. This postulate is of extreme importance for the methodology of social science. What makes it possible for a social science to refer at all to events in the life-world is the fact that the interpretation of any human act by the social scientist might be the same as that by the actor or by his partner.[100]

Such a criterion for adequacy of interpretation and explanation of course raises an additional problem, the objection that such a model is so committed to the participants' account of events that they are given the last word in explanation. Thus the remaining problem with this approach is not, as some critics would have it, that it produces merely subjective meanings. On the contrary, since they are shared, such meanings are in fact intersubjective. Rather the problem is that if the interpretation remains locked within the participants' perspective, no one else can challenge the meanings they have agreed upon. Without the possibility of distance from the participants' own meanings, there is no room for critique, no perspective from which to analyze the function of power in language, or to acknowledge what is repressed and concealed in communication.[101]

However, if we take seriously Habermas's argument that language is the medium not only of cultural meaning but also of power and labor, we are driven to a perspective distant from, but not outside of, the realm of language. That is, recognizing the way language not only constitutes but is constituted by material conditions suggests that we require a perspective distant enough from tradition—yet never fully outside of it—from which to study and critique those relationships. In the context of the Habermas-Gadamer debate, this argument is advanced in abstract and metatheoretical language, but it has practical implications for the task of interpretation. It means that while an interpretation must be hermeneutically informed, we also require a perspective sufficiently distant from shared meanings that we may attend not only to what is in any one interpretation, but also to what has been subjugated, distorted, or concealed by it. In this way, we leave open the distinct possibility that even the participants may at times misunderstand or misrepresent their own experiences.

Habermas's own attempts to address such questions are not unproblematic.[102] However, Habermas is useful here in the way his emphasis on the role of distortion, or violence in communication, underscores "the need for an objectivating "outsider's" perspective to get beyond shared, unproblematic meanings and their hermeneutic retrieval."[103] It signals in some sense what we already know, that is, that what we require is a kind of distance from the social practices we study, or in which we are engaged. Such distance enables an outsider's perspective that is in history but detached from it. It thus depends upon a distinction between the positivist notion of objectivity that presupposes a position outside of power and language from which to see the truth "unfettered," and a conception of distance more like impartiality than neutrality. As Arendt puts it:

> As distinguished from this "objectivity," whose only basis is money as a common denominator for the fulfillment of all needs, the reality of the public realm relies on the simultaneous presence of innumerable perspectives and aspects in which the common world presents itself and for which no common measurement or denominator can ever be devised. . . . Being seen and being heard by others derive their significance from the fact that everybody sees and hears from a different

position. This is the meaning of public life, compared to which even the richest and most satisfying family life can offer only the prolongation or multiplication of one's own position with its attending aspects and perspectives. The subjectivity of privacy can be prolonged and multiplied in a family, it can even become so strong that its weight is felt in the public realm; but this family "world" can never replace the reality rising out of the sum total of aspects presented by one object to a multitude of spectators. Only where things can be seen by many in a variety of aspects without changing their identity, so that those who are gathered around them know they see sameness in utter diversity, can worldly reality truly and reliably appear.[104]

Arendt here shows how distance is created by way of a kind of shifting impartiality derived from the move across and among various viewpoints. This notion of shifting impartiality rather than positivist neutrality provides space to entertain the possibility that the participants can misunderstand or misrepresent aspects of their own behavior. As actors often disagree among themselves about meanings, the interpreter thus assumes the stance of a partner in learning. The interpreter can disagree with the participants, not as a neutral, scientific observer, but as a participant in an evolving and hypothetical discussion.

Despite Habermas's insistence on attending to the role of power in the explication of meaning, the question remains: who, ultimately, has the power to determine the amount of distortion in dialogue? As I have argued, in a postcolonial world these "dialogues" across cultures often take place under conditions of radical inequality, for example, between "center" and "periphery," that is, within a system of international capitalism where accumulation at the center impoverishes the periphery. Moreover, as Pheng Cheah notes, uneven neocolonial globalization, that is, the "uneven accumulation of capital and distribution of wealth and resources on a global scale exacerbates the unequal distribution of political power and economic resources within decolonised countries. At the same time, globalization is accompanied by the spread of a political culture that historically emerged in the West: human rights, women's rights, equality, democratization, and so on."[105] Thus despite the fact that radically different peoples have been subjected to similar socioeconomic processes, modernization and now globalization often confront postcolonial and/or "peripheral" nations not with greater parity but rather with a more deeply entrenched inequality: as Marshall Hodgson puts it, it is not that colonialism has transformed a "pristine precolonial order" but rather that as modernization (and, I would add, globalization) proceeds, Muslims must build "not from economic and social advantages based on yet earlier advantages, but rather from disadvantages based on yet earlier disadvantages."[106] Such inequalities, in all their dimensions, "enframe" the arguments of participants in the conversation and work to authorize some experiences and arguments while disqualifying others.[107] This points to the difficulties of diminishing distortion even in a dialogic model of understanding, for cross-cultural conversation alone cannot produce genuine compromise without attending to the cultural, economic, and political inequalities that shape the conditions and terms of the dialogue.

Nevertheless, it is my contention that as we cannot escape the hermeneutic circle, the dialogic model recommends itself not because it is invulnerable to distortions of power but less susceptible to them than the social scientific models parasitic on rationalist discourse I have analyzed here. For in attending to socially mediated understandings, this approach remains permanently open to awareness of the inequality of participants in dialogue in a postcolonial world and, concomitantly, to the inevitable implication of power, and lack of power, in interpretation. If it is imperative to seek understanding, and to seek the best understanding possible, we are, paradoxically perhaps, best served by methods attentive to the finitude of our capacity to understand complex matrixes of meaning in part constituted by systemic inequalities of power.

Toward an Understanding of Islamic Fundamentalism

This brief discussion suggests that to understand Islamic fundamentalism we must begin with an interpretive account of the power of fundamentalist thought rather than with categories outside the fundamentalist worldview that marginalize fundamentalists' own ideas about the movement's meaning and purpose. As I have argued, without such an account, imposed meanings are privileged by default: meaning is derived from function, and function is enframed by and deduced from Western analytic categories inattentive to cultural and historical difference. Indeed, I have suggested the ways in which modern rationalist discourse is carved from the West's dialogue with its own past, a dialogue in which the very meanings of "modernity" and "modernization" were defined against a prior age characterized by the centrality of God, religious authority, and tradition. In the attempt to compass the world of Islamic fundamentalism, then, approaches embedded in this rationalist tradition are shaped and constrained by the assumptions of the discourse, assumptions constituted by culturally specific experiences concealed by claims to universality. The image of fundamentalism produced by them may thus yield an understanding of Western conceptions of truth, modernity, political fears, and cultural unease as much as they capture what fundamentalism "really is."

If this image says as much about Western discourse and methods of interpretation as it does about Islamic fundamentalism, what, exactly, is it saying? In part, it is evidence that modern Western rationalist discourse continues both to frame and to create our notions not only of ourselves, but also of the world around us. In Said's language, it elaborates a dimension of cultural power. As Said claims about Orientalism, "it not only creates but also maintains; it *is*, rather than expresses, a certain *will* or *intention* to understand, in some cases to control, manipulate, even to incorporate, what is a manifestly different world" (emphasis in the original).[108] In part, then, current scholarship on fundamentalism is an exercise in power: the power to construct and control a subject that has little opportunity to contest either the interpretation or the terms of the discourse; the power to dictate the parameters of the field, from which experts regularly pronounce the identity, meaning, and function of a movement without reference to the adherents' own understanding of the connection between action and meaning. It is not that any one scholar expresses such an intention but rather that, in the very attempt to understand fundamentalism, authors embedded in the rationalist tradition I have described cannot but construct fundamentalism according to the assumptions of the discourse.

But this image is more than an exercise in the power of a Western discourse to define its subject, the fundamentalist "Other." Indeed, to suggest that rationalist analyses are an exercise in power is to repeat what has become a staple of scholarship at least since Foucault. The question of power turns on a prior question regarding impetus: What drives the will to construct Islamic fundamentalism along these lines? And what is it about Islamic fundamentalism, in particular, that evokes these kinds of analyses? In part, such constructions enable the Western rationalist narrative to survive, for much as "European culture gained in strength and identity by setting itself off against the Orient as a sort of surrogate and even underground self," within rationalist discourse, Islamic fundamentalism serves as the irrational Other to our intelligible Self.[109] Bigo suggests that the persistence of such binary oppositions in a post–Cold War multipolar world in particular expresses the need to have an enemy against which we can define our national identity, and originates in "a struggle between experts in the security field who try to impose their argumentation and classification as the real theoretical framework, the only possible view of the world being in terms of 'who scares us.' "[110] Bigo continues: "In any case, it is neither an explanatory principle nor even a description *but a process of adjustment of actors in the security field facing changes that they have difficulty admitting.* It provides them with a justification against peripheral critics and permits them to reconvert the techniques used in East/West relations for use in North/South relations"[111] (emphasis in the original). As Aziz al-Azmeh points out, in its politicized forms, Islam "is constituted within a polarized system of binary classification in which 'the West' is taken as a normative meta-language from which are generated, by negation, the tokens that together constitute the properties of 'Islam': fanaticism, irrationalist traditionalism, atemporality, and their many metonyms, each betokened by common images, such as crowds, the veil, postures of prayer, and so forth." [112] Thus rationalist dichotomies function in part to generate a sense of vast distance between "us" and the "irrational Other"—whether it is the "East," "Islam," or "fundamentalism"—thus furnishing an irrational counterpart to our rational self-image.

In this view, fundamentalism is a vehicle for reactionary, fanatical sentiment, which, given slightly different historical and political circumstances, might just as easily express itself in Marxism, or any other ideology similarly equipped to register the cry of the extremist. [113] It may be that fundamentalists would surely "believe and behave as we do, if only they were as mature and enlightened as we are," [114] but as they are "antidemocratic," "antimodern," "cultlike," "nativist," "fearful," "reactionary," "totalitarian," "insecure," "angry," and most of all, increasingly powerful, they are, at a minimum, extremely threatening. As I argued in the introductory chapter, the fears of such a threat are played out in images of fundamentalism as the "green peril," the new modern scourge of "global democracy" replacing the "red menace," a danger rivaled only by that of other resurgent particularisms such as ethnic nationalism. [115] It is not the case that religious inspiration is anathema to modern Western political life; on the contrary, religious commitments are often operative in and through the politics of particular actors. Yet, in its most explicit registers, post-Enlightenment thought defines modern politics in terms of a public realm that is or should be (at least formally) animated either by apparently objective socioeconomic interests or secular ideals, or both; by contrast the very definition of irrationalism is historically and culturally linked with the authority of religion, faith, and tradition. [116] The attempt to remake the public realm in terms of religious imperatives, to (re-)define the boundary between public and private, to (re-)interpret the collective good in terms of a divine mandate comes to seem no less than an attempt to destroy the foundations of modern politics itself. Islamic fundamentalism thus becomes the repository of many modern, Western anxieties about the religious, the irrational, the foundationalist in modern political life, a projection of both old ambivalences in Western thought and new fears about the growing power of such practices in "the heart" of the West, whether it is the religious Right in American politics or the resurgence of ethnic nationalisms in post–Cold War Europe. Fundamentalism has in many ways become a negative mirror reflecting back on Western life that which it would leave behind; it signifies the resurgence of the irrational in what much of Western culture has come to regard as the age of rationalization.

By contrast, I have suggested that a dialogic model of understanding may lend greater insight into the power and appeal of Islamic fundamentalism. Importantly, the interpretation central to such an approach cannot claim to be the only and finally objective account; yet the dialogic model provides criteria that make it possible to differentiate between "better" and "worse" interpretations. "Better" interpretations are those that approach the subject as one would a dialogue, an orientation that presupposes the possibility of a reciprocal and transformative "fusion of horizons" and thus carves out an analytic space for the voices of the fundamentalists themselves. "Better" interpretations do not aim at arriving at the final, objective (in the positivist sense) truth of the matter but rather are those that are at one and the same time aware of their own conditionality and are open to the distortions occasioned by conditions of radical inequality in the postcolonial world. "Better" interpretations are readings in which the subject might recognize himself or herself, his or her meanings, his or her actions, and might even agree. And "better" interpretations are those that are simultaneously attentive to participants' self-understandings and to the way power functions in language, that is, interpretations that make central the explication of the subjects' meanings without concluding that there is no perspective adequately distant from them from which to criticize the actors' account of their own experience.

Moreover, it is plausible to argue that such understandings must be central not only to an interpretation of the meaning of fundamentalist ideas but also to causally adequate explanations of the increasing strength of Islamic fundamentalism. This argument does not require that we relinquish standards of objectivity, nor does it negate the possibility that participants' have themselves misunderstood their own experiences. A model of dialogic understanding assumes, not that all interpretations are equal, but that interpretation is a reciprocal, transformative, and, perhaps above all, ongoing process. In other words, the idea of the "inexhaustibility" of the meaning of texts does not signal a rejection of all criteria by which to evaluate interpretations but rather an abandonment of a positivist criterion in particular, that is, standards of "right" and "wrong" that implicitly or explicitly presuppose a relationship to truths accessible only by standing outside of historical or cultural contexts.

By extension, then, the dialogic model suggests not that rationalist analyses of fundamentalism are false—in some sense of not corresponding properly to objective, as yet undiscovered truths—but rather that they cannot provide a complete explanation of the power of Islamic fundamentalism in the modern world. They are not false because, of course, positivist notions of truth and falsity that depend upon a one-to-one correspondence of truth to "linguistically naked" facts in the world are particularly problematic when applied to the "human sciences." More immediately germane to the discussion at hand, they are not false because the value of any one interpretation of Islamic fundamentalism is related to what it claims to explain. The question then becomes: What, if anything, do they help us understand? The rationalist explanations of Islamic fundamentalism surveyed here explicitly seek to answer one kind of question but often answer a second kind altogether. The first kind of question involves gathering what are regarded as "brute data" about fundamentalists, that is, carefully documented empirical information about fundamentalist movements that are least vulnerable to challenging interpretations: Who are the fundamentalists? From what class do they come? What are their professional orientations, their ages?[117] Yet more often than not, such empirical information is organized to sustain another kind of proposition altogether, that is, a causal explanation with implicit claims to objectivity: Islamic fundamentalism is growing stronger, for example, because urbanization, disenfranchisement, industrialization, and unemployment continue to enlarge the group of malcontents that feed into it.

I have argued that the fact that knowledge is always mediated by language does not mean that we cannot conceive of knowledge or data about actual social processes. In Foucault's work, there is a constant tension between understanding the subject as a primarily discursive construction and the possibility that there is a reality "out there" to which discursive representations may refer.[118] Unlike Foucault, Said never questions whether there is, in fact, an Orient "out there" that is independent of Western discursive representations.[119] My own position is that Orientalist discourse is indeed a way of producing and managing something called the Orient, but it also may be something more; the story of cultural hegemony may not exhaust what Orientalism is. The fact that Orientalist analyses are implicated in imperialist power is not a sufficient reason to disqualify or negate the knowledges they produce. Texts that serve imperialist interests may simultaneously reveal the workings of European-Atlantic power *and* capture a dimension of life in "the Orient." By the same token, exploring the ways in which Western rationalist categories in part create our understandings of fundamentalism does not presume that the knowledge they produce is fatally tainted by distortion; rationalist analyses of Islamic fundamentalism are not prima facie useless to the task of understanding because they simultaneously express the power of a dominant discourse.

Consequently, while this chapter has charted the rationalist "production" of fundamentalism, it does not foreclose the possibility that the currently hegemonic image of fundamentalism generated by these explanations help us understand its meaning. Indeed, it is my contention that social science understandings of Islamic fundamentalism can provide compelling answers to narrower questions, such as those concerned with the realm of "brute data," and those concerned with the empirical study of material processes. In particular, this information serves to document a socioeconomic backdrop to the emergence of fundamentalism; it establishes conditions of discontent and disaffection that may accompany the growth of revolutionary movements. Developments such as modernization, urbanization, industrialization, rising unemployment, and increased literacy may indeed explain the urge toward revolutionary expression, or, at the very least, the urge to challenge prevailing conditions and the powers and processes that produced them.

Thus it is important to know that insecure Middle Eastern regimes have a penchant for closing down leftist and secular channels of representation, and that contemporary fundamentalists tend to be children of the petite bourgeoisie, young, well-educated, disproportionately in the natural sciences. Such facts do not, however, constitute meaning: the fact that leftist channels of expression are unavailable does not fully explain the particular draw of fundamentalist ideas. Nor does the fact that many fundamentalists come from a particularly reactionary class with specific historical experiences shed much light on why so many are drawn to fundamentalist as opposed to, for example, fascist or Marxist political solutions. To recognize the corruption of Middle Eastern elites, the authoritarianism of Middle Eastern regimes, the high national debts and low rates of employment is to say much about political, social, and economic conditions in the Middle East, some about the alienation that can accompany certain structural changes, and substantially less about the particular draw of fundamentalism itself as opposed to any other system of ideas.

We are thus left with the question as to why fundamentalism, as opposed to any other set of ideas, is the increasingly popular vehicle to register the protest. Indeed, this is a question posed by a number of the scholars I have discussed. "The question therefore boils down to why it is that, in Egypt and the Arab world, people with roughly the same social profile have flocked into militant Islamic movements more readily than they have into, say, leftist or outright Marxist groups?"[120] The answer offered in these accounts of Islamic fundamentalism is that all other such ideologies have been tried and have failed economically, politically, and culturally. Ibrahim and Ayubi both point to the Egyptian middle classes' rejection, respectively, of liberalism (1922–1952), nationalist socialism (1952–1970), and quasi-liberal autocracy (1970–1980) as proof that alternatives to Islamic politics have registered failure, a failure that resounds not only in Egypt but throughout the Middle East. "Thus it should not be surprising to observe people resorting to Islam as a result of what they would consider the failure of other options."[121] The implication is that given such failures, Islam appears to be the remaining rational choice, the ideology that promises to achieve the economic justice, political liberation, and international redress that other ideologies have failed to deliver.

This argument is often coupled with two other, somewhat incompatible explanations for the appeal of Islamic ideas. After suggesting that Islamic ideology owes much of its appeal to the manifest failures of the alternatives, it is also argued that its power stems from the fact that leftist channels of expression are more easily shut down by insecure regimes than are religious ones: thus "revolt takes an Islamic expression because quite often there are no other outlets left in the society for channeling political demands."[122] Indeed, Ayubi argues elsewhere that resistance to state power takes on a specifically religious form because the "modern territorial State has adopted secularism and taken on the language of rationality and modernisation. . . . It was natural then for the excluded and the disappointed to adopt a counterideology that is stark in its opposition to the official ideology."[123] The claim that Islamic ideology is the most rational (i.e., effective) alternative is thus conjoined to the suggestion that, quite practically, it may be the only alternative. These two arguments are then oddly linked to yet another claim, this one about authenticity: fundamentalism is somehow the more inevitable form of social protest because it is experienced as more authentic than identifications based on class or nation or common individuality. Indeed, Ayubi argues that as the drive toward emancipation becomes increasingly popular, it shows a "tendency" to become more religious.[124]

In sum, the dominant answer to the question "Why Islam?" is a combination of the failure of ideological alternatives, the unavailability of competing political channels, and the authenticity that accrues to religious, and specifically Islamic, identifications in the Middle East. I am, of course, skeptical of arguments that do not explicitly attend to the complexity of notions such as the "authenticity" of Islamic identifications; there are too many questions about what is authentic, how something comes to be experienced as authentic or imposed, or if there is any such thing as an "authentic identity" once identity is understood to rest on an inevitably selective and eclectic narrative about history, politics, and culture. Placing the authenticity argument aside, however, the two other claims regarding the failures and the unavailability of alternatives are certainly plausible, yet they ultimately skirt the question Ibrahim rightly posed above. For as Sami Zubaida contends, "social entities are not given to politics having been formed by social processes elsewhere; as political forces and concepts, they are formed through the political process itself."[125] Moreover, it is surely not the case that moral beliefs are selected as are tools in a hardware store, chosen only for their efficiency, or because the store was out of all other brands. Although it is certainly true that ideas are often adopted and discarded for a variety of reasons, including instrumental ones, religious convictions—as are all convictions worth the name— are far too complex to be either reduced to an option in the marketplace of ideas or minimized as a "refuge that provides emotional peace and comfort."[126]

CHAPTER THREE

A View from Another Side: The Political Theory of Sayyid Qutb

> At this time an outcry has arisen everywhere, a warning alarm about the fate of humankind in the thrall of a materialist civilization devoid of faith and human spirit—the white man's civilization. The alarms are various: at times, they warn of the descent of all humanity into the abyss; others warn of its descent into Marxism; still others have made various suggestions to prevent these manifold dangers. But all of these attempts are futile because they do not deal with the foundation of the problem, they do not attack the vast and extensive roots of the problem which lie buried beneath European soil. All these outcries and all these remedies just make clear to us the deficiencies and myopia of the European mentality and its vision.
>
> —Sayyid Qutb, *al-Mustaqbal li-hadha al-Din*

PERHAPS the most common observation in Middle Eastern scholarship concerns the intimacy between religion and politics: the Prophet was both the recipient of the Qur'anic revelation and the founder of the first political community in Islamic history. The first year of the Islamic calendar is not the year of Muhammad's birth or the date God's word was revealed but rather marks the ascendence of the Muslim community in Medina. This actualization of God's will on earth is the prototype for all Muslim political communities, the ideal in whose shadow Islamic political theory, jurisprudence, and ethics developed. This nexus of Islam, history, and politics that organizes much of Middle Eastern scholarship has become the beacon signaling unfamiliar territory to Western eyes, the fundamental difference that must be attended to in order to understand much of what follows. This is so not because such convergence is alien to the history of Western politics and theory, but because it *has become* alien to a Western tradition that, in its most explicit registers, insists upon the ethical necessity of the autonomy of religion and politics. Orientalists, among others, have identified this intimacy between religion and politics as the timeless "essence" of Islam, one brought into sharpest relief in contrast to the "essentially secular West."[1] In benign formulations, such claims have served to demarcate the fundamental difference and distance between Islam and the West; at their worst, such claims have underwritten arguments about Islamic backwardness and the urgency of remolding the "Muslim world" in the image of Western rationalism.[2]

In light of such claims, we might consider that radical Protestantism worked "not because it furthered the separation of church and state, but precisely because it did not."[3] In *Politics and Vision*, Sheldon Wolin provides a reading of Calvinist Protestantism that suggests a profound intimacy between religious and political theory:

> The totality of these problems [concerning the Church] constituted more than a theory of an ecclesiastical polity; it was nothing less than a comprehensive statement covering the major elements of a political theory. Here was a vision of a rightly ordered society and its government; here, in the sacramental mysteries and in the preaching of the Word, lay a new symbolism; a new set of sustaining "myths" to cement the society together; here . . . was the shaping hand to mould the members to a common outlook and instruct them in the lessons of a common good; and here in the promise of salvation was the perfecting purpose toward which the particular wills of the members were to be bent. The central message of the whole was of man's necessary relationship to a determinate order.[4]

We might also consider, for example, the interplay of religion and political identity in Ireland, Poland, Holland, and Spain, cases of established religion such as the Anglican church in England, the concordats in Italy, and religiously based political movements, from the civil rights movement in the United States to the liberation churches in Latin America.[5]

By the same token, there are important historical discontinuities and exceptions to the insistence that the Islamic essence lies in the identity of religion and politics. For example, medieval Islamic thought came closer to a de facto separation of religious and civic power than classical Islamic theory; indeed, H.A.R. Gibb even suggests that a doctrine equivalent to the Western *raison d'etat* reached a "new climax" during the Umayyad Caliphate.[6] As opposed to the original insistence on faith as the regulator of all aspects of life, the ascendancy of temporal power in medieval Islamic history generated an interpretation of religion "almost as coordinate with other aspects of the world's life, rather than as their coordinator."[7] It is also the case that from the classical period onward, "other-worldly" groups such as Sufi mysticism have flourished in Islam. As opposed to its "inner-worldly" counterpart, Sufism has tended to advocate a turn from the corruption of politics, cultivating instead an emphasis on the individual rather than the social, the eternal rather than the historical or political.[8]

Historicizing such notions about "essential cores" suggests that the relationship between religious and political thought in both traditions is not easily captured, and, concomitantly, that the putative distance between "Islam" and "the West" is not so easily defined and measured. Indeed, in my discussion of Western critics of modernity in chapter 5, a picture emerges that complicates the simple opposition between the secularism of modern Western thought and a uniformly antisecular Islamic political thought. Yet here I want to focus less on the accuracy of such claims about the essence of Islam and the West than on the most recent and politically significant expression of them. Interestingly, such claims are today most emphatically embraced by fundamentalists for whom precisely this "essential Islam"—and its absolute opposition to an equally essentialized "West"—is both premise and argument. Such essentialism presupposes a particular reading of history: as Aziz al-Azmeh argues, it is "predicated on the notion of a historical subject which is at once self-sufficient and self-evident. . . . History therefore becomes an alternance in a continuity of decadence and health, and historiographical practice comes to consist in the writing of history as a form of classification of events under the two categories of intrinsic and extrinsic, the authentic and the imputed, the essential and the accidental."[9]

This essentialism is central to the political theory of a highly influential Islamic fundamentalist thinker, Sayyid Qutb (1906–1966), that is the subject of this chapter.[10] Islamic fundamentalists such as Qutb advance essentialist versions of "Islam" and "the West," yet in this context such essentialism inverts Orientalist arguments: for Qutb it is precisely the essential, universal, constant, and a priori unity of religious and political authority in the authentic Islam that redeems it from the bankruptcy and fragmentation that plagues the rationalist, secular West.[11] In the course of this chapter, then, I advance a reading of Qutb's fundamentalist political thought in general, and his emphasis on divine sovereignty in particular, as a rebuttal of and antidote to the perceived impoverishment of post-Enlightenment rationalist discourse itself, that is, the Western discourse defined by the commitment to reading the political world as understandable, explicable and knowable by way of human reason and methods.[12] While providing a window onto the supposedly pathological world of Islamic fundamentalism, this reading lends additional force to the argument of the last chapter. For it suggests that the rationalist categories that dominate current social scientific scholarship on Islamic fundamentalism are particularly problematic because the more our stories about politics—about authority and what constitutes legitimate political action—are wedded to a rationalist epistemology, the more difficulty we may have in compassing the significance of practices and ideas guided by and defined in terms of belief in divine truths unknowable by purely human means.

Another implication of this argument is that I may not be on dangerous ground to suggest that inasmuch as Qutb's political thought is itself animated by questions about the nature of legitimate sovereignty, the relationship between moral and political life, and the individual to the community, he is (among other things) a political theorist.[13] Along with others, Edward

Said has rightly cautioned against the imposition of specifically Western constructs to interpret non-Western culture;[14] arguing that Qutb's thought may be understood in terms of a Western discipline such as political theory might raise just such worries. In light of this concern, it is well to keep in mind the fact that there is a long Islamic tradition in which questions about the nature and legitimacy of political authority, for example, have been repeatedly raised and debated; these questions arise not only from Western cultural experience. This is not the same as saying that these questions can be asked because they capture perennial dilemmas that arise out of a universal human nature. But neither can we assume that such questions are a Western possession alone simply because we may first encounter them within a Western theoretical tradition. As Hamid Enayat notes, "if the dispute as to *who should rule?* and *why should we obey the rulers?* is the hub of politics, no conscious Muslim can study his history even in the most casual fashion without feeling the urge to ask these questions."[15] In addition, the fact of Western cultural hegemony in the context of colonialism meant that texts of Western "political theory" were, as Aziz al-Azmeh puts it, "very much in the air" in nineteenth- and twentieth-century Egypt.[16] Indeed, Qutb refers to such philosophers as Plato, Aristotle, Descartes, Bertrand Russell, Comte, Marx, Hegel, Fichte, and Nietzsche, and he quotes at length from French scientist and Vichy collaborator Alexis Carrel's (1873–1944) *Man, the Unknown*.[17]

More importantly, however, such a move is suggested by the distinctive ambitions of Qutb's own project: rather than advocating a religious movement that somehow stands outside the political realm, Qutb's Islamic fundamentalism retrieves and reinterprets the lessons embedded in an "original" Islamic ideal as a guide to radically restructure modern political and social conceptions of the world. Religion is thus the standard by which communities are judged, ethics are formulated, and justice is realized; it is "the final arbiter of all that is."[18] Neither separate from culture nor part of it, religion is, as Haddad aptly puts it, both the "framework within which all aspects of life are to be designed and the measure by which they are judged. Religion moulds and shapes culture."[19] Thus the very scope of what constitutes religious authority for Qutb renders the line between political theory and Islamic thought somewhat permeable. An argument about divine authority becomes an argument about sovereignty in the ideal political community, and debates about Islamic jurisprudence become discussions of law and society.

The point here is not that Qutb is something called an *Islamic* political theorist but rather that as Qutb's work is itself animated by questions and concerns that have defined political theory as a field, a "conversation" with him (in Geertz's sense of the term) is perhaps best conducted *in terms of* political theory. Such an argument is double-edged. It presumes that as political theory provides distinctive ways of interrogating and reflecting on the premises of political life, it can and should play a unique role in the study of concrete political phenomena often considered beyond its jurisdiction. Indeed, given the increasing power of fundamentalist ideas, it is imperative that political theorists not retreat from this distinctive role: Qutb's political thought and the thought of those like him are not just a matter of intellectual interest or enrichment, but of urgent political realities. But conversely, Qutb's perspective on the intimacy between religious and political concerns implicitly contests and enlarges the boundaries that, with several notable exceptions and reversals,[20] have defined political theory as a primarily Western and secular discipline at least since the Enlightenment. Asking political theory questions of Qutb's text thus enables us to understand his work through its own categories without insisting either that such categories result in a completely enclosed world of meaning, or that his answers be our answers. Engaging Qutb's political thought may not be quite the experience of "looking for friends in history" that Salkever and Nylan describe, but then again, knowledge comes from friends and foes alike.

SAYYID QUTB: RADICAL AND MARTYR

> After a meeting of nearly all the members of the Islamic Youth in Rabat, I was offered the book of Sayyid Qutb, *Ma'alim fil-Tariq* [*Signposts along the Road*]. I read practically the whole book that night, and it overwhelmed me. Thanks to him, I began to understand things. He completely changed my life. I decided to give myself to . . . I don't like the word to militate, I prefer the word *Da'wa* [the call] or *Jihad*.[21]

The upsurge of Islamic fundamentalist activism in the Middle East has defied a chorus of predictions throughout the last fifty years that fundamentalism was a passing ideological fad, a reactionary movement that had momentarily harnessed the frustration engendered by state failures to register what was primarily a protest vote.[22] In debates about democratization in the Middle East, many observers now worry that open elections in several countries would register not a minority protest vote, but a majority. Consequently, where there previously had been little scholarship there are now countless studies that take close note of the strength and composition of fundamentalist groups in the Middle East. In part, what has emerged from these analyses is a record of a heterogeneous collection of fundamentalist political ideas that seem to cohere around a commitment to Islam as an identity, a revolutionary ideology, and a framework for moral reform despite serious juridical disagreements and differences in political contexts and strategies. As the martyr whose manifesto helped inspire and formulate many of these commitments—thereby becoming perhaps the most influential thinker for the religio-political insurgency of the Egyptian Muslim Brotherhood, and of Sunni[23] Islamic fundamentalism more broadly—Sayyid Qutb has now taken center stage.[24]

Qutb's prominence seems an accepted fact among scholars of Muslim fundamentalism. Yvonne Haddad claims that "few Muslim thinkers have had as significant an impact on the reformulation of contemporary Islamic thought as has Sayyid Qutb."[25] Mahdi Fadl Allah calls Sayyid Qutb the most famous personality in the Muslim world in the second half of the twentieth century.[26] Shahrough Akhavi argues that Qutb's significance for contemporary Islamist movements is "even greater than that of Ayatollah Khomeini."[27] Richard Mitchell deems Qutb "the center as well as the main ideologist of the Muslim Brotherhood,"[28] and Samir Amin argues that Qutb's work "remains unparalleled: the recordings of Ayatollah Khomeini, the long educational talks that the Arab television stations, from Morocco to the Gulf, offer their viewers, the religious education propagated by the militants, the endless range of books and pamphlets shelved in bookshops under the Islamiyat label, have added nothing to the master's thinking."[29] Translations of his most influential book, *Ma'alim fil-Tariq* (*Signposts along the Road*), have appeared in Urdu, Turkish, Malay, Persian, and a variety of European languages. Indeed, *Signposts* is in many ways the manifesto for the Sunni Islamic movement. Its language, arguments, and contradictions have shaped the ideologies of the Islamic groups we read about daily, among them the Islamic Salvation Front in Algeria; Sheikh 'Umar 'Abd al-Rahman, the cleric convicted of "seditious conspiracy" in 1995 in connection with the World Trade Center bombing in New York City; Hamas in the Occupied Territories; and Islamists in Saudi Arabia, Egypt, Jordan, Syria, Iraq, Lebanon, and Turkey.[30] Qutb is even credited with influencing 'Ali Shari'ati, a writer some scholars have dubbed the "ideologue of the Iranian Revolution."[31]

Yet it would seem that Qutb's significance is defined less in terms of originality than of impact. He has stepped onto a stage largely constructed by the intellectual and political work of others. Indeed, the last two hundred years have witnessed a procession of Muslim thinkers who saw in a revitalized Islam the necessary response to the decline of the Ottoman Empire and the rise of the imperialist nation-states of Europe. As I will show in the following chapter, as early as the nineteenth century, Islamic "modernists" had argued for the reform and revival of Islamic foundations to strengthen Islam in the midst of a political arena where Western powers had come to dominate a fractured Muslim world.[32] Furthermore, it was Hasan al-Banna who founded the Muslim Brotherhood in Egypt in 1929, and it was al-Banna who first prescribed a regiment of Islamic activism and renewed Qur'anic commitment to rearm Islam in the face of political paralysis and British colonial domination of Egypt.[33] Under al-Banna's guidance, the Brotherhood insisted on Islam as the universal and comprehensive arbiter of all aspects of life, a definition developed, in part, in opposition to the perceived growth of nihilism, materialism, and secularism in Egyptian culture.[34] Al-Banna, however, was more activist than theorist; he committed little systematic doctrine to paper. Hence, when he was assassinated in 1949, he left both a vital Islamic organization and what Gilles Kepel calls an "ideological vacuum" in his wake.[35] Qutb's role was that of a successor: to fill this vacuum, forging al-Banna's legacy into a systematic ideology that would outlast the passing of his charismatic leadership.[36]

Qutb also borrowed liberally from the earlier works of the Pakistani jurist Abu al-Ala al-Mawdudi in formulating his own political theory. Indeed, Qutb's most powerful organizing concepts are Qur'anic terms that Mawdudi had revived for contemporary use years before.[37] In addition, some scholars suggest that Qutb's emphasis on the illegitimacy of non-Islamic law is perhaps more properly understood as the contemporary legacy of a theologian named Ibn Taymiyya, who had introduced this criterion for judging rulers in his theory of a "right to revolt" as early as the fourteenth century.[38] That Qutb's influence is undisputed is, perhaps, due to his capacity for synthesis, a timely passion, and an evocative life story. His importance is clearest in the extent to which he has altered the very terms of Islamic political debates concerning the legitimacy of authority, the nature and necessity of political activism, and the characteristics of the just community.

MODERNITY AS PATHOLOGY: ANALYSIS AND EXHORTATION
IN *SIGNPOSTS ALONG THE ROAD*

> Humanity is standing today at the brink of an abyss, not because of the threat of annihilation hanging over its head—for this is just a symptom of the disease and not the disease itself—but because humanity is bankrupt in the realm of "values," those values which foster true human progress and development. This is abundantly clear to the Western World, for the West can no longer provide the values necessary for [the flourishing of] humanity.[39]

So begins the first chapter of Qutb's last book, *Signposts along the Road*, the culmination of a nearly twenty-year-old political and intellectual journey. This passage alone captures the tone and substance of *Signposts*, a text that is both a call to a revolutionary Islamic vanguard and an indictment of the modern world. It is an exhortation to recognize the imminence of disaster and an insistence that the only possible solution lies in the actualization of the just Islamic community in history. Indeed, it is several books in one: a guide for the virtuous Muslim, an Islamic commentary, a manifesto for revolution, a discourse on the nature of authority, and anti-imperialist propaganda. I have suggested that Qutb's thought can serve as a window into

the world of contemporary Islamic fundamentalist political practice; as
Qutb's most influential and radical book, *Signposts* is the text that has significantly influenced such practices.

Muhammad Tawfiq Barakat offers a three-part periodization of Qutb's
work: a liberal period, a period of general Islamic direction, and a period of
specifically Islamic writing.[40] *Signposts* is generally taken to represent the
concluding stage of this journey of radicalization, yet it retains the imprint
of the prior stages of his intellectual, political, and spiritual life and commitments; indeed, the book literally contains much of his earlier works.[41] This
evolution from critic to revolutionary must be understood in the context of
the political and personal experiences of his life, experiences that are, in
turn, located within a broader intellectual and historical context. In the
course of the following analysis, then, I draw upon this larger context, but
not to suggest a causal relationship between personal, political, and historical events and specific moments in Qutb's political thought, as if there were
a meaningful dichotomy between thought and context whereby a body of
work reflects the political and historical context in which it is produced.
Rather, I invoke this larger context to show the intertwining of thought and
context, to explore how the experiences of his life and the moment in which
he worked constrain and frame the dynamics of his political thought. Indeed, the very power and appeal of *Signposts* cannot be fully understood
without considering the ways in which the events of Qutb's life and death
have become an extension and symbol of his life's work, a guide almost as
potent as his written words. For Qutb witnessed firsthand the failures of
both Egyptian liberal and socialist regimes—in later years from behind the
bars of Nasser's prisons[42]—and it was after the publication of *Signposts* in
1964 that Qutb was arrested for the third and final time, accused of heading
a conspiracy against the Nasser regime. In fact, *Signposts* was used as evidence against him. After a quick trial in August 1966, Qutb was hanged on
the gallows and buried in an unmarked grave. He was sixty years old and had
written ten works of Islamist doctrine, five while incarcerated. Martyred by
his execution, Qutb's life history endowed the already potent *Signposts* with
added power and appeal, which would increase posthumously to reach an
international audience.[43]

Jahiliyya *and the Just Community*

The focus of the *Signposts along the Road* is a tripartite analysis of contemporary political communities that consists of a diagnosis of the ills of modernity (*jahiliyya*), a cure (rebellion, followed by the establishment of sovereignty based on Islamic Law), and a method of implementing the cure
(organizing a counter-community, *jama'a*, and spreading it through *jihad*,

which literally means struggle, but also holy war). *Jahiliyya*, a term taken directly from the Qur'an, specifically refers to the period of pre-Islamic ignorance in Arabia. As revived by Mawdudi, and subsequently used by Qutb, *jahiliyya* becomes a condition rather than a particular historical period, a state of ignorance into which a society descends whenever it deviates from the Islamic way. Whereas ancient *jahiliyya* was a function of simple ignorance, modern *jahiliyya* is a conscious usurpation of God's authority.[44] All contemporary ills are the product of this foundational transgression of human hubris. The problem of modernity, then, is essentially the problem of *jahiliyya*:

> We are today immersed in *jahiliyya*, a *jahiliyya* like that of early Islam, but perhaps deeper, darker [*azlam*, more unjust]. Everything around us expresses *jahiliyya*: people's ideas, their beliefs, habits, traditions, culture, art, literature, rules and laws. Even all that we have come to consider Islamic culture, Islamic sources, philosophy and thought are *jahili* constructs. This is why Islamic values have not taken root in our souls, why the Islamic worldview [*tasawwur*] remains obscured in our minds, why no generation has arisen among us equal to the calibre of the first Islamic generation.[45]

Yet the problem of human hubris is not peculiarly modern. The Bible is replete with parables of human arrogance, and the very word recalls the ancient Greek belief that excess of hubris incites the gods' wrath. Indeed, in *Social Justice in Islam*, Qutb seems to acknowledge as much in detailing what he terms the "first assault" against Islam, the corruption of the Islamic caliphate by the greed, arrogance, and moral corruption of the Ummayyad dynasty in early Islamic history.[46] Qutb's critique here, however, centers on a particular form of hubris, that is, the claim that sovereignty is legitimate in part *by virtue* of the exclusion of divine authority. This is different from the theory (also illegitimate by Qutb's standards, but perhaps less essentially *modern*) that human sovereignty is legitimate insofar as it claims to be God's representative on earth. Qutb's complaint seems to be that this aggressively secular formulation of legitimacy is a peculiarly modern form of transgression and is particularly widespread in the contemporary world.

The *jahili* society is thus one that refuses to submit to Allah's sovereignty (*hakimiyya*)[47] in the realm of belief, worship, and law, through a denial of his existence, restriction of his authority, or dilution of his sovereignty with false gods. Its essence is a rejection of Allah's sovereignty in favor of a philosophy and epistemology that claims for humans the right to create values and to legislate rules for collective behavior.

> But what is "*jahili*" society? . . . *Jahili* society is any society that is not a Muslim society. If we want a specific definition we can say: every society is *jahili* that is not dedicated to servitude to Allah alone and does not embody this servitude in its

worldview and beliefs, its rituals of worship and in its laws. With this specific definition, all established societies today on earth are actually encompassed by this "*jahili*" framework.[48]

How is it possible to recognize and combat a disease that has insidiously invaded human beings' very thoughts, shaping their understanding of the good life such that their values, their very imagination, are themselves diseased? Qutb argues that we must not rely on perception but must instead redefine true progress, true civilization, true justice, and genuine freedom. This entails a rejection of the Western-inspired measurement of civilization in terms of material, scientific, and technological progress. The only civilized community, to Qutb, is the moral one; real freedom is moral freedom, and true justice is Islamic justice. Hence, Qutb argues that Western hegemony has ended, not because it is materially or militarily poor, but because the authority of science produced by the Enlightenment worldview has proven incapable of promoting real progress, that is, moral progress.[49]

Importantly, Qutb felt that he himself had witnessed firsthand the moral bankruptcy of the modern West in the form of postwar America. His sojourn in the United States was precipitated by the displeasure of King Faruq: an employee of the Egyptian Ministry of Education in the 1940s, Qutb began after the war to churn out scathing analyses of contemporary political and social problems—not the least of which was the Egyptian defeat in Israel's 1948 War of Independence—joining the ranks of those critical of the political paralysis of Egypt's constitutional monarchy.[50] Not surprisingly, King Faruq took exception to Qutb's attacks and sought to incarcerate him; instead, he was sent into nominal exile in America, ostensibly to study U.S. education on behalf of the Egyptian Education Ministry, but also to be exposed to the appeal of "modern life" in America. In the United States, Qutb was assaulted by what he perceived as anti-Arab stereotypes, unequivocal support of the new Israeli state, and a moral corruption evinced by flagrant sexuality and excessive consumption of alcohol.[51] Instead of becoming "Americanized," Qutb returned to Egypt and joined the Muslim Brotherhood in 1951. Describing his decision, Qutb later said, "I was born in 1951."[52] Although he had written *Social Justice in Islam* even before this trip (although it was published months later), he returned from the United States absolutely convinced that "modern life," far from providing a solution to modern problems, was in fact the cause of them. The systems of the modern world, individualist and collectivist, he concluded, have established material and technological progress as ends in themselves, and it is because the rest of the world has largely followed the West's definition of the good in terms of economic prosperity that human beings are now almost incapable of perceiving the real threat to their existence. So fierce was his newfound realization that Qutb was forced to resign from the Egyptian Education Ministry in 1952.

In his indictment of *jahiliyya*, Qutb is largely unconcerned or unaware of the ways in which the charge of "false consciousness" has reflexive force. Although he is quite alert to the complex of influences and circumstances that condition interpretations with which he disagrees, Qutb's tendency to regard truth and falsity as self-evident inures him to the conditionality of his own interpretation. When he discusses *jahili* society, he is attentive to the ways in which a nexus of material, cultural, and political circumstances conditions not only how we see the world but also our capacity to envision alternatives to that world. Qutb argues, persuasively I think, that we are locked in a worldview that has colonized the human imagination itself. Yet without a hint of self-consciousness, Qutb claims to see clearly what the rest of us cannot, that is, both the conditions that entrap us and the truths they obscure. In *Social Justice in Islam*, he makes it absolutely clear that "what we are saying about Islam is not a new fabrication, nor is it a reinterpretation of its truth. *It is simply plain* Islam" (italics added).[53] In placing himself beyond the dominion of appearances, Qutb need not attend to the potentiality of multiple interpretations. Indeed, although he insists on the importance of carefully delimited *ijtihad* (personal or independent interpretation) in administering Islamic law, in general he eschews interpretation itself as a mode of understanding because it is appropriate to grasping surfaces rather than apprehending self-evident truths. In so doing, Qutb assumes for himself (and for perhaps a few other select Muslims) the status of one who has ceased to watch shadows on the wall, one who has ascended beyond the mouth of the cave and into the blinding light of the sun.

On the basis of such clarity of vision, Qutb argues that communist society is clearly a *jahili* society, and he seems to employ it as a prototype for all modern secular regimes, liberal and socialist. To Qutb, the most obvious danger, and the one unique to Marxist thought, is the blatant denial of the existence of God. However, of equal and perhaps broader importance is the ascendance of the party as sovereign in the place of God and a philosophy of history in which God plays no role. This usurpation of divine authority by man-made authority[54] unites communist, liberal, socialist, and nationalist systems. In all of these *jahili* systems, legislative authority is ultimately located in assemblies and legislative institutions: "these regulations and laws are . . . not from God's authority, but are . . . derived from the worship of priests, astrologers, magicians, the nation's elders, or are derived from civic, secular institutions that control legislative authority without reference to divine law. These institutions claim supreme sovereignty in the name of the people, or the party or in the name of some other being, but in reality, sovereignty belongs to God alone."[55] For Qutb, once man-made authority supplants divine sovereignty, humans are deprived of a context in which (paradoxically, perhaps) they can exercise their unique capacity for moral discernment. They are thus reduced to the status of beasts.

Crucial to Qutb's argument here is that this threat to humanity characterizes all contemporary societies, even, or perhaps especially, those that claim to be Islamic. For when Muslims struggle to imitate alien models, they inevitably replicate the ills of Western society in the Islamic world.[56] The "New *Jahiliyya*" may have originated in the experience of British imperialism, but it has become the defining characteristic of Egyptian society, and it is precisely when the threat to Islam comes from within that the danger is the greatest. Importantly, Qutb had both witnessed and experienced personally the immediacy and extent of the threat: in the brief six-month period following the Free Officers Revolution in 1952,[57] Gamal Abdel Nasser invited Qutb—now a prominent member of the Egyptian Muslim Brotherhood—to work with the Revolutionary Command Council. The Free Officers soon antagonized Qutb in a dispute about the ethical and social foundation for the new republic.[58] When the Free Officers voted to reject his proposal for an Islamic state, Qutb left. The antagonism between Qutb and the Nasser regime quickly deepened: the regime arrested Qutb three times, subjecting him to interrogation, torture, and more than ten years of incarceration on accusations of conspiracy. Already frail, Qutb reportedly endured torture so extreme that he was admitted to a military hospital in 1955 to be treated for chest ailments, arthritis, and cardiac problems; he had two heart attacks while incarcerated. It was after the publication of *Signposts* in 1964 that Qutb was arrested for the third and final time, accused again of heading a conspiracy against the Nasser regime.

From behind the bars of Nasser's prison, Qutb joined contemporary politics to Ibn Taymiyya's theory of legitimate authority to argue that all supposedly "Muslim" societies in the contemporary world are *jahili* societies as long as their leaders claim legislative authority for themselves, and construct social life on the basis of "modern science" while paying lip-service to Islamic belief. Islamic society, Qutb insists, is not one in which people follow their own version of Islam. There is no such amalgam called "progressive Islam":[59] "Islam does not look at the labels, titles or banners that these various societies have assumed. They all share one common truth: their way of life is not established on complete submission to Allah alone. In this respect they share the same characteristic of other societies, the characteristic of *jahiliyya*."[60]

Qutb argues that there is but one immutable version of Islam, and the prototype lies in the actions and events of Muhammad's mission in Mecca and Medina. Although the Islamic *tasawwur* (worldview) can be manifested in many different forms according to the needs of the time, its actual program and method (*manhaj*) must be culled from the history of the first generation of Muslims that gathered around the Prophet. In contrast to those who have read the contemporary world as too corrupt to realize the original Islamic *Umma*,[61] Qutb insists that it is precisely the extent of moral corruption that lends the struggle its urgency. The purity of the original *umma* is not a remote ideal. The *umma* can be revived at any historical juncture, when true Muslims grasp the necessary knowledge and path. Moreover, Qutb claims the traditionally elite prerogative to judge rulers for himself and for all virtuous Muslims, much as the Reformation sought to make the Biblical text accessible to laymen.[62] Thus, Qutb insists that Islam is a universal message whose success is not inherently dependent upon the presence of the Prophet (nor for that matter, on the judgment of the *'ulama'*). If this were the case, Islam could not be what God intended it to be: a religion for all humankind at any point in time. As used by Qutb, the *umma* is thus a transcendent, ahistorical ideal waiting to be actualized at any moment in history: it is "a demand of the present and a hope for the future."[63] In this insistence, Qutb detaches the ideal Muslim community from its historical moorings, investing Islamic texts with a new immediacy.

> The Islamic community, then—with respect to its form, scope and way of life—is not a fixed historical picture, rather its existence and civilization are based on fixed historical values. So when we say "historical" we mean only that these values were known in a specific period in history, not that they are a *product* of history. They are not related by nature to a particular time; rather they are a truth that has come to humanity from a divine source, from a realm beyond the human, and beyond material existence.[64]

Qutb emphasizes that the Qur'an reveals only one foundation for the just Islamic community: faith, grounded in the belief in the unity *(tawhid)* and sole authority of God, and witnessed in the proclamation *La ilaha illa Allah* (There is no God but Allah). As Qutb goes to great pains to document, there are many other ways that God could have instructed the Prophet to establish an Islamic community. For example, the Prophet could have united all Arabs under the call of Arab nationalism, class war, or economic reform and, once united under his authority, Muhammad could have made them submit to Allah. But the key here is that the call must be for submission to God alone and not to the authority of any man, even the Prophet, even in the name of Islam. That, Qutb insists, is simply replacing one kind of tyranny with Arab tyranny. There is no concession to realpolitik here; any compromise to manmade authority, even for a just end, is illegitimate and becomes indistinguishable from tyranny. The end does not justify the means; the means have become coextensive with the end.

Submission to God alone is expressed in the establishment of *shari'a* (Islamic Law) as the sole source of sovereignty.[65] Islamic law is the collection of prohibitions and regulations derived from the Qur'an and Traditions.[66] While it may appear that Qutb's focus on law as the essential attribute of sovereignty is a very narrow understanding, it is important to emphasize that *shari'a* covers a broader area than that suggested by its English translation:

it encompasses but is not limited to matters of law as it is understood in the West. In fact, *shari'a* is perceived as infallible legislation for almost all aspects of human existence and so governs the seemingly disparate realms of religious belief, practice, and observance of the law. *Shari'a* thus has equal authority over realms often divided into "public" and "private": in principle it "covers every possible human contingency, social and individual, from birth to death," including matters relating to administration, justice, morality, ritual washing, dispensation of property, and political treaties.[67] This is the scope of sovereignty as Qutb employs it, and a state in which such sovereignty prevails is the only state sanctioned by God. The citizens of the Islamic state are thus moral by virtue of membership in it, and all of their behavior is brought into conformity with God's will through daily adherence to laws large and small.

By definition, then, belief in the unity of God entails total submission to his authority in both the sphere of worship and that of sovereignty.[68] Hence, betrayal of that belief is evinced both in worship of other gods and in obedience to all sovereignty other than the divine. Both are *shirk*, that is, associating false gods with Allah. Political obedience is in this way equated with worship, and acquiescence to human sovereignty becomes a challenge to the hegemony of the one God. Any society built upon human authority has deified human beings, elevating some over others, regularly exacting an obedience to human laws and judgments akin to worship. As Ellis Goldberg points out, Qutb consistently conflates "idolatry" (*taghut*) and "tyranny" (*tughyan*).[69] This may be an intentional elision designed to revive the Qur'anic equation of political obedience and worship. To obey a tyrant means assuming a posture of submission due only to God. Just so, the word for worship, homage, and servitude of God (*'ubudiyya*, which is not a Qur'anic term) is the same one that means slavery and bondage. The extraordinary implication of such an equation is that servitude is only slavery when obedience is given to men rather than God.

Liberty and Equality

By contrast, Qutb claims that real civilization, Islamic civilization, is based on the freedom and equality of every individual in the community. What, to Qutb, do real freedom and equality mean? Qutb seems to intend freedom to encompass what Isaiah Berlin would divide up into positive and negative liberty.[70] More specifically, it means freedom *from* obedience to tyrannical rule, which Qutb defines as the absence of restraint on the part of the sovereign; such tyranny is not an occasional evil but rather an intrinsic characteristic of human sovereignty. But it is also the freedom *to* submit to membership in God's community, to repudiate the dominance of passion and license that has passed as freedom, and thus to become fully human.

The purpose of this righteous guidance is the good and prosperity of humanity: the good that springs from the return of mankind to its Creator, the prosperity that emanates from the congruence between the movement of humanity and the guidance that would navigate one specific, independent course. [Such congruence] would elevate [mankind] to the noble stature that God intends, freed from the dominance of desires.[71]

Likewise, equality is only possible under a divine sovereign, where each member is equal by virtue of their common submission to God. This is not the Lockean idea of equality whereby all persons are free and equal in that each has a natural right to life, liberty, and property. Rather, it is the case that since all are equally subject to God's call, they are *therefore* equal: "The 'citizenship' Islam intends for men is a citizenship of belief through which all . . . are equal under the banner of Allah."[72] In *Social Justice in Islam*, Qutb seems to define such natural equality in the sight of God primarily in terms of racial equality, and equality in status, origin, and station.[73] Yet, like Aristotle and Rousseau, Qutb goes on to argue that such equality does not and should not deny the existence of inequalities in natural endowments such as intellect, strength, beauty, or, as I will discuss below, inequalities resulting from such "natural" differences as gender. To ignore such natural inequalities is to level differential talents down to the lowest common denominator. Furthermore, despite his marked concern for economic justice, Qutb takes an almost Aristotelian position by suggesting that such inequalities of natural endowments are a justification for proportional justice: "we must not close off the outlet for these endowments and do them the injustice of reducing them to the weaker abilities. . . . Islam has left the door open for attaining preeminence through effort and hard work."[74]

The concern for economic equality that so dominates *Social Justice in Islam* is not abandoned in *Signposts* but rather is subsumed within Qutb's focus on the foundations of sovereignty. The shift in emphasis reflects, in part, a rejection of the accommodationist stance in the earlier text. But it is also an outgrowth of an increasingly organic vision of the Islamic state, a vision where the health of the body politic is determined by the nature of sovereignty rather than any particular policy regarding economic or social equality. Qutb argues in *Signposts* that, once sovereignty is established in its proper scope, social justice, equality, and freedom will naturally follow.[75] In sum, then, both freedom and equality are premised upon submission to God's will through membership in his community, a transformative act that is both the precondition to and fulfillment of the actualization of the Islamic *umma*.

When the highest authority is God alone—and is expressed in the dominance of divine law—this sovereignty is the only kind in which humans are truly liberated from slavery to men. Only this is "human civilization," because human civilization requires that the basis of rule be the true and perfect freedom of man and the absolute dignity of each individual in society. There is no true freedom and no dignity for men, or for each and every individual, in a society where some individuals are lords who legislate and others are slaves who obey.[76]

In this way, the proclamation "there is no God but Allah" is a direct challenge to all forms of human sovereignty and, by implication, to all political constructs whose authority and logic are founded on something other than God's absolute omnipotence and omniscience. Instead of natural rights, for example, Qutb proposes equality of submission; in lieu of freedom from constraints, Qutb offers the exchange of unjust slavery for righteous servitude. And in place of police coercion and constitutional regulations to constrain social behavior, Qutb argues that conscience, God's wrath and pleasure, and the reward of Paradise are the only constraints that can adequately control both social behavior and the condition of the soul. In the end, Qutb even seems to suggest that the community of the first Islamic generation illustrates that profession of faith can make even the punishments prescribed by God unnecessary. And much as Marx argues that the actualization of the communist society would render the state superfluous, Qutb further implies that if Islamic law is strictly applied, even the Islamic state may ultimately be unnecessary. In this case, there would be no need for institutions of representation, which Qutb regarded as a source of the corruption of legitimate sovereignty.

Gender and Race

According to Qutb, one of the most salient examples of Western moral bankruptcy is the deterioration of the family unit in the West. In *Social Justice in Islam* he argues that it is through the strength of the family unit—specialization of work between the sexes, mother as primary caretaker, sex in the context of legitimate, which is to say legal, relationships—that the morals of the next generation are inculcated and reinforced. When a woman becomes a sexual object, that is, when men objectify her or when she asserts her sexual identity; when she abandons the natural division of labor between the sexes and enters the workforce; when the relationship between men and women is a matter of lust and impulse, society has ceased to be part of what he terms "civilization." In fact, Qutb goes so far as to say that the relationship between the sexes is the key to the entire character of a society. It determines whether a society is civilized or backward.[77]

Qutb's arguments about gender changed in the course of his life. During his "liberal" phase, he tended toward a view more in keeping with American conservatism than with the view of women current among Islamic fundamentalists: in early articles, Qutb supports the education of women but objects to coeducation; he does not support veiling but is cautious with regard to women's place in the public realm. By the time he wrote his later works, however, Qutb's view of gender relations had changed considerably, having become more "radically conservative."[78] Nevertheless, throughout his writings, Qutb consistently emphasizes that the traditional family unit is the repository of everything from intergenerational continuity to the moral status of an entire civilization, and that a woman's responsibility in society is synonymous with her biological function in life: rearing children. Her role as caretaker of children within this family unit thus defines her identity, importance, and dignity.

Qutb's most extensive treatment of gender and politics appears in his discussion of equality in *Social Justice in Islam*. In this text—Qutb's more "liberal" treatise—he seems eager to rebut the accusation that Islam regards men and women as fundamentally unequal (as a reflection of his move away from an "accommodationist" stance, Qutb betrays no such concern in his later *Signposts*).[79] He does so in two ways. First, Qutb attempts to deflect the charges by arguing that women are valued less in Western societies than in Islamic ones. For Qutb, the evidence of this denigration of women in the West is obvious. By forcing women to work for pay outside the home, Western societies reveal their contempt for women while demonstrating men's failure as caretakers. Qutb does not here consider the possibility that the denigration of women might originate in the objectification of women by men rather than residing in the mere fact of women's labor; therefore he does not entertain the possibility that the remedy might require changing men rather than restricting women.[80]

Second, Qutb insists that women are equal in the most important regard, that is, with regard to piety and religiosity, and that consequently, inequalities in gender in Islamic societies stem from practical and social circumstances rather than any claim in the "inherent superiority" of men over women in Qur'anic law. But if such inequalities are merely consequences of society rather than of Islam or nature, how does Qutb's distinction here square with the Qur'anic passages which clearly state, for example, that men have "precedence" over women; that men are to receive double the inheritance of women; and that the testimony of one man equals that of two women? To render them consistent, Qutb must make interpretive judgments regarding the relative weight and meaning of some Qur'anic passages versus others. Such interpretation is not inherently problematic, yet Qutb must achieve it by sleight of hand given his repeated claim that "what we are saying about Islam is a not a new fabrication, nor is it a reinterpretation of its truth. It is simply plain Islam."[81]

Qutb thus confronts two dilemmas with regard to gender. First, he must show that certain Qur'anic passages mean something different from what they seem to say. And second, he must convince his readers that such a task is not an act of interpretation but is, in fact, the discovery of the "true Islam." These dilemmas are similar to the one evident in his critique of *jahiliyya* where he sought simultaneously to argue that interpretation is nothing more than fallible human opinion, and to maintain that his (re-)interpretation is objective truth and thus not an interpretation at all. In an attempt to make the Qur'anic passages on women mean something other than what they seem to say, Qutb takes up the question of equality between the sexes as an extension of his distinction (discussed above) between the natural equality of all men—and, it would seem, women—under the sight of God, and inequalities with regard to natural endowments and capabilities.

> As for the relation between the sexes, Islam has guaranteed to women complete equality with men in regard to sex, and it has allowed no discrimination except in some incidental cases relating to endowments, customs or responsibilities, none of which affect the actual situations of the two sexes. So whenever endowments, customs and responsibilities are equal, the two sexes are equal, and whenever they are different, discrimination between the sexes follows accordingly.[82]

In the matter of inheritance, Qutb argues that discrimination between genders is simply an expression of proportional justice. That Islamic law grants men double the share of inheritance as women is due to the fact that, in his view, men conventionally bear the economic burden of sustaining the family, whereas a single woman has only to provide for herself, and a married woman is sustained by her husband. Yet the attribution of such discrimination to convention quickly slides into a compound of social *and* biological inequalities. In Qutb's treatment of the Qur'anic passage that states that "men are overseers of women," for example, he argues that men supervise women by virtue of a natural physical superiority compounded by an intellectual superiority that even Qutb acknowledges as conventional rather than natural. That is, as men are freed from the cares of the household, they develop intellectual powers such as reflection and thought that women, by virtue of their "natural" restriction to the household, cannot. This socially inculcated "emotionalism" thus accounts for the equating of the testimony of two women to that of one man: "due to the nature of family duties, the emotional and passionate side of the woman grows and develops . . . so if she forgets or gets carried away by her emotions, the other woman will remind her."[83]

Both Sylvia Haim and William Shepard emphasize Qutb's care for women and high regard for their function as the guardians and nurturers of what is the "human essence."[84] While this assessment may beg crucial questions about what exactly is meant by "care" and "regard," it is worth noting that Qutb's analysis of women is not entirely reducible to an argument "by nature." Rather he argues that women are schooled in the emotions and passions by convention, a convention that he endorses as the vehicle through which men and women do what they are best suited by nature. Qutb thus attempts to conceptualize a principle of gender (in)equality that is at once inhospitable to arguments that women are inferior "by nature" and supportive of the differential treatment of men and women in the Qur'an. While Qutb's arguments about women strain to cohere, it is interesting to note that he brooks no such intellectual sleight of hand on matters of race, a subject he treats briefly in the same section of *Social Justice in Islam*, entitled "Human Equality." Here Qutb not only rebuts arguments from nature but goes on to reject any social conventions or institutions that express a principle of racial inequality. Using passages from the Qur'an, Qutb unequivocally rejects the idea that there are intrinsic inequalities among races and affirms the argument that the inherent equality of all Muslim individuals with regard to religious status makes race irrelevant. The implications of this emphasis on religious equality do not bode well for religious minorities, however, as I will suggest below.

Science and Epistemology

Qutb's critique of *jahiliyya* is clearest in his discussion of science and epistemology, for it is through the exposition of the nature and opposition of an originally Western rationalist epistemology and the truths of Islamic revelation that Qutb's terms and targets are most carefully delineated. Indeed, despite the radical shifts in his thought over the years, for Qutb the tension between these two approaches to knowledge remains a consistent preoccupation and constant source of anxiety.[85] This is perhaps unsurprising. Like many others in the colonized Muslim world, Qutb's early life was marked by the tension between Western influence and Islamic traditions: the growing influence of secular education, liberalism, and nationalism in Egyptian life, and the increasing importance of maintaining an indigenous Islamic identity as a bulwark against cultural and political encroachment. Qutb's early education in Musha, a village in Asyut, Upper Egypt, exposed him to both Sufi mysticism and Qur'anic training;[86] at an early age, then, Qutb had both memorized the Qur'an and adopted anti-British nationalist sympathies. Yet Qutb was later sent to what has been called a "modern"[87] rather than a traditional religious school by his father, al-Hajj Qutb Bin Ibrahim, an initially prosperous farmer who later fell on hard times, but who was also a delegate of Mustafa Kamil's National Party. After the nationalist revolution of 1919, Qutb studied at Dar al-'Ulum, a nonreligious teacher training institute that Hasan al-Banna had attended seven years before.[88]

While in Cairo, Qutb's uncle introduced him to 'Abbas al-'Aqqad, a leading Egyptian "liberal"[89] journalist whose work, like that of many other prominent intellectuals at the time, reflected the Western-inspired politics and thought pervading Egyptian public life and educational system. When Qutb graduated from Dar al-ʿUlum in 1933, he worked as an elementary school-teacher of Arabic in Egypt's modern education system. At this time, Qutb's intellectual orientation tended toward the individualist, secularist, and ratio-nalist views of his mentor; Abu Rabiʿ goes as far as describing Qutb's work at this time as anti-Islamic and anti-traditionalist.[90] And much like ʿAqqad, Qutb began as a member of the Wafd Party but later distanced himself from party politics. During an eight-year tenure at the Ministry of Education fol-lowing his teaching, Qutb became an avid contributor to the literary debates dominating Egypt's intellectual circles, often aligning himself with ʿAqqad and the "liberals" of an older generation against younger, more religiously inclined poets.[91]

Yet it is clear that from the beginning, Qutb evinced a preoccupation with the moral life and the spiritual realm that distinguished him from ʿAqqad, and his anxiety about the threat to faith remained with him throughout his life. It was perhaps this tendency that eventually led him away from his mentor to a philosophy, epistemology, and politics that virtually negated his earlier thought, culminating in his analysis of *jahiliyya* in *Signposts*. Perhaps this journey was precipitated by shifts in the political atmosphere at the time: along with many "liberal" intellectuals who were reared on the prom-ises of Western culture, Qutb was forced to reassess his political orientation and intellectual alliances in response to British policies during World War II and the establishment of Israel in 1948.[92] Perhaps it also betrays the effort of a student intent upon distinguishing himself from a powerful teacher.[93] Yet I am also suggesting that in this journey generally, and in his arguments about epistemology in particular, we can see the dynamics of a lifelong ten-sion between radically different approaches to and experiences of truth working themselves out, constraining and framing his political thought.

Challenging Islamic thinkers of a prior generation who had sought to rec-oncile reason and revelation, Mawdudi had insisted that, "instead of claim-ing that Islam is truly reasonable, one should hold that the true reason is Islamic."[94] In *Signposts*, Qutb follows Mawdudi's lead:

> He who feels a need to defend, justify and apologize is not capable of presenting Islam. Rather, he is one who lives in *jahiliyya*, a life that is hollow, full of contradic-tions, defects and flaws. This is one who, in fact, wants to search for justifications for *jahiliyya*. These are the people who attack Islam, forcing some of its adher-ents—who are ignorant of its true nature—to defend it, as if Islam somehow stood accused, in need of defending itself, like a prisoner on trial.[95]

Qutb rails against both the arrogance of modern science and the Arab intellectual movements catering to it. Given his Manichaeanism, it is per-haps not surprising that Qutb's critique of science begins with a dichotomy.

There are two types of sciences, he argues, physical and philosophical. The former, which includes physics, astronomy, medicine, military arts, and technology, is not only permissible but necessary for the functioning of a modern Islamic society. Indeed, Qutb regards pursuit of material progress as a divine command, since such prosperity is a prerequisite for social justice and a condition of human vice-regency (*khalifa*). Further, it seems that the use of such knowledge is built into his understanding of vice-regency itself. In *The Islamic Conception and Its Characteristics*, Qutb defines "vice-regency" in two different ways: one actual, the other ideal. The practical sense in which humans are vice-regents of God is their control over the Earth and all its resources, or what Qutb also refers to as "managing the affairs of the Earth."[96] The second sense in which humans are Allah's "deputy" is the way they must use such resources to transform the world according to Qur'anic precepts. Both practical and ideal dimensions of such vice-regency distinguish humans from beasts.[97]

As no less than a condition of human vice-regency on earth, then, mastery of such practical sciences is a "collective obligation" (Qutb uses the phrase *fard al-kifaya*, a term from Islamic law).[98] Such obligation is collective in the sense that it is necessary for the functioning of society as a whole, but it may be delegated; it is not an obligation that all must fulfill individually. Moreover, Qutb argues, first, that much of Western science originated in Islamic universities prior to European ascendance and, second, that such knowledge does not entail a challenge to the fundamental concepts of Islamic belief. Indeed, Qutb argues that all the physical sciences "lead toward Allah,"[99] provided they remain within the bounds of natural experiments and do not attempt philosophical speculations that render human history and the universe devoid of divinity: "a Muslim may examine all facets of *jahili* activity, but not in order to belong to its worldview and knowledge, but rather to come to know how *jahiliyya* is corrupting, and to learn how to rectify these distortions of humanity. [We must study *jahiliyya* only] to restore humanity to its true foundations in accordance with the principles of the Islamic worldview and the truths of the Islamic faith."[100]

Qutb thus embraces science and technology provided they are confined to the study and mastery of the material world.[101] This is in stark contrast to the philosophical sciences, which Qutb argues are the cornerstone of *jahili* authority. This relationship between philosophy and *jahiliyya* is greatly illuminated by an examination of Qutb's direct attack on the methodology and epistemology of Western, Greek, and Islamic philosophy in *The Islamic Conception and Its Characteristics*. While this earlier text, like *Social Justice in Islam*, can be brought into a discussion of *Signposts along the Road* only with caution, it is illuminating because Qutb states clearly that the purpose of *The Islamic Conception* is not social critique or exhortation to revolution, but the explication of the "Islamic Conception" itself.[102]

In the first chapter of *The Islamic Conception*, Qutb argues that Islamic philosophy developed as a way to negotiate and resolve religious disputes arising from the spread of Islam and the concomitant influx of new cultural mores and concerns into an ever-expanding Islamic community. Over time, these developments produced a class of philosophical experts that in turn defined philosophy as an activity of intrinsic worth and reward, autonomous from the Qur'anic sources and Islamic community that had formerly delimited and legitimized it. For Qutb, such autonomy expressed two significant disasters for Islam and for humanity in general. First, Qutb argues that the emergence of an autonomous subject called "philosophy" reflected the successful penetration of non-Islamic methods and concerns—Greek philosophy in particular—into what Qutb regarded as a pure Islamic conception of life, that is, a conception that in its so-called original form had been defined by clear geographic, cultural, and theological boundaries. Thus, for Qutb, the very emergence of philosophy as an intellectual enterprise, Islamic or otherwise, was already an expression of the corrosion of Islam by foreign cultures.

The second disaster philosophy precipitated in Islam is tied to the first: under the shadow of non-Islamic influences, the very enterprise of "philosophy" expanded the legitimate range of human speculation to encompass questions of existence itself. It opened to human inquiry the "whys" as well as the "hows" of the universe. Put another way, philosophy became an enterprise not entirely reducible to theology and, in so doing, redefined the scope of human reason.[103] For Qutb, all philosophy—Islamic, Greek, or Western—is intrinsically corrosive to Islam because it presumes that the meaning of human existence is a legitimate field of human inquiry rather than a mystery known only to God. This presumption is corrosive in part because it is transgressive: it represents human encroachment on the realm of divine authority. But it is also corrosive because it subjects what are essentially self-evident, divine truths to interpretation through human reason, which is by definition limited and fallible. For Qutb, by contrast, the only legitimate function of reason, that "great and valuable tool," is to enable us to understand and enact God's precepts and thus to fulfill the role of God's vice-regent on Earth.[104]

This development [of our mind] is connected to man's duty on Earth as Allah's vice-regent, and [vice-regency] requires that the creation of man's mind is according to this design because it is the most suitable one for the performance of this role. Man will advance in grasping the laws of matter and exploiting them at the same time that he advances in the knowledge of various aspects of 'man's reality,' moving beyond what he had known before. But the secrets of man's existence, the secret of life and death and of his soul, will remain hidden, beyond the scope of his reason, because the knowledge of all these things is not necessary for the performance of his basic role.[105]

For Qutb, reason is the faculty that enables us to think systematically and logically about the parts of the world we can apprehend, that is, the realm of practical knowledge; it is also the faculty that enables us to recognize the limits of our own knowledge. In recognizing the limits of reason, we are prepared to acknowledge God's truths as self-evident, as beyond rational proof:

> Indeed, "reason" isn't rejected, disregarded or banished from learning through revelation and understanding what it receives; it comprehends what is necessary as well as surrendering to what is beyond its scope. But it cannot be the ultimate "judge." As long as there is an exact text, that explicit meaning of that text—without any speculation—is the ultimate judge of interpretation. The mind then derives its decisions from the meaning of this explicit text.[106]

Given Qutb's insistence on the limits of human reason, philosophy thus appears both methodologically and epistemologically antagonistic not only to Islam but to the very truths of human existence. Nowhere is this opposition clearer than in modern Western philosophy, which is distinguished by explicit rather than merely implicit antagonism to religion.[107] According to Qutb, the result is tantamount to a deification of reason, that is, the use of reason as a means of simultaneously expanding and legitimizing the range of human knowledge, thereby discrediting the authority of religious truths: "The hostility of European thought to religion and to the religious approach lies not only in the subjects of study, philosophical systems and schools of thought that were established by European thought, but in the core of this thought, and in the methodology by which it acquires knowledge."[108] Reason in this way becomes a method and justification for the completeness of human knowledge. It not only determines how human beings come to know the world but also defines what is worth knowing as that which is knowable to human beings. As a result, Qutb maintains that what is now considered worthwhile knowledge is only knowledge of worldly phenomena; we have ceased even to acknowledge the unseen world, the source of real truth. The result is a truncated concept of the world.

Whereas *Signposts along the Road* reveals Qutb's outrage at the arrogance of human claims to knowledge and the usurpation of God's rightful authority, in *The Islamic Conception and Its Characteristics* there is a subtext of pathos in Qutb's critique of philosophy. Here Qutb suggests that there is something besides transgression at stake; the ascendence of philosophy also represents a profound loss. For although humans cannot wholly grasp either God's existence or his plan, the eclipse of religious meaning deprives humanity of the only spark of true knowledge available. This knowledge is what Moussalli aptly calls "true allusions to truths which are inaccessible to us."[109] Unlike rationalist philosophy in which the development of nature and existence is reduced to scientific theories of causality, competition, and chance, Qutb argues that religious truths and Islamic truths in particular contain the meanings for which human beings by nature yearn, answers to such basic questions of human existence as why we are born, for what purpose we live, and why we die.

> [T]he Muslim realizes that his existence on Earth is neither unplanned nor transitory; rather, it is foreordained and destined, his path planned, his existence designed with purpose. He has come into being in this world in order to act and work for his own sake and for the sake of others around him . . . and he cannot show his gratitude to God for the blessing of his existence and his true faith, nor can he hope for redemption from God's appraisal and punishment, unless he fulfills his positive role as God's vice-regent on Earth.[110]

Without such "true allusions to truths," Qutb contends, all human knowledge is by definition incomplete and fragmentary, a distortion of nature. Indeed, Qutb implicitly suggests that without the possibility of unitary knowledge—and in particular acknowledgment of a moral unity in terms of which we can organize human life—humanity is cut adrift, doomed to a knowledge that is purely positivistic and instrumental. What is perhaps most distinctive for Qutb about the modern condition, or the "new *jahiliyya*," is the way in which such distortion and fragmentation is obscured by the investment "modernists" have in the authority of such knowledge and the methods that produce it. Modern science, Qutb argues, is now a totalizing worldview intent on preserving its own truths. As such, it is not only wrong but pernicious, for Qutb sees its aggressive worldliness as both the impetus for and a product of the denial of God's importance and existence. "This *jahiliyya* is not 'abstract theory' . . . it is always embodied in a dynamic movement . . . it is an organic society, [built upon] the unity, harmony and cooperative interplay of its individuals, and with a will that, consciously or unconsciously, strives to preserve its own existence, to defend its essence. [It is always ready] to annihilate dangerous elements which threaten its very being."[111]

For Qutb, the rationalism of the philosophical sciences is the core of the *jahiliyya* worldview and the source of its inexorable drive to destroy Islam. To underscore the sense of danger, Qutb reifies *jahiliyya*, endowing it not only with material existence but with agency. *Jahiliyya* is at once the embodiment and instrument of slavery, alienation, fragmentation, and cosmic disharmony; it is also the veil that cloaks such evils in the language of freedom, progress, and personal fulfillment. This moral threat is far from abstract: in the Islamic world at least, military defeats, political disunity, corruption, and genuine poverty are the concrete results.

Political Action

As in his treatment of *jahiliyya*, Qutb moves between describing Islam as a set of guiding principles and portraying it at times almost as an agent with purpose and will. To Qutb, then, history is an arena of battle, a story punctuated and defined by the cosmic struggle between faith and disbelief, Islam and *jahiliyya*, tyranny and justice.[112] Qutb argues, for instance, that Islam "acknowledges" those qualities that human beings share with other creatures yet recognizes, nurtures, and enhances those capacities that set humanity apart from beasts. The Islamic religion (*din*) thus "addresses" the call (*da'wa*) to the human being qua human being, to an essential quality of humanity that is ahistorical and universal. This paradigm of warring opposites recalls the Qur'anic model of the perennial battle between the forces of God and those of Satan (*Iblis*) and, paradoxically, mirrors the rhetoric of the clash of civilizations discussed in the introductory chapter. But Qutb's view of history also echoes Marx's argument that the victory of communism is both necessary—in the sense of being inevitable and desirable—and contingent on human action. For Qutb implies, as Haddad puts it, that the virtuous society is realized only "through human participation in the flow of history."[113] Qutb here grafts the Western concept of progress onto the ideal of the Islamic community; importantly, however, change is not the inevitable result of, for example, the march of history but a potential grant from God contingent on human effort and technological progress.[114] In other words, Qutb calls not for mere renewal and (re-)affirmation of faith, but active participation in the realization of the Islamic way on Earth. Thus, in a familiar paradox, Qutb argues that God's will alone guarantees the victory of the *umma*, but it is a necessity that human beings coordinate their activities with those of the divinity.

> [Allah's wisdom] guarantees that believers will see the signposts along the road clearly and starkly, for [God's wisdom] establishes the course for those who wish to traverse this road to its end, whatever that end may be. Thus, the fate of their mission and of their very lives will be whatever Allah wills. . . . If God intends to actualize His mission and His religion, only He will do so, but not as recompense for human suffering and sacrifices.[115]

Once the individual has overcome the alienation intrinsic to *jahiliyya*, Qutb argues, the "signposts" are clearly marked. Such an individual should have "already fought the greater battle (*al-jihad al-akbar*) within himself against Satan, against his whims, desires and ambitions and the interests of his family and nation—against anything that is not Islamic."[116] Once this battle is won, the conclusion is inevitable. The individual's struggle both presages and inaugurates the worldly endeavor to realize Islam as a social system. Qutb's penultimate focus is this-worldly; human beings must change themselves so that they may change the world. Like Max Weber's account of Calvinists' relentlessness in pursuit of the elusive certainty of grace, Qutb's account of this struggle cautions that there is no guarantee of rewards in this life, or in the next. He emphasizes instead the intrinsic value of pious martyrdom, for it is a Qur'anic injunction not only to implement Islam within one's own life, but to strive to destroy *jahiliyya* wherever it appears in the world. Understanding the nature of *jahiliyya* thus calls for a struggle by the righteous to recognize *jahiliyya*'s multiple sources of power: moral, educational, and technological, as well as explicitly coercive. The lessons of modern power are not lost on Qutb, nor on those influenced by him; it is thus unsurprising that the contemporary Islamic movement advocates both veiling of women and mastery of modern weaponry, mass media, and the cassette tape.

The form of this activism is *jihad*. *Jihad* is an injunction of the Qur'an that had, over time, fallen into disuse.[117] While Mawdudi was the first to stress the imperative of *jihad* for contemporary Muslims, Haddad argues that Qutb took the concept to its radical conclusion. For Qutb, *jihad* is the liberating force that both sets humans free and enables them to help bring about the Kingdom of God on Earth. It is not defensive as several Muslim "apologists" have argued. On the contrary, it is unapologetically offensive, the necessary response to an increasingly strident enemy. In this way, *jihad* simultaneously defines the range of legitimate action and endows such action with existential weight, for despite humans' status as vice-regent of God on Earth, Qutb insists that the vice-regency of human beings is neither automatic nor fulfilled by words alone. Instead Muslims must perform righteous deeds. Action in the context of *jihad* thus realizes the promise of human vice-regency by bringing all endeavors into accord with God's will. Such action has several stages: before engaging in such *jihad* there must be a group of Muslims (*jama'a*) that coalesces around the commitment to *jihad* and thus initiate change, and there must be a stage where this group removes itself (*hijra*, that is, separation) for a period of time from the corrupting influences of *jahili* society. As Goldberg points out, this understanding of *jihad* shifts the very understanding of what it means to be Muslim, for it represents the denial that being Muslim requires only formal membership in the visible community of believers.[118] It also shifts the focus of *jihad*. While the traditional concept of *jihad* concerned the relationship between Muslims and non-Muslims, Qutb insists that it must also apply to the relationships among Muslims—that is, among those individuals Qutb would distinguish as "true" Muslims and so-called Muslims.

Jihad is thus the means to eradicate a *jahili* society in favor of an Islamic society that exercises sovereignty in God's name by applying the prescriptions of revelation. *Jihad* operates on two levels, the ideological and the practical, and employs tools appropriate to each dimension. Preaching and persuasion are the tactics in the realm of ideas and beliefs, and the sword is necessary to remove the political, social, and economic obstacles to the establishment of the Islamic community. The sword is justified not only by the events in the Prophet's life and quotes from the Qur'an, but also by the nature and mechanisms of the power of the secular state in the contemporary world. As Qutb notes with a bit of sarcasm, the oppressors of Allah's servants and the usurpers of Allah's authority on Earth will not relinquish their power merely through argument and rhetoric.[119]

How can Qutb justify war against essentially all non-Muslims and most Muslims to establish an Islamic community given that the Qur'an states (2:256) that "there is no compulsion in religion"? In an argument reminiscent of Rousseau's claim that human beings must be "forced to be free," Qutb maintains that coercion is justified in the pursuit of liberation from slavery: Islam has not only the right, but the obligation to realize human freedom. After all, the Qur'an states that "oppression is worse than killing" (2:217). Islam means freedom from *jahiliyya*, freedom from the enslavement of one individual to another, freedom to exercise the freedom to choose. But freedom to choose what? Islam, of course. The paradox is that Qutb (along with many other theists) both claims for Islam the status of liberator from oppression and insists that freedom be exercised in acceptance of Allah's sovereignty.

Qutb justifies this move by arguing that, after the constraints of *jahiliyya* are eradicated, the only choice is the sovereignty of Allah. For only this authority makes choice itself possible. While stating that an individual can adopt any belief he wishes, Qutb also insists that the nature of the Islamic *din*—religious way of life—precludes the possibility of following one's own beliefs while under divine authority. Ultimately, he falls back on a quotation from *In the Shade of the Qur'an* implying a division between personal and public belief: "[One should always keep in mind] the principle that there is no compulsion in religion; so *after* the removal of the rule of men and the sole authority of Allah is established—because, of course, the totality of religion belongs to God—*then* there is no compulsion to adopt the faith" (my emphasis).[120] Islam, he says, attacks institutions and traditions to liberate humanity, but does not force individuals to accept its beliefs. But, of course, Qutb's understanding of the nature of those institutions precludes such a space for freedom of faith: the political community is premised upon an act of belief. In the ideal Islamic community, belief is never just a matter of individual conscience, but an issue of sovereignty. Qutb attempts to negotiate this contradiction by claiming that while it is part of a divine "program" (*manhaj ilahi*) to establish the Islamic system based on the authority of Allah, once done, the matter of "personal faith" is protected under a vague concept of "freedom of conscience" (literally, "freedom of sentiment," *hurriyat al-wijdan*).[121] However, given the scope of Islamic sovereignty as Qutb defines it, such a distinction seems at best disingenuous, at worst, meaningless.

Morality and Politics

For Qutb, just as the telos of history lies in the actualization of the *umma* on Earth, so, too, there is a final resting place of all human activity: harmony. Qutb assumes that the universe is a unitary substratum of existence that is naturally coherent. It is an organic machine whose many parts are balanced, controlled, and motivated by divine will. Human beings' involuntary existence—life, death, health, and disease—is governed by the same system of divine law that rules the entire universe. Qutb does not provide an exact definition of universal law, but he does clearly state that these laws govern humans' biological being, their involuntary functions; *shari'a* is part of this universal law; and the physical laws of nature embody these laws. In short, universal law is divine law and it seems to be embedded in physical and biological phenomena, much as natural law was for Western theorists. The task Qutb sets his audience is both to recognize this underlying unity and to act in order to realign human behavior—both individual and collective—with the functioning of all creation.

To achieve this end, Qutb argues, the Muslim must realize that the good of humanity is embedded in the *shari'a*, and not in limited human knowledge. "Do you know best or does Allah?" asks the Qur'an. "Allah knows and you do not know. . . . You have been given only a little of the [true] knowledge."[122] A clear Qur'anic text is decisive and must always supersede *ijtihad* (independent personal interpretation). Where there is no such text, personal judgment may play a role, guided always by divine principles governing *ijtihad*.[123] This is so because only divine legislation can bring concord between physical needs and social behavior: "There is no conflict between man and his nature because the *shari'a* of God harmonizes the realm of external behavior with that of man's internal nature with ease. From this congruence emanates another: all relations between men and their actions are harmonious because they all proceed together under one system, which is itself a part of the laws that govern the universe."[124]

Because the benefits of such harmony are realized not only in the hereafter—although it is in the afterlife that such sublime concord reaches perfection—its establishment demands a distinctively activist interpretation of Islam. The imperative to establish divine harmony on Earth carries an added urgency given the modern condition, a condition that Qutb likens to schizophrenia. The division of the realm of human beings' voluntary existence from the sphere ruled by God, the division of humans from themselves, and the division of humans from the universe; this is the legacy of *jahiliyya*. By contrast, action in the name of Islam becomes the path to cosmic harmony: the righteous *jama'a* (body of believers) is the "vehicle of redemption for the society," and "the *umma* and its destiny . . . supersedes all individual considerations."[125] Individual commitment and faith are strengthened though participation in such action, and the *umma*, in turn, creates righteous relationships on Earth, lends power to the community in its confrontation with hostile forces, and imbues life with special significance. Endowed with God's vice-regency on Earth, humans occupy a place above other creatures, yet human knowledge is circumscribed by the limits of their nature and task. There is an essence called "humanity" that is immutable and of divine creation; the *shari'a* judges human behavior deficient or worthy in terms of this standard. Although men and women everywhere degrade that which is most fully human in themselves by existing in a state of unbelief, through membership in the righteous community, human beings' noblest intellectual, moral, and spiritual characteristics find their fullest expression. Indeed, Qutb suggests that as Allah's vice-regent on Earth, humans nevertheless have the potential to soar to heights even beyond those of angels.

The Islamic State

"[Islam is] just like a strong, towering tree which casts a long shadow, its intertwined branches striking the sky. By nature its roots penetrate deep into the earth, extending to its farthest recesses, in proportion to its splendor and greatness."[126] For Qutb, the metaphor for the Islamic community is a tree. Comprised of different, living parts, the tree nonetheless grows in accordance with a single pattern, an unchanging worldview that allows for variation in application depending on circumstances and needs. Such variation means that there can be no specific theory of an Islamic state. There are no specifics to address, Qutb insists, because Islam is not theory, but practice. Of course, when Qutb refers to "theorizing," he does not mean the formulation of a set of ethical principles guiding a community—for in this sense, his whole project is "theory"—but rather the process of mapping out specific forms of institutions. Actualization of an Islamic community that believes "there is no God but Allah" of necessity precedes elaboration of organizational details. Only when the community's needs are known, given the conditions of the time, can a system of rules and regulations become necessary, indeed, even possible: "[Islam] does not posit hypothetical problems in order to prescribe solutions for them. Rather it considers tangible conditions in a concrete society that has already submitted to God's law."[127]

Olivier Roy contends that the "poverty of Islamist thought on political institutions is striking, considering the emphasis Islamism places on politics."[128] Yet Qutb's refusal to provide a blueprint for the institutions of an Islamic state expresses his unwillingness to play an intellectual game wherein the rules are determined by the enemy. Rather than expand on his vague references to the state in *Signposts*, Qutb develops a principled opposition to the very terms of the debate. For Qutb, such concerns are no more than the misguided obsessions of the dominant discourse: those who ask of Islam to provide a theory of the state seek to degrade Islam by insisting that it be cast in the same terms as man-made theories of sovereignty. To engage in what Qutb implies is a kind of scholastic sophistry would be to rend the essential connection between Islam and action. Since building belief is coextensive with building a community, theorizing is a *jahili* tactic designed both to distract believers and to neutralize the essential practicality of the Islamic worldview.

Qutb always conceives of Islam as a dynamic and continual movement, a "program" particularly attentive to the transformative capacity of action. The echoes with Marxist theory here, as elsewhere, are striking. Like Marx, Qutb sees tyranny as a function of state power and, also like Marx, eschews theorizing as an expression of the dominant interests, in this case, Western and *jahili* interests. Consequently, this reading evokes the Marxian understanding of praxis as both a "tool for changing the course of history and a criterion for historical evaluation."[129] Indeed, Qutb argues that Islam is beyond intellectualism, beyond the theory and practice divide: it is a religious doctrine that is "oriented to praxis."[130]

> Islam is a living faith which, by the imperatives of its own nature, must be embodied in a dynamic and organic reality. We should not reduce Islam to "theory," [thereby] transforming it into a mere abstraction to be studied, a subject for intellectual mastery, merely because we want to counter impoverished human constructions of "Islamic theory." We must realize that such attempts are not only misguided but dangerous.[131]

Importantly, Qutb's emphasis on "praxis" is directed not only against theorizing as a tactic of *jahiliyya*, but against the authority of Islamic jurisprudence. For Qutb, human traditions are by definition fallible and need to be continually revised to accommodate the changing social and material conditions of each historical period.[132] In so doing Qutb distinguishes between *shari'a*—the divine and unchangeable law—and human legal interpretation (*fiqh*), an argument that allows him to critique the latter without challenging the authority of the former.

Given the antitheoretical tone pervading *Signposts*, it is perhaps not surprising that the few suggestions of a nascent "theory of the state" are located not in Qutb's political manifesto but in his earlier book, *Social Justice in Islam*.[133] The hints here, however, are less than illuminating. Qutb states that government must be participatory, a collaborative effort between ruler and ruled, a requirement culled from several Qur'anic passages concerning the principle of *shura* (consultation).[134] For example, the Qur'an exhorts believers to "settle their affairs" by "mutual consultation" (42:38) and admonishes them to "seek counsel" from their brethren in all affairs (3:159). But as Qutb himself admits, the *shari'a* does not specify the form of such consultation, leaving it open as to who will participate, when they will participate, and how they should participate.[135] He suggests that such collaboration is a fundamental principle of Islamic politics but provides no blueprint for institutions to ensure such participation. Indeed, despite Leonard Binder's suggestion that Qutb can be seen as harbinger of a "philosophical path for the cooperation of fundamentalists and contemporary political movements of both the right and the left," in the first chapter of *Signposts* Qutb insists that democracy (among other systems) is bankrupt in the West, and useless anywhere else.[136]

As might be expected, *Social Justice* makes it clear that, whatever the regime, the nature of government authority—though not its scope—must be vastly circumscribed. Since all human activity is regulated by divine law, government is no longer the source of legislation, but only of administration, much as Plato's Philosopher-Kings were more "selfless instruments of timeless truths" than actual legislators.[137] In practice this means that the purpose of government is simply to enact into state law and to enforce preexisting rules and regulations that, when clear, are beyond human question and interpretation. These include rules related to prayer and worship; prohibitions against usury, monopolies, gambling, drinking, and prostitution; punishment of thieves by cutting off their hands; excommunication of rapists; and public stoning to death of adulterers.[138] Consequently, although the ruler receives his power from "one source, the will of the governed," such power depends always upon the ruler's commitment to upholding the *shari'a*, not allegiance to the governed.[139] The responsibility of the ruler to the ruled and ruled to ruler is thus mediated by the *shari'a*: justice flows from adherence to Islamic law alone, not from adherence, for example, to the terms of a political contract. Because the ruler's authority is entirely derivative, he has no claims to hereditary succession, special privileges, or elevated status. There is, of course, a realm subject to the ruler's discretion. When there is no guiding precedent to be found in law, the ruler may pursue the welfare of the community as he sees fit. Such actions are justified in terms of two principles: that of "public interest" (*maslaha*)—welfare measures for which there is no decisive Qur'anic text—and that of "blocking of means"—which Musallam describes as "obstructing the means to illegitimate ends by prohibiting acts which would otherwise appear permissible by Qur'anic precepts."[140] But even then, such broad powers are tempered by both the letter and the spirit of the *shari'a*: reform and innovation are legitimate only to the extent that they can be justified by reference to Islamic principles and facilitate the realization of the ethico-political worldview implicit in Islamic law. Deviation in these guidelines signals the lapse of authority and the release of subjects from the requirements of obedience.

Likewise, the economy must be ruled according to the principles and prescriptions of Islamic Law. In *The Politics*, Aristotle both defends private property and argues that its use and quantity must be guided by the needs and moral ends of the polis.[141] Similarly, Qutb argues that Islam allows private property, but since such ownership is conceived of as mere stewardship of common property, the Islamic government retains the right to redistribute such wealth as it sees fit.[142] By implication, this is a rejection both of the ideal of a "free market" and of the existence of a self-contained set of economic laws of accumulation and exchange. For if all economic transactions must by guided by the moral and religious ends of the community, the idea of a "free market" appears to be a contradiction in terms.[143] Qutb thus emphasizes Qur'anic prescriptions with economic implications in a modern context, invoking moral and religious ends to advocate the nationalization of public resources, the "taking of overabundant wealth out of the hands of bloated capitalists," the establishment of minimum wages and social security, and the provision of free medical care and education.[144]

Ultimately, Qutb implies that the state's primary purpose should be understood in terms of social justice. The community is morally responsible for the maintenance and protection of its weakest members, an obligation enforced by both law and common morality: "The whole community is to blame and deserves harm and punishment in this world and in the next if it keeps silent when evil is done by some of its members. Thus it is charged with the duty of watching over every one of its members."[145] As Qutb takes great pains to emphasize, Islamic social justice is the natural expression of an organic worldview: it is but one practical corollary of the universalistic ethics of unity, mercy, love, and mutual responsibility. Thus, for Qutb, Islamic justice entails equality in the social, political, and spiritual realm simultaneously, and he contrasts this with reduction of justice to economic equality in Marxism. Justice in each sphere reflects on the other. Attentiveness to social justice is the path to Allah's pleasure and avoidance of his vengeance both for the individual and, importantly, for the community. Justice is an expression of and catalyst for the solidarity inherent in the nature of human beings.

In his emphasis on social justice, I would like to suggest, Qutb is drawing upon two distinct traditions, Qur'anic and Marxist.[146] The Qur'anic revelation exhorts the community to ensure that each Muslim be able to earn a living. One of the five pillars of Islam is an obligatory poor-tax (*zakat*, literally meaning purification, but also charity), a property tax that functions to provide a kind of safety net for the poor.[147] The Qur'an states: "So observe your devotional obligations, pay the *zakat*, and obey the Apostle so that you may be shown mercy" (24:56). Generosity is a function of piety that both ensures a minimal care for the poor and militates against the love of gain that is inherent in human nature. In this Qutb shares with several Western theorists a view of human nature as inherently self-interested. Yet he argues that both the individual and the collectivity must resist such impulses in order to construct the just society. Hence, Qutb condemns monopolies and usury and, in *Signposts*, explicitly vilifies capitalism.[148]

But while Qutb's emphasis on social justice is couched in Qur'anic verses,[149] his concerns are also informed by the politics of his time in Nasser's Egypt. Indeed, Shahrough Akhavi argues persuasively that Qutb has read back into the Qur'an and Sunna a distinctively modern emphasis on the *social* dimension of justice not in fact present in the texts.[150] In the context of widespread poverty, Nasser's socialist redistributive programs had amassed a wide appeal.[151] Thus, Qutb's pronounced and repeated concern for material equality seems an example of his tendency to absorb the very terms and concerns of his opponent, incorporating contemporary political truisms into a refurbished Islamic vision. That is, Qutb's categories and concerns echo precisely those of the communist and Arab socialist systems he reviles.[152] Qutb implicitly acknowledges such echoes in his very attempt to dismiss them; in at least one passage, he argues that any similarities between the socialist and Islamic worldviews are eclipsed by a wealth of larger differences. It is thus perhaps appropriate to apply to Qutb's view of social justice Roy's more general conclusion that "it is Marxism that is the mirror and foil of the Islamist effort."[153]

Qutb's vagueness regarding the structure of an Islamic state raises a number of problems, not least of which is the status of religious minorities in a state where membership is defined by religion. While Christians and Jews—"People of the Book" (*ahl al-dhimma*)—are historically protected peoples in Islam with rights grounded in public law, in practice and in theory they are nevertheless unequal. Such inequality is evinced by their differential treatment in the realms of taxation, military service, and job opportunities, as well as in popular suspicion of religious minorities.[154] And Qutb's polemics against the "Zionist conspiracy" and Christianity provide no remediation. Yet despite his xenophobia, Qutb claims that the just Islamic society will be characterized by diversity, an inclusiveness that incorporates and builds upon a plurality of histories, cultures, and identities united by each individual's equal relationship with the Creator.[155]

This language of pluralism, however, may be misleading. For Qutb's concern is unity, not diversity; solidarity, not plurality. In *Social Justice in Islam*, he explains that the equality of all individuals is a function of their common humanity, but the incorporation of all into the Islamic community seems contingent on a kind of assimilation rather than integration. I have argued that Qutb attempts to reconcile his broad understanding of sovereignty with the Qur'anic injunction that "there is no compulsion in religion" by reference to a vague concept of "freedom of conscience" (*hurriyyat al-wijdan*, also meaning "freedom of sentiment"). Even the sketchy outlines of the Islamic state offered in *Social Justice in Islam* reveal this reconciliation to be superficial at best: for when economy, government, and society are all regulated alike by the dictates of Islamic law; when citizenship itself is established by the declaration of faith in the one God; when criminal punishments are derived from the Qur'an; when all actions enjoined or prohibited in Islamic law are thereby invested with religious weight, any concept of religious freedom is gutted of meaning. This is because the implication of Qutb's arguments is that religious minorities are to be tolerated to the extent that their belief is not expressed in action that runs contrary to the injunctions of Islamic law or, in other words, that "freedom of sentiment" is largely limited to the realm of private conscience only. But it is crucial to Qutb's own argument that religious belief constitutes not just a moral attitude but a way of life with inherently political dimensions; this drives his critique of political systems whose authority is premised upon the plausibility of "privatizing" religion. To claim such scope for the Islamic religion while restricting all other belief to matters of the mind simply reinscribes, albeit along different lines, the religious intolerance he imputes to aggressively secular regimes.

Qutb's emphasis on forging unity out of diversity is thus more an expression of his vision of a community that has transcended the "base" divisions of class, clan, tribe, race, and country than a discussion of tolerance in the Lockean sense. Indeed, Qutb states explicitly that the diversity and differences characteristic of humanity are intended to give way to harmony, uniformity, and solidarity.[156] Qutb's organic account of the state here speaks from and to two different strains of thought: on the one hand, his view of the state as the vehicle to transform natural harmony into communal solidarity challenges political theories that build upon a conception of human nature as inherently contentious and define progress as the outcome of tension and discord between species, classes, or interests. At the same time, Qutb's monism builds upon a distinctively Islamic memory of early tribal and clannish factionalism, a divisiveness that not only pitted Arab against Arab but also presented a formidable obstacle to the spread of Islam. Evoking the powerful cultural symbol of chaos (*fitna*, which means a state of rebellion or war against the divine law, but also implies a moral chaos that ensues when Muslims' purity of belief is threatened),[157] Qutb can underscore the importance of transcending divisiveness in a unity possible only where membership is defined by belief.

Yet the question remains: what, in the end, will the Islamic state look like? Given Qutb's view of theory, such a question is itself illegitimate. Nevertheless it is worth drawing together Qutb's disparate and often fragmentary statements regarding government institutions to see if they suggest the rough contours of an Islamic state. In addition to his well-established antipathy to democracy, liberalism, communism, socialism, and nationalism, Qutb insists there is no legitimate "priesthood" or intermediary between God and the pious Muslim, and he argues that theocratic rule by those who would legislate God's will is illegitimate.[158] Monarchy is therefore unjust to the extent that it grants sovereignty to men and does so on the basis of kin and clan rather than piousness, ability, and impartiality.[159] In a letter to the Egyptian press in 1952, Qutb advocates what he calls a "just dictatorship."[160] On the basis of these very sketchy statements, it would not be unreasonable to suggest that Qutb leaves us with an image of rule by an institution, a group, or a person that can only be likened to a Platonic Philosopher-King. For it is rule that draws its legitimacy not from a contract between the people and the state but from superior piety, knowledge of Islamic law, moral integrity, and judiciousness than that found in the greater Muslim *umma*. However, such qualities are exercised solely in the recognition and application of laws that are by definition beyond human interpretation; justice flows from the common obedience of both ruler and ruled to divinely ordained truths. The result is ultimately a form of rule Ayubi aptly calls "nomocracy," that is, "the reign of the Word and the Rule."[161]

On the basis of Qutb's rather free-form interpretations of "clear" Qur'anic passages, his distinction between practical sciences and philosophical knowledge, and his attack on inequalities of rank, race and wealth, it seems possible to identify several features of Qutb's Islamic state. It would be committed to the acquisition of modern technology, the pursuit of scientific advancement, free education and health care, and the eradication of poverty and extreme wealth. There is also evidence to suggest that Qutb's state might embrace a version of meritocracy, one where preeminence is determined by work rather than social standing and wealth is accrued through labor rather than through "preferential treatment."[162] These speculative conclusions indicate that Qutb's Islamic state would not represent an attempt to recreate the structure and organization of seventh-century Mecca. On the contrary, they point to an embrace of many of the social and economic processes commonly associated with "modernization" as defined by social science. Yet this should not obscure the radical implications of Qutb's theocratic framework: all economic, social, and political policies and actions are defined by and judged in terms of the Islamic ends of the community as adumbrated in Islamic law. Usury is illegal, as is drinking alcohol. Criminal punishments range from excommunication to public stoning. And citizenship would formalize the political supremacy of the male Muslim not only over Muslim women and adherents of minority religions of both genders, but also over any Muslims unwilling to endorse Qutb's definition of what it means to be a Muslim.

RATIONALISM AND REENCHANTMENT

Two seminal analyses of Islamic fundamentalism, Sivan's *Radical Islam* and Kepel's *Muslim Extremism*, interpret Qutb's later writings as a direct political critique of the absolutism of the Egyptian regime under which he lived.[163] As we have seen in Qutb's focus on socialism, his opposition to Nasserism is indeed a dominant strain in his work. The antagonism is hardly surprising given Nasser's brutal repression of the Muslim Brotherhood, and the danger an Arab nationalism couched in symbols, of Islamic legitimacy posed to Qutb's insistence on the moral necessity of divine sovereignty. But I would suggest that Nasserism is just the most historically immediate target in a multidimensional critique that takes on not only Egyptian socialism, but also the transcultural historical and philosophical context in which it flourished.

Despite the Islamic rhetoric employed by Nasser's nationalist regime, his absolutist rule claimed a hegemony over the public sphere only possible in the context of the de facto separation of government and religion, the same development that, in Qutb's language, had brought the West to its current state of moral decline. For while Nasser's explicit intention was not secularization but the modernization of the official Islamic institutions in an attempt to transform them into an effective "transmission belt for state ideology,"[164] Arab socialism turned out to be a "dangerous Trojan horse of secularism, even of atheism."[165] Qutb, for one, did not find this surprising. He regarded an affinity between nationalism and secularism as the natural and inevitable product of a common European origin.[166] Indeed, his insistence on Islam as arbiter not only of the religious, but also of the political and social sphere in *Signposts along the Road* is a critique of precisely this transcultural investment in the legitimacy of the separation of religion and government.

While Qutb here intends to recapture the timeless "essence" of Islam, his insistence on the undiluted supremacy of divine authority is a return to Islamic foundations in only a limited sense. For while his explicit task is a resurrection of a past historic ideal, his very project—its language, symbols and focus—is defined as much by his contemporary interlocutors as by the "origins" of Islam.[167] That is, Qutb is preoccupied with such distinctively "modern" phenomena as Enlightenment philosophy, socialism, and liberalism, unintentionally incorporating many of the terms and concerns of those discourses while insisting on philosophical "purity." His work is thus not the expression of some kind of "pure," unadulterated Islamic thought: consider, for example, the reification of Islam, the understanding of social systems in terms of dynamic, social processes, the incorporation of an idea of progressive (if contingent) historical change, the pronounced concern for social justice, the embrace of modern technology and meritocracy, his modified historicism, the dialectical vision of history, and the very concept of modern *jahiliyya*.[168] These are the intellectual products of the interaction of Qutb's version of Islamic thought with the contemporary world, a world where colonialism and the influence of Western cultural thought had set the terms of debate even for those who sought to critique such influence. Despite the fact that authors such as Sivan often characterize Qutb as antimodern, he is a distinctively modern fundamentalist: he is a thinker whose work is a complex blend of modern pragmatism and nostalgic idealism and whose writing is a montage of Qur'anic quotes and contemporary aphorisms.[169]

Of course, the multiplicity of meanings embodied in the word "modernity" makes its use in relationship to Qutb suspect at best. Should modernity be taken to connote an emphasis on modern technology, progress, and worldliness, Qutb is essentially modern. Should it be understood to imply an openness to Westernization, or a commitment to secularism, Qutb is deeply antimodern. Should modernity be taken in a deconstructionist formulation, "modernity" may not correspond to objective phenomena at all. Yet given the universalization of the Western experience of modernity, the very meaning of "modern" authority has been defined in terms of the right of human beings—either through a leader or representatives or directly—to rule the public sphere, and in opposition to theocentric systems of social organization and knowledge that obtained in times designated as "premodern." Consequently, Qutb may be considered "antimodern" in this one qualified and contingent sense: his uncompromising opposition to all contemporary sources of legitimacy as man-made usurpations of God's sovereignty. All such "man-made" sources of authority assume that sovereignty is autonomous from the authority of the spiritual realm.

Herein lies the larger dimension of Qutb's critique, the target lurking behind his aversion to the Nasserist regime per se: Qutb engages not just the institutional and historical reality that is secularism, but the epistemology and worldview upon which it is founded. I am arguing, then, that Qutb's insistence on the exclusivity of divine sovereignty constitutes a repudiation not only of the corruption of Middle Eastern regimes and their failure to deliver on political, social, and economic promises of reform, and the dominance of Western political, cultural, and economic power, but also a moral indictment of post-Enlightenment political theories such as Marxism, nationalism, liberalism, and socialism that assume the exclusion of religious authority from the political realm. From Qutb's perspective, these theories require but one name—*jahiliyya*—because they are fundamentally united by a theory of human sovereignty legitimated by a modern, rationalist epistemology.[170] As I have noted, such rationalism regards human comprehension as the determinant not only of how we come to know the world, but also what constitutes legitimate knowledge. In this way, men's and women's ability to reach the truth through reason is linked to an explicit repudiation of religious authority over politics.[171]

As I have attempted to show in the preceding analysis, Qutb is located in a position from which such claims would inevitably be experienced as both nonsensical and pernicious to the very possibility of acknowledging the metaphysical truths upon which all meaning in the world is dependent. For Qutb the consequences of such abstract claims are thus immediate and grave. The triumph of rationalism entails a denial of divine sovereignty, and the denial of divine sovereignty is the source of moral corruption, fragmentation of knowledge, and the corrosion of meaning; all contribute to the greed of Egyptian elites, social and economic inequality, internal disunity, and military defeats. In this way, Qutb's critique of modern political theories of sovereignty is ultimately a rebuttal to the epistemological assumption that truths about the world can be reached by way of human faculties and methods without divine intervention, and that knowledge of such truths can legitimate mastery over nature and human nature.

The point here is not that Qutb is somehow *right*. Indeed Qutb's rigid distinctions between East and West, truth and opinion, "real" Islam and "false" Islam, women and men are at best highly problematic. Nor is the aim here to render Qutb more palatable, reasonable, *rational* than he is. His arguments are at times quite disturbing, and to recast Qutb as "rational" would do violence not only to Qutb's project but also to my own. What I do want to suggest, however, is that this reading extends the argument advanced in the previous chapter by showing that what is problematic about Qutb's political thought cannot be captured by the language of irrationalism, pathology, and antimodernism. It cannot be captured in this language in part because such rhetoric does not allow for the tensions embedded in the complex of influences and allegiances that shape and inform Qutb's thought. Moreover, the very language of irrationality and antimodernism replicates the very mistake Qutb makes so often in his critique of modernity by ignoring its own conditionality. For lost in this rhetoric is acknowledgment of the culturally specific experiences and values embedded in the term "modern," and the ways in which the accusation of "irrationality" renders illegitimate all commitments and actions constituted by belief in truths not fully and immediately accessible to human reason and methods.

It is perhaps more illuminating to characterize Qutb's work as an embrace of the nonrational, that is, an argument for the authority of knowledge that is by definition beyond human reason. As I will argue, such an embrace is neither pathological nor unfamiliar to the West but may be usefully seen as one part of a larger effort to "reenchant" a world defined by disenchantment, one attempt among many to seek an overarching moral unity as an antidote to what is seen as the subjectivism, atomism, and fragmentation of contemporary life. Understood in this way, in Qutb's work we are witnessing not antimodernism but rather another perspective on and attempt to redefine what it must mean to live in the modern world, a perspective that challenges the so-called imperatives of modern rationalism in the name of other possible modernities. Understanding Qutb in this way escapes what Foucault called the "blackmail" of being "'for' or 'against' the Enlightenment," that is, the glib equation of "critical reservations about modernity with a virulent antimodernism and antirationalism."[172] Paradoxically perhaps, Qutb's perspective thus underscores what Rousseau's "Discourse on the Origins of Inequality" suggested over two centuries ago, that the "modern condition" is itself characterized by serious ambivalences toward "modernity."

It is my contention that what is particularly problematic about Qutb's political thought lies not in this search for moral unity and reenchantment but with, first, his insistence, that the only true unity lies in Islam and, second, his denial that his own interpretation of Islam is an act of interpretation. This antihermeneutic stance in particular is problematic in part because it locks him within an untenable contradiction. For he insists that the proper scope of reason is apprehension of the material world and receptivity to the self-evidence of divine truths expressed in the Qur'an and Sunna. While Qutb insists on the necessity of adapting the Islamic worldview to changing conditions and circumstances, such adaptation is deductive only: changing circumstances do not alter his version of the essence of Islam. Certain aspects of the fixed, pure, and unchangeable Islamic framework are simply realized in a variety of ways and through a variety of institutions given the conditions that obtain at that particular moment in history.[173] Interpretation and speculations about the basics of these fixed, self-evident truths are thus unnecessary, fundamentally transgressive of divine authority, and deeply misguided: unlike the clarity of divine truths, human reasoning about that which is beyond human reason is faulty and pernicious.[174] This is why he claims repeatedly that his version of Islam is not a "version" at all. It is *the* essence of Islam, an Islam undiluted by the influences of alien cultures and *jahiliyya*.

Yet his entire project is an act of interpretation, and, as I have argued throughout this chapter, it is an interpretation that betrays the influence of the very categories and concerns he reviles as alien and corrupting. Indeed, the Islam here does not entail a return to the time of the Caliphs "but is a new Islam of commitment to an abstract concept of community and moral authority."[175] Moreover, Qutb's is an interpretation of the most "philosophical" (in his meaning) and speculative sort. It is designed to respond to the yearning for meaning that inheres in the human condition, and the *modern* human condition in particular. Indeed, his readings of the Qur'an often vitiate his own standards. In his discussion of gender, for example, he is not merely offering a literalist reading of a particular Qur'anic passage, but defending the passage against contemporary accusers and accusations by way

of an interpretation that, to put it generously, stretches the fairly unequivocal Qur'anic passages beyond their outermost limits.

Revealing Qutb's contradictions is, however, substantially less interesting
and less important than exploring the political and moral implications of his
selectively antihermeneutical position. Denying that his own work is an act
of interpretation places him in an epistemologically privileged position despite his attempt to "democratize" the act of Qur'anic interpretation, to
wrest that privilege from Islamic jurists and engage Muslims without specialized training. Not only does Qutb claim for himself the knowledge required to see clearly the self-delusions of Western societies and religions,
deploying the charge of "false consciousness" to silence all challenges or
complications, but he makes himself the sole authority of what it means to be
a Muslim, of what authentic Islam is and always has been. Thus he simultaneously denies that his Islam is just one among many "remakes of things
traditional" and effectively forecloses the possibility of productive dialogue
among Muslims about what it means to be a member of an Islamic community in the modern world. This is a question that, as I will show in the
following chapter, has many possible answers.[176] Indeed, as I suggest in the
introductory chapter, the denial that an interpretation is an interpretation is
a crucial characteristic of what it means to be a "fundamentalist." The claim
to specialized knowledge, perhaps embodied most vividly in Plato's Philosopher-Kings, silences all critique, closes discussion on basic questions of living together such as: What is the good life? What is the purpose of politics?
What is legitimate authority? Such claims can serve to justify quite dangerous political practices. If we take public contestation not only about specific
policies but also about the very nature and purpose of collective life as the
stuff of politics, it is also the case that such claims are essentially antipolitical
as well.

CONCLUSION: BEYOND ORIENTALISM

Qutb's text is one highly influential picture of the Islamist worldview. It is
not definitive but illustrative of the critique of post-Enlightenment modernity and epistemology current in much of Sunni Islamist political thought.[177]
This picture cannot stand in for an account of the ways in which Islamist
activists read Qutb, or of why any one individual "becomes" a fundamentalist. Yet Qutb's continuing influence over the ideas and actions of contemporary Islamists make his text particularly illuminating for any attempt to
understand the movement's meaning. There is a moral power to fundamentalist ideas that cannot be explained only by variables outside of the ideas.
This is not the same as arguing that fundamentalism can be understood
solely by reference to ideas and without attention to the ways structural
conditions significantly shape and enframe such ideas. On the contrary, the

corrective to overly functionalist accounts of fundamentalist ideas is not an exclusive emphasis on the explication of meaning—as if meaning could somehow be abstracted from historical, cultural, political, and economic context. As the dialogic model discussed earlier suggests that meaning and function are dialectically and mutually determinative, such an emphasis merely reproduces—albeit along different lines—a false dichotomy between action and ideas, function and meaning. Consequently, I am not arguing that such explanations are "wrong" or irrelevant, but rather that they have inverted the task of interpretation: located in and defined by a particular context, the horizons of meaning of the phenomenon must be taken to "determine both the nature of the political body and its function in society, and not vice-versa."[178]

The power of fundamentalist ideas is certainly not unrelated to the political, cultural, and economic conditions so well documented in empirical studies of fundamentalism; as a critical, utopianist, and revolutionary movement, fundamentalism is dialogically and functionally related to the conditions that obtain around it. But as I argued in the previous chapter, saying that fundamentalism is intimately connected with material conditions and disaffection, for example, is different from arguing or implying that such conditions explain the appeal of fundamentalist ideas. Social science understandings of the material context from which fundamentalism emerges are thus integral to, yet do not themselves constitute, a full explanation of the resurgence of political Islam. It is my contention that fundamentalists' own understandings of the movement's meaning and purpose render the specific appeal of fundamentalism intelligible. If my analysis of Qutb is plausible, Islamic ideas are compelling in part because they are a powerful challenge both to the legitimacy of secular, modernizing Middle Eastern regimes and to the Western rationalist and imperialist ways of understanding and thus organizing political life.

Yet given my criticisms of the way rationalist assumptions reflect and express Western fears and experiences as much as they illuminate Islamic fundamentalism, and given that I, too, am a "situated interpreter," what claims can I make for my reading of Qutb and, by extension, my explanation of Islamic fundamentalism? I argue that a dialogic model of understanding challenges the notion of an archimedean point outside of language and politics to which we can refer our disputes about interpretation and determine the truth of the matter "once and for all." Thus, I do not claim that this is the final, objective account: this reading may not be *the* interpretation of fundamentalist thought, nor may it exhaust the range of possible truths about Qutb's own understanding of the movement's meaning and purpose. Yet to acknowledge that this is not the only possible reading of Qutb's political theory and of the power of Islamic fundamentalism more generally is not necessarily to argue—as Ernest Gellner argues postmodernists argue—that all interpretations are equal.[179] Like Gellner, I want to maintain that we can and must be able to judge among rival interpretations. Indeed, I want to claim that this interpretation is better. But I do so on very specific grounds: I suggest that "better" interpretations are those that approach the subject as one would a dialogue; those that at one and the same time are aware of their own conditionality and are open to newness; those attentive to participants' self-understandings—and, concomitantly, ones in which the subject might recognize herself, her meanings, her actions.

Understanding fundamentalist ideas requires locating fundamentalists not "beyond the pale" but firmly within a human predicament we recognize, if not endorse. This entails an attempt to understand the "Other's" voice on as close to its own terms and categories as humanly possible, which in turn requires that we preserve the common humanity of the subject. Yet "better" explanations must also be attuned to the possibility that actors may misunderstand or misrepresent their own experiences, and thus that critique and evaluation are not only possible but necessary. As Isaiah Berlin illustrates by argument and example in "Joseph de Maistre and the Origins of Fascism," interpretive understandings do not preclude critique, but rather make critique possible by making genuine understanding possible.[180] Thus Berlin argues that for theorists such as Kant or Mill, rational argumentation constitutes both the substance and form of their work; their arguments stand or fall according to the standards of such argumentation. But for more metaphysical, poetic, or romantic thinkers such as Qutb, or the protofascist de Maistre (or Hegel or Plato, for that matter), understanding requires immersion in the universe of the theorist more than, or prior to, a point-by-point evaluation of his or her logic.[181] In this sense, Qutb's project may be usefully understood in the context of what Wolin has termed the "epic tradition of political theory," one "which is inspired mainly by the hope of achieving a great and memorable deed through the medium of thought. Other aims that it may have, such as contributing to the existing state of knowledge, formulating a system of logically consistent propositions, or establishing a set of hypotheses for scientific investigation, are distinctly secondary."[182] Berlin's point regarding de Maistre, and mine regarding fundamentalist theorists such as Qutb, is not that they eschew argumentation; rather, the point is that it is not by such arguments that they are judged.

> For their essential purpose is to expound an all-embracing conception of the world and man's place and experience within it, they seek not so much to convince as to convert, to transform the vision of those whom they seek to address, so that they see the facts "in a new light," "from a new angle," in terms of a new pattern in which what had earlier seemed to be a casual amalgam of elements is presented as a systematic, interrelated unity. Logical reasoning may help to weaken existing doctrines, or refute specific beliefs, but it is an ancillary weapon, not the principal

means of conquest: that is the new model itself, which casts its own emotional or intellectual or spiritual spell upon those who are converted.[183]

This chapter attempts to render just such an interpretive yet critical reading of Qutb's worldview. If my argument that this hermeneutically informed interpretation is both defensible against others and plausible on its own terms, what then about the inverse objection, that is, that all interpretation—including my own reading of fundamentalist thought—is an exercise in power that inevitably distorts or disfigures that which it claims to illuminate? Put more contentiously, are cultures locked in hermetically sealed boxes of meaning such that we in the West, as both outsiders and former colonialists, are doomed to employ interpretive categories that at best distort, and at worst demean, the voices and meanings of the participants themselves? As I argued in chapter 2, no interpreter stands clear of a discourse, myself included. Indeed, I have argued that given the prevalence of Western texts and discourses in Cairo, and his own "modern" education, Qutb is not only engaged in a rereading of the Islamic past but also profoundly influenced by Western experiences of modernity and rationalism, and shaped by the facts of Western colonialism and imperialism. So just as the West is itself a product of multiple identities and traditions, the "view from the other side" evident in Qutb's fundamentalist thought is itself a culturally syncretic perspective, a complex and eclectic amalgamation of Western ideas and reinterpreted Islamic traditions. Consequently, my interpretation of Qutb's work is the result of an interaction between the perspective that I bring to the project and his own, already mediated worldview.

That politics is implicated in the production of truth is inescapable; that truth is reducible to politics is untenable, but not because, as Ernest Gellner would have it, truth is constituted by those irrefutable realities that by definition exist beyond power, beyond politics, beyond human interests.[184] The question, then, is not whether an interpreter is "located," but how the interpreter makes use of the knowledge that she is "located." Again using Gadamer's description of hermeneutically informed interpretation as a guide, the point is not to abstract oneself from one's own prejudices, but precisely the opposite: interpretation is like a conversation where the interpreter must acknowledge her own prejudices, remain open to the meanings of the Other, and can find a language that is appropriate to such meanings without violating her own linguistic worldview. Such reciprocity means that a vision of interpretation as an evolving "fusion of horizons" supersedes the image of cultures locked in sealed boxes of meaning. This process does not eradicate distortion but opens the possibility of obtaining genuine knowledge of others through the self-conscious attempt at careful listening. In the end, then, I want to argue that this reading of Islamic fundamentalist ideas and of the resurgence of Islamic fundamentalism is compelling because it begins with an attempt to provide an interpretive account of the power of fundamentalist thought rather than with categories outside the fundamentalist tradition that have subjugated the importance of fundamentalists' own ideas about the movement's meaning and purpose. I defend this reading as less distortionary than others because this interpretive account is one that, I submit, the subject himself would recognize; because, I advance it without recourse to a notion of truth and facts unmediated by language, but without relinquishing all standards by which to evaluate interpretations; because it does not claim to replace but rather to complete causal explanations; and because, in the final analysis, it does not claim to tell the truth about the text or the phenomenon once and for all, but rather to offer a richer, more compelling understanding of it.

CHAPTER FOUR

A View across Time: Islam as the Religion of Reason

I HAVE approached Qutb as a political theorist because, I have argued, his own preoccupations with the moral foundations of political authority are the preoccupations of political theory as a field, and, moreover, his political thought is significantly shaped by the experience of Western colonialism and cultural influence. In emphasizing this kind of context for Qutb's work, I have tried to illustrate an approach that, to borrow and perhaps subvert Clifford Geertz's language about interpreting culture, works to expose what is familiar in the unfamiliar without denying its particularity.[1] Within the proposed framework of comparative political theory, such exposure is potentially double, for it simultaneously provides a window into the world of Islamic fundamentalism and holds a mirror up to our own world. Yet at the same time that Qutb's perspective on "the modern condition" illuminates the extent to which modern ideas we value are experienced and redefined in other cultures, the cultural syncretism of Qutb's thought blurs the boundaries between Islam and the West. In this way, his work comes to seem less a perspective of radical difference than a different perspective on what it does and must mean to live in the modern world.

Yet the attempt to expose familiarity in unfamiliarity risks orienting Qutb's thought, and the agenda of Islamic fundamentalists more generally, in terms of "our" concerns: the very paradigm of familiarity inevitably measures Qutb's intelligibility in terms of his accessibility, or inaccessibility, to Western worlds of meaning. This is a concern despite the fact that those worlds of meaning have substantially framed Qutb's own political thought. In the following discussion, then, I contrast nineteenth-century Islamic "modernist"[2] arguments for the compatibility of Islam and reason with Qutb's insistence that such arguments are both false and corrosive to Islamic authenticity. Indeed, in *Signposts along the Road* and *The Islamic Conception and Its Characteristics*, Qutb explicitly repudiates such arguments as an apologia for Western dominance, and therefore as a prescription for further decay rather than renewal. For Qutb contends that the emphasis on the importance of reason in Islam, and arguments for the compatibility of modernity and Islam, rationality and revealed law, are simply poorly masked attempts to justify Islam against both the obscurantism of Islamic scholars and attacks from Western and Eastern secularists.[3] The underlying premise and implication of such apologetics, Qutb argues, is that Islam is on trial because it is somehow "guilty" and therefore in need of exoneration.[4] This defensive posture is a position not of strength and certainty but of power-lessness. As we have seen, while Qutb does not eschew the exercise and importance of human reason for understanding aspects of the world, he is outraged by the claim that reason and scripture are equally important for knowledge and guidance when it is self-evidently true that

> [divine revelation] came down to be a source which human reason must consult, to be the standard in terms of which all judgments, knowledge and concepts of human reason are evaluated, and to correct the deficiencies and distortions pro-duced by reason. There is, no doubt, congruence and harmony between the two but on this basis alone: the absolute supremacy of divine revelation over human reason, not a posited equality or commensurability between them.[5]

What has alternately been called Islamic "modernism," Islamic re-formism, or at times referred to by the term *salafiyya*—a word deriving from the Arabic root meaning "predecessors" or "forebears"—provides a point of sharp contrast to Qutb's rejection of rationalist ambitions to understand hu-man nature and purposes.[6] In general, Islamic modernism refers to an intel-lectual stream of nineteenth-century Islamic thought that took shape in the shadow of the slow decline of the Ottoman Empire and the expansion of European political and economic power. Such thought posited a golden age in the earliest generations in Islamic history and sought simultaneously to revive and reform Islam in the image of that golden age,[7] thereby providing a bulwark against the encroachments of Western imperialist and colonialist power upon a decaying Islamic community. This historical and political con-text had also shaped a prior generation of Muslim intellectuals— writers such as Rifa'a Badawi Rafi' al-Tahtawi (1801–1873) and Khayr al-Din Pasha (1820s–1889)—yet at that time, the disparity in power had not yet lent what Sharabi calls a "menacing aspect" to European growth. For this earlier group of Muslim thinkers, European ascendence was "less of a threat and more of a promise."[8] Thus, although the gradual but steady growth of Euro-pean influence in the workings of the Ottoman Empire in particular had been a matter of concern among Muslim intellectuals for some time, in the mid-1800s "they had not yet become so great as to constitute the central problem of political life, and the main problem was still what it had been for the Ottoman writers of the seventeenth and eighteenth centuries—internal decline, how to explain and how to arrest it."[9] The years 1875–1882 radically altered that landscape: by 1877 Russia had attacked Turkey, Tunisia was occupied by the French four years later, and by 1882 Egypt was occupied by the British. "The problem of inner decay still exercised men's minds," Hour-ani observes, "but there was grafted on to it a new problem, that of survival: how could the Muslim countries resist the new danger from the outside?"[10] Although Islam had always moved through repeated cycles of renewal and reform, what distinguished the modernist movement of the late nineteenth century from earlier attempts at Islamic "purification" was its profound engagement with the external threat posed by Europe.[11]

The movement is perhaps most closely associated with the work of Muhammad 'Abduh (1849–1905), but it arguably includes, or was significantly presaged by, the anti-imperialist philosophy and activism of 'Abduh's sometime collaborator, Jamal al-Din al-Afghani [al-Asadabadi] (1839–1897).[12] For many scholars of Islam, the influence of Afghani and 'Abduh is an established fact, and the importance of their political thought and activism for understanding subsequent developments in Middle Eastern politics is undisputed. For example, Charles C. Adams cites approvingly biographers who have described 'Abduh as "one of the creators of modern Egypt" and "one of the founders of modern Islam";[13] Badawi calls Afghani the Socrates of the Islamic Reformist school; and Wilfred C. Smith argues that it was Afghani who first stressed the "Islam-West" antinomy, and the first important figure with "nostalgia for the departed earthly glory of pristine Islam."[14] Yet since the 1960s, a number of scholars have challenged the standard account of Afghani and 'Abduh as pioneering Islamic reformists, casting doubt upon their sincerity and emphasizing their failure systematically or significantly to reformulate Islamic doctrine.[15] Yet even these critics portray Afghani and 'Abduh as inaugurators of Islamic revival broadly understood. For example, a leading scholar on Afghani, Nikki Keddie, notes that while some scholars have exaggerated Afghani's direct influence over subsequent movements and ideologies in the Middle East, and that Afghani in fact wielded little political influence during his lifetime, it is also true that "Afghani was one of the first influential figures to try to restate the Muslim tradition in ways that might meet the agonizing problems brought by the growing encroachments of the West in the Middle East."[16] Sylvia Haim concurs in her overview of Arab nationalism by stating that Afghani offered the most "significant" and "influential" defense of Islam and can be credited with transforming Islam into an ideology. She concludes: "His political activity and teaching combined to spread among the intellectual and official classes of Middle Eastern Islam a secularist, meliorist, and activist attitude toward politics, an attitude the presence of which was essential, before ideologies such as Arab nationalism could be accepted to any degree."[17] The lively and unceasing debate over the significance, impact, and originality of both thinkers and their work assures, and indeed presupposes, their importance in Islamic political thought.

As this analysis takes Qutb's criticisms of Islamic modernism as a point of departure for examining arguments of the modernists themselves, this chapter does not attempt an analysis of Afghani's and 'Abduh's lives and thought in full, nor does it aspire to be a full account of Islamic modernism. Lastly, this analysis cannot stand in for a genealogy: indeed, it is one of the paradoxes of the contemporary Islamist movement that while 'Abduh is explicitly rejected as the modernist who "let reason in the back door," as it were, Afghani is celebrated as a great anti-imperialist defender of Islam, an argument that, as we shall see, privileges some of his writings over others.[18] As with my analysis of Qutb, I approach Afghani's and 'Abduh's thought with a particular set of purposes: to highlight the extent to which these responses to the challenge of Western cultural and political power are premised upon the assumption that rationalism not only is compatible with Islamic teachings but is actually enjoined by such teachings when rightly—which is to say rationally—understood.

AFGHANI AND ISLAMIC PHILOSOPHY

> The father and mother of science is proof, and proof is neither Aristotle nor Galileo. The truth is where there is proof, and those who forbid science and knowledge in the belief that they are safeguarding the Islamic religion are really the enemies of that religion. The Islamic religion is the closest of religions to science and knowledge, and there is no incompatibility between science and knowledge and the foundation of the Islamic faith.[19]

Any analysis of Jamal al-Din al-Afghani's political thought, no matter how carefully delimited, immediately encounters the difficulty of locating him, both geographically and intellectually. Afghani wanted it known that he was born and raised as a Sunni Muslim in Afghanistan, but it has been persuasively established that he was most likely born into a family of sayyids (descendants of the prophet) in Asadabad, Iran, near Hamadan in 1839. Thus he was raised and educated as a Shi'ite Muslim at home until he was ten, when he continued his religious education in Tehran and in the shrine cities of Iraq.[20] Afghani's Iranian origins are for Elie Kedourie a sign of the duplicitousness and manipulation that tarnishes not only his life but his intellectual agenda as well. In contrast, M. A. Said Badawi argues that given the historical tensions between Sunnis and Shi'ites, Afghani's pan-Islamic commitments necessitated a Sunni identity.[21]

The confusion surrounding his origins is only exacerbated by the complex interplay of his intellectual, political, and religious commitments. For example, he apparently made different arguments to different audiences. Consequently, much of the secondary literature on Afghani is preoccupied with determining the "real" versus the merely strategic in Afghani's writings. Nikki Keddie has argued in several books, including a seminal biography, that Afghani's reputation as a pioneering *Islamic* reformer obscures the extent to which his commitment to Islam often served rather than shaped his political interest in strengthening the Muslim world against Western power.[22] Kedourie goes as far as portraying Afghani as an almost Machiavellian figure whose commitment to Islam was entirely utilitarian. Kedourie further argues that examination of both the substance and function of Afghan's and 'Abduh's shifting Islamic commitments reveals a heterodoxy tantamount to irreligiosity.[23]

While it is difficult if not impossible to determine definitively in retrospect what Afghani "really believed," it is possible to argue that his political writings are consistently characterized by the tension that defined his life: the repudiation of Western imperialism in all its forms and the conviction that Western rationalist methods and the technological and scientific expertise they produced were necessary for political strength and for the survival of the Islamic community. Afghani's anti-imperialism in particular is a remarkably consistent thread in his life: after a childhood in Iran, Afghani spent most of his peripatetic life agitating for pan-Islamism[24] and against European imperialism. His first recorded political activities are in India, where he apparently moved from Iran in 1855–1856. It was in India that his exposure to British imperialism had a profound effect, and there that he came into his first direct contact with the sciences and mathematics of Europe. Afghani came to Afghanistan for the first time in 1866 and appears on the political scene in his late teens already as a decidedly anti-imperialist, anti-British activist. In what was to become a pattern in his life, Afghani was expelled from Afghanistan in 1868 when the new Amir of Afghanistan grew suspicious of him. He made his way to Istanbul by 1869 and found favor with the reformer and leader Ali Pasha. But he was expelled on the grounds of heresy in 1870 after he delivered a public lecture drawing upon his training in Islamic philosophy and comparing prophecy to philosophy, "the highest of crafts."[25]

The arguments of this lecture, as well as those of his other writings on philosophy, illustrate the centrality of Afghani's conviction that the decay of the Muslim *umma* (community) and its manifest weakness in relation to European ascendence are inextricably tied to the neglect of science and philosophy. In contrast to Qutb's insistence that to be truly Muslim means acknowledging the limits of human reason in matters metaphysical and moral, for Afghani the survival of Islam depends not on the repudiation of rationalism but on the employment of it against the real enemy: imperialism. Thus while Qutb argues that the intrusion of ancient philosophy and rationalism inaugurated a corruption of Islam completed by the aggressive secularism of the Enlightenment, Afghani attributes the decay of Islam to the negation and neglect of reason and philosophy, both of which are transhistorical imperatives for knowledge.

Afghani thus seeks to disentangle the prevailing equation of rationalism and the West so that the free exercise of reason appears neither inimical to Islamic truths nor tantamount to Westernization. Toward this end, Afghani's "Lecture on Teaching and Learning" (delivered in Calcutta in 1882) establishes a distinction between the power of science and the power of particular cultures or nations whose successes have been facilitated by science. As science and philosophy are the means by which human beings obtain truths about the world, such truths and the methods used to obtain them are not the product of the West but of human endeavor generally. The subject of science is universal, and the truths it reveals are self-evident. All wealth and riches are products of these universal truths, truths that encompass not only the functioning of nature and human nature, but, by extension, the requirements for living and living well.[26] This means that scientific truths do not now reside in European culture any more than they did in Egypt or Phoenicia at the pinnacle of their civilizational strength. Science, constituted and guided by the ultimate science, philosophy, is the source of real power in the world. Thus, according to Afghani, "[t]here was, is, and will be no ruler in the world but science."[27] Although rationalism is currently associated with Western culture, Afghani insists that Islam has contributed substantially to the evolution of human rationality and that, in addition, the very universality of rational methods and the truths they produce belies constructions of Islam as inherently incompatible with rationalism.[28]

Thus Afghani contends that "real" Islam encourages the use of reason, even or especially when interpreting scripture to guide human action. Doing so, moreover, is the precondition to both truth and the strength of the Islamic community. But, Afghani argues, Muslim scholars have insisted on dividing up the world into "Muslim science" and "European science," not understanding that "science is that noble thing that has no connection with any nation. . . . [E]verything that is known is known by science, and every nation that becomes renowned becomes renowned through science. Men must be related to science, not science to men."[29] For Afghani, to bifurcate science in this way entails the claim that Islam is incompatible with self-evident knowledge. Because this knowledge is both the precondition to and expression of any culture's wealth and power, such bifurcation not only positions Islam in opposition to truth, but also condemns Islam to decay and weakness.

> [A] science is needed to be the comprehensive soul for all the sciences, so that it can preserve their existence, apply each of them in its proper place, and become the cause of the progress of each one of those sciences. The science that has the position of a comprehensive soul and the rank of a preserving force is the science of *falsafa* or philosophy, because its subject is universal. It is philosophy that shows man human prerequisites. It shows the sciences what is necessary. It employs each of the sciences in its proper place. . . . That community without the spirit of philosophy could not deduce conclusions from these sciences.[30]

For Afghani, scientific knowledge and the philosophy that governs its discovery progress over time and flourish in different places and cultures at different moments in history. In emphasizing an understanding of knowledge as dynamic and evolutionary, Afghani challenges the view that there is in the universe a fixed sum of knowledge, a "solid and immobile" mass to be acquired "not by analysis, induction and experiment but by the simple amassing of what already existed or, at most, by deductive reasoning from accepted axioms."[31] This evolutionary view of knowledge underlies his contention in the "The Benefits of Philosophy" that the *umma* needs philosophy because it is the precondition not only to scientific knowledge but also to moral development. For in *The Refutation of the Materialists* Afghani argues that men (women are not mentioned) are by nature cruel, greedy, and ignorant, and that the closer they are to their true nature, the closer they are to animals.[32] Given human nature, then, morality reflects an arduous and ongoing battle against the pull of bestial nature, a battle in which habit and education are therefore crucial.[33] Insofar as philosophy facilitates the exercise of reason, it broadens the scope of human thought from mere instinct to reflection and insight, thereby making possible the emergence not only of virtue but of civilization itself. Philosophy is thus what distinguishes human beings from animals.

If philosophy is the crux of human development, moral and scientific, what, then, is the point of religion for Afghani? His arguments in this regard must be situated in the context of his political activities for, as Kedourie persuasively argues, Afghani's paramount concern with imperialism often relegated Islam to secondary significance, both in thought and practice, as the means to political, economic, and scientific mastery of the material world. Indeed, it is often noted that Afghani seemed willing to work anywhere, with anyone—sultan, despot, or colonialist—who would advance his anti-imperialist objectives. After Afghani was expelled from Istanbul for his lecture on philosophy, for example, he began an eight-year stay in Cairo, living on a government pension arranged by Riaz Pasha, whom Hourani dubs a "minister of liberal views."[34] During this time Afghani became the center of a group of young Egyptian intellectuals, including Muhammad 'Abduh, drawn to Afghani's anti-imperialism and his use of Islamic philosophy to render Islam compatible with scientific, technological, and political progress. Initially on good terms with the heir to Egypt's monarchy, Afghani was deported to India in 1879, once Tawfiq wrested power from his profligate father with the help of British and French intervention.

After a time in India and Paris, Afghani visited London in 1885 at the invitation of Wilfrid Blunt, a highly placed Englishman sympathetic to Irish, Arab, and Indian nationalist aspirations. Through Blunt's auspices, Afghani negotiated with British statesmen in an unsuccessful attempt to encourage the British to leave Egypt. In an echo of the circumstances that marked many of Afghani's previous "departures," Blunt eventually asked him to leave his house when two of Afghani's friends argued somewhat violently there. Afghani then went to Iran, Russia, and then back again to Iran, where he served as adviser to Shah Nasir al-Din. But the shah eventually expelled Afghani for his involvement in the Tobacco Uprising of 1890–1891, a mass protest against the shah's concession of a monopoly over the Iranian tobacco industry to a British company.[35] Afghani then traveled to Istanbul at the request of the Ottoman Sultan Abdülhamid, but soon incurred the sultan's enmity and distrust by expressing support for an Arab caliphate, an implicit challenge to Ottoman authority. Moreover, one of Afghani's Iranian disciples had killed the Shah of Iran in 1896, arguably at Afghani's urging; not surprisingly, this contributed to Abdülhamid's growing sense that Afghani posed a danger to his authority. Anxious to retain a measure of control over Afghani's political activities, the sultan denied him permission to leave Istanbul several times. Afghani spent the final years of his life, until he died from cancer in 1897, a virtual prisoner at the sultan's court.

It was after his expulsion from Egypt that Afghani returned to India for two years and there wrote one of the rare documents of his views on religion, *The Refutation of the Materialists*. In this attack on a growing group of Westernizing modernists in India called the *neicheris*, or "followers of nature," Afghani emerges perhaps for the first time as a staunch defender not only of the integrity of the Muslim community but of Islam per se against the challenges of the unorthodox and Muslims overly imitative of the West. In the introduction, Afghani states that religion is a crucial link in the development of knowledge, in the advance of civilization, and in the very possibility of morality. Indeed, evoking the language of disease and cure that characterizes Qutb's assessment of modernity, Afghani has been quoted as saying that "every Muslim is sick, and his only remedy is in the Qur'an."[36] Although Afghani readily acknowledges the defects of Islam, he insists that such defects do not inhere in Islam but are the products of current understanding and practice. For Afghani, an understanding of the true Islam means recognizing that the achievements of philosophy are not defined in opposition to the truths of religion. Religion in general, and Islam in particular, has facilitated the transformation of human beings from ignorance and savagery to knowledge and civilization, and it has done so by encouraging the free exercise of human reason. Proper reading reveals the extent to which rationalist methods and philosophical truths are not only encouraged by, but actually contained in, the Qur'an and the traditions. The Qur'an and the Prophet exhort Muslims by word and example to pursue "knowledge, wisdom, learning, reflection, thought, and insight" and include moral guidance entirely in keeping with the truths of philosophy. With the Qur'an, Allah "planted the roots of philosophical sciences into purified souls, and opened the road for man to become man. . . . [T]he Precious Book was the first teacher of philosophy to the Muslims."[37] Religion properly understood both enjoins and makes possible human perfectibility. This capacity is "the greatest deterrent to men's rending each other to pieces like tearing lions, raging wolves, and biting dogs. It is the greatest obstacle keeping men from having the low and base qualities of animals. It is the best incentive for intellectual activity and the use of man's mental faculties. It is the most influential factor in purifying souls of impure vices.[38]

In tying religion not only to moral but also to scientific progress, Afghani makes religion essential to human survival and advancement, and hence to "modernity" itself. In this view, modernity and Islam properly understood are mutually constitutive. Indeed, Afghani affirms the superiority of Islam to all other religions because Islam rightly understood is absolutely unique in exhorting believers to exercise their reason and prohibiting them from "blind submission."[39] This suggests that Afghani's objection to Muslim scholars is not that they bow to divine authority but that they misinterpret such authority and its truths as antithetical to the philosophical reasoning and insight that are necessary to all progress, scientific, political, and moral. Moreover, in *Refutation of the Materialists*, Afghani asserts that the Enlightenment makes exactly the reverse mistake: the *philosophes* posited an opposition between reason and revelation only to resolve the contradiction in favor of reason. In this way reason became linked to the negation of divinity, religion, and custom. For Afghani, both theology and Enlightenment philosophy are misguided because the very opposition between rationalism and religion that underlies them is false. Luther's reformism, which Afghani claims has simply drawn on Muslim examples, demarcates a "third way," or, more accurately for Afghani, the only way:

> [T]he members of each community must found their beliefs, which are the first things written on the slates of their minds, on certain proofs and firm evidence. In their beliefs they must shun submission to conjectures and not be content with mere imitation (*taqlid*) of their ancestors. For if man believes in things without proof or reason, makes a practice of following unproven opinions, and is satisfied to imitate and follow his ancestors, his mind inevitably desists from intellectual movement, and little by little stupidity and imbecility overcome him—until his mind becomes completely idle and he becomes unable to perceive his own good and evil; and adversity and misfortune overtake him from all sides.[40]

Afghani often does not sufficiently engage or resolve many of the questions raised by his own arguments. He does not fully consider the possibility that science and philosophy may produce transhistorical and universal truths yet still be constitutive of Western cultural and political power. Nor does he consider that his insistence on the "true Islam" begs innumerable questions about what constitutes the essence of Islam and what does not. But perhaps the most pressing issue arising from Afghani's insistence on the rationality of Islam is, what happens with scripture contradicts reason? Afghani's contention that the Qur'an and traditions are already consistent with philosophical truths seems to preclude even the possibility of such an occurrence. Yet Afghani's emphasis on the attainment of scriptural meaning by way of reason implies that "when scripture apparently contradicted reason or science, . . . scripture must be reinterpreted."[41] Such a conclusion is anathema to Qutb and those like him, who argue that reason is determined by scripture and that divine revelation is the "source which human reason must consult," the "standard in terms of which all judgments, knowledge and concepts of human reason are evaluated."[42]

Afghani's writings generally reflect this attempt to reconcile the imperatives of human reason with those of scripture, the teachings of philosophy and those of Islam, with one startling exception: Afghani's response to the French philosopher Ernest Renan's 1883 article, "Science and Islam," in which Renan argues that Arab "backwardness" was a direct product of Islam. Having left India—voluntarily—in 1882, at this time Afghani was living in Paris, working with Muhammad 'Abduh on an Arabic newspaper devoted to anti-British and pan-Islamic philosophical analyses and political polemics. His response to Renan, written in French, initially seems to be a radical departure from the rest of Afghani's project. For in language reminiscent of the *philosophes* he criticizes elsewhere, Afghani contends that all religions resemble each other, and that all religions are equally and fundamentally incompatible with philosophy. "Religion imposes on man its faith and its belief," Afghani writes, "whereas philosophy frees him of it totally or in part. . . . It will always be thus. Whenever religion will have the upper hand, it will eliminate philosophy; and the contrary happens when it is philosophy that reigns as sovereign mistress." Afghani goes so far as to agree with Renan's assessment by acknowledging that Islam historically has tried to "stifle science and stop its progress" and has halted the "philosophical or intellectual movement and [turned] minds from the search for scientific truth."[43] But he insists that Islam is not the sole culprit; all religions have at some time similarly impeded the pursuit of truth.

One reading of the apparent contradiction between this "Response" and his other work is that Afghani was simultaneously committed to the Islamic *umma* and unsure about his faith, and that the "Response," not intended for a wide readership, expressed precisely such uncertainty.[44] By contrast, Kedourie sees Afghani's "Response" as a fatal blow to his reputation as a believing Muslim reformer, a confirmation of the revisionist picture of Afghani as manipulative and duplicitous.[45] Kedourie's interpretation suggests that Afghani's real views are revealed in this address to the Western intelligentsia—written, it must be noted, a year before his defense of Islam in *The Refutation of the Materialists*—and not in his decidedly more emotional *Refutation*, written to be read by Muslims generally. Indeed, Keddie argues that Afghani adopted from Islamic philosophy, and from al-Farabi (875–950) in particular, the tendency to vary his words and arguments when speaking to elites—including a Western and Westernized intelligentsia—and when

addressing "the masses."[46] In this view, only the educated are able to understand rational argumentation, while the masses must be brought to the truth
by way of rhetoric, authority, and sentiment. For Keddie as for Kedourie,
such differences support the argument that Afghani valued Islam for its usefulness as a source of a cohesive political identity for the uneducated masses,
rather than as a true religion. Thus, when writing for a general Muslim audience, Afghani would inflame them with emotional rhetoric about the evils of
Western encroachments. In contrast, when speaking to members of the intellectual elite such as Renan, Afghani emphasizes the utility of religion to
facilitate the movement of human evolution out of its infancy.

These multiple readings reveal the difficulty of placing the "Response" in
the context of Afghani's other writings. The task becomes even more complicated considering the ways in which the "Response" at times even contradicts itself.[47] It is perhaps unsurprising, then, that while Renan celebrated
Afghani's response as the work of an intelligent and "enlightened Asiatic,"
many in the Islamic world have cited it as a defense of Islam.[48] Indeed,
despite the "Response," Hourani concludes that Afghani

> not only believed that Islam was as true or false as other religions, but that it was
> the one true, complete, and perfect religion, which could satisfy all the desires of
> the human spirit. Like other Muslim thinkers of his day, he was willing to accept
> the judgment on Christianity given by European free thought: it was unreason-
> able, it was the enemy of science and progress. But he wished to show that these
> criticisms did not apply to Islam; on the contrary, Islam was in harmony with the
> principles discovered by scientific reason, was indeed the religion demanded by
> reason. Christianity had failed—he took Renan's word for it; but Islam, being
> neither irrational nor intolerant, could save the secular world from that revolution-
> ary chaos, the memory of which haunted the French thinkers of his time.[49]

While the picture of Afghani as a political manipulator and intellectual
Machiavellian is no doubt overstated, the apparent rejection of any compatibility between religion and philosophy in the "Response" at the very least
complicates the reading of Afghani as a defender of the theological, as opposed to cultural, dimension of Islam. However, this is largely consistent
with Afghani's commitment to defining Islam as a cultural and political identity fully compatible with philosophy and rationalism. It is possible, then,
that the contradiction between Afghani's general defense of Islam and his
rejection of religion in the "Response" is more apparent than real. As some
scholars have suggested, Afghani's response to Renan may be an indictment
of Islam as it is, following the rejection of rationalism by Islamic theologians,
rather than the Islam that has been and could again be if philosophy is rein-
corporated into it.[50] This reading is particularly plausible given Keddie's
argument that Afghani's emphasis on reason in Islam is in fact a revival in a
modern context of early rationalist arguments such as those of the *Mu'tazila*,

who were the first to use the methods and categories of Hellenistic philosophy to advance an Islamic rationalism in the late eighth and first half of the ninth century.[51] For the *Mu'tazila*, rationalism did not entail the marginalization of Islamic revelation. On the contrary, they regarded themselves not as philosophers but rather as theologians who "represent the true orthodoxy, in other words . . . the correct interpretation of the Kur'anic revelation."[52]

This context suggests an answer to another lingering question: if Afghani's project entails the transformation of Islam from a set of revealed truths to a political and cultural identity compatible with reason, what, exactly, does Afghani mean by rationalism? By reason? By philosophy? It is here that the mythology surrounding his origins bears directly upon his political thought. The fact that Afghani was born and raised in Iran rather than in Sunni Afghanistan is significant because his education in Iran exposed him not only to the traditional Shi'i Islamic disciplines but also to Islamic mysticism and Islamic philosophy. By all accounts such an education would have been much less likely in Afghanistan given that Sunni Islam tended to regard such teachings as heretical.[53] The schools of Islamic philosophy—particularly that of Abu 'Ali ibn Sina (Avicenna, 980–1037) and of the later Persian philosophers—were more accessible and alive in Iran than in Sunni Islamic countries.

As Keddie notes, Afghani often employs the Arabic word *hikma*, meaning philosophy or wisdom in a broad sense, interchangeably with *falsafa*, which means medieval Islamic philosophy with a Hellenistic base in particular. The conflation of wisdom generally with Greek-inspired Islamic philosophy substantiates the argument that Afghani's claims about the significance of philosophy and reason are deeply indebted to Islamic philosophy, which was, in turn, influenced by Aristotle and neoplatonism. W. Montgomery Watt characterizes this Islamic neoplatonism in particular as "an attempt to produce a version of Greek Philosophy for Muslims."[54] Afghani's embrace of Islamic philosophers as the exemplars of rationalist reasoning and argumentation thus incorporates the Greek epistemological assumption that knowledge about nature and human nature can be reached by way of demonstration and rational proof. Yet Afghani follows the Islamic philosophers in a crucial departure from Greek thought: as Keddie persuasively argues, given the societies in which the Islamic philosophers lived, they could not afford to assume the supremacy of reason over scripture and so developed arguments that such rational truths and divine laws were entirely compatible: "the means [for such reconciliation] adopted by the great philosophers from Farabi and Avicenna down through the later Persian philosophers, who also influenced Afghani, involved the belief that literalist revelation was necessary for the masses, but that the higher truth was to be uncovered by rationalist interpretation of scripture."[55] Thus Afghani's rationalism is wedded not only to a faith in human reason as the means to unlock the secrets of nature, and the (Platonic) link between virtue and knowledge, but also an emphasis on a rationalist interpretation of religion for those with such special knowledge, and the conviction that the majority of believers are not sufficiently capable of such philosophical understanding.

Yet while embracing Islamic philosophers' arguments regarding human nature, the role of special knowledge, and the unfettered exercise of critical reason for the exceptional of mind, Afghani also turns his own critical reason against his masters. He argues that when it comes to the Greeks, the Islamic philosophers fail to apply their own prescriptions. For example, Afghani argues that the Islamic philosophers' uncritical acceptance of Greek philosophy eclipsed the contribution of earlier "Eastern" cultures to the evolution of such knowledge. According to Afghani, Muslim philosophers believed all too readily that "each one of those ancient philosophers had invented some branches of philosophy . . . without the help of others. . . . They disregarded the fact that the philosophic sciences, like the other sciences and arts, have achieved their aim through the succession of ideas and the progress of beliefs" from India to Babylonia to Egypt well before the rise of Greek culture and the Roman Empire.[56] And in "The Benefits of Philosophy," Afghani argues that the acceptance of Greek philosophy in its entirety meant accommodating Greek polytheism as well, a criticism not unlike Qutb's contention in *The Islamic Conception and Its Characteristics* that Islamic philosophy is tainted by the paganism and idolatry pervading ancient Greek thought. But unlike Qutb, Afghani objects to such polytheistic idolatry not on the grounds of its falsity or its usurpation of God's rightful authority, but on the grounds that Greek theology was both presented and accepted without rational proof or argument. Afghani thus judges the Islamic philosophers as he judges theologians, that is, by the extent to which they either advance or retard the exercise and evolution of reason through rational proof and argumentation. This is perhaps why Afghani concludes his critique of Islamic philosophy with the absolute conviction that while "incomplete," Islamic philosophy is essential because it embraces the free exercise of reason in ways contemporary Muslim scholars do not. For the intellectual elite and the civilization of which they are both an expression and a harbinger, the exercise of reason makes possible a level of reflection that at once frees humans from the rule of animalistic instinct and guides them to the truths about how to live and to live well. Such a radical premise will find fuller, if more cautious, expression in Muhammad 'Abduh's modernism.

'ABDUH AND *THE THEOLOGY OF UNITY*

"The light of this Glorious Book which used to be followed by science no matter where it went, East or West, must inevitably return to its full splendor and rend the veils of error. It will return to its original place in the hearts of Muslims, and will take shelter there. Science will follow it, for it is its only friend, its sole support."[57] Unlike Afghani's work, which is less theology or political theory than political and social criticism, Muhammad 'Abduh's work is theological and philosophical in nature. This distinction is perhaps the reason why Qutb singles out 'Abduh—and his student, Rashid Rida—in his most direct criticisms of Islamic modernism. Yet any analysis of 'Abduh's modernism must attend to Afghani's profound influence upon it. For like Afghani, 'Abduh aims at revitalizing Islam as a resource for moral and communal strength to meet the challenge of modern developments and European power. 'Abduh, like Afghani, seeks to delineate an understanding of Islam not as it is currently practiced, but as it is when rightly understood. And, like Afghani, 'Abduh criticizes believers who eschew reason and rationalists who repudiate Islam for failing to understand that the true Islam is the religion of reason. Thus for 'Abduh and for his sometime collaborator, Islam is the "first religion to address human reason, prompting it to examine the entire universe, and giving it free rein to delve into its innermost secrets as far as it is able. It did not impose any conditions upon reason other than that of maintaining the faith."[58]

Yet unlike Afghani's literal and figurative homelessness, 'Abduh's life and thought were defined by a commitment not only to Islam generally but also to the politics of his native Egypt. There is no mystery surrounding 'Abduh's origins or the substance of his education: he was born in 1849 in an Egyptian Delta village to a family of the peasant class.[59] Like Qutb, 'Abduh memorized the Qur'an at an early age, and when he was only thirteen years old he was sent to the Ahmadi mosque at Tanta to continue his religious training. Unhappy with what he saw as the impenetrable methods of instruction he encountered there, 'Abduh ran away on two separate occasions and hid for several months with various uncles. Ultimately, he fell under the influence of a paternal uncle, Sheikh Darwish Khadr, trained in Islamic Sufism. Through sheer persistence Khadr initiated him into the Sufi approach to Islamic instruction and practices. 'Abduh then voluntarily returned to Tanta deeply committed to and infused with Islamic mysticism.[60] Fired by love of religious instruction, 'Abduh continued his traditional religious education at al-Azhar from 1866 to 1877, graduating with the degree of 'alim.

It was during this time at al-Azhar, in 1869, that 'Abduh first met Afghani and became a fervent disciple. Although 'Abduh was in the midst of his studies in traditional Islam, he found in Afghani a fellow mystic, yet a mystic who both led him to greater engagement with worldly affairs, and exposed him to the works of the Islamic philosophers. 'Abduh's association with Afghani was to cause him great trouble over the course of his life. There was, for example, a tension between the traditionalism of his teachers at al-Azhar and the more heterodox influences encouraged by Afghani. Consequently al-Azhar authorities attempted to withhold 'Abduh's teaching license, although he was eventually granted the license through the intercession of the university rector. After obtaining his degree, 'Abduh began teaching at al-Azhar and in 1878 was appointed a teacher at Dar al-'Ulum, the newly founded "modern" teaching college that both Hasan al-Banna and Qutb would attend more than thirty years later. Yet when Afghani was expelled from Egypt in 1879 by the new Khedive, 'Abduh was fired from Dar al-'Ulum and ordered into retirement because he was a known associate of Afghani.

After his dismissal from Dar al-'Ulum, in the early 1880s 'Abduh became an active critic of the growing European influence in Egyptian politics and of the corruption of a ruling elite that had increased Egypt's dependence upon foreign powers. A supporter of and key player in the nationalist opposition to the Egyptian monarchy, 'Abduh was imprisoned and then tried along with other nationalists by Khedive Tawfiq, who had been restored to power by the British. 'Abduh was sentenced by the court to three years of exile from Egypt, forbidden to return without the permission of the Khedive. In 1884 'Abduh went to Paris at Afghani's invitation. There he collaborated with his radical mentor in producing revolutionary articles against British imperialism and became embroiled in Afghani's anti-British intrigues.

It was during this exile from Egypt that 'Abduh gave a series of lectures in Beirut—updated and given again at al-Azhar—that were later revised and published by his student Rashid Rida as *Risalat al-Tawhid* [The Theology of Unity] in 1897. In this text, perhaps his most famous, 'Abduh argues that Islam, properly understood, starts from the premise that reason is a feature of human nature, and human nature is created by God. Consequently, reason is no less a gift from God than is revelation: "God has endowed us with senses and implanted in us faculties that we employ in all their dimensions entirely as a gift of God."[61] As both revelation and reason are divine creations, a contradiction between the laws of God expressed in the Qur'an and traditions and those of God embodied in the natural world is an impossibility.[62] Those who infer an essential enmity between Islam and the exercise of critical reason from the history of Islamic practice have mistaken a debased Islam for the true faith. The "real" Islam has never ceased to exhort Muslims to use their reason. Thus Islam cannot be antithetical to the fruits of human reason, the discoveries of modern science. Indeed, 'Abduh argues that the Qur'an and traditions encourage the pursuit of knowledge of the material world as the means necessary for survival and well-being, and actually anticipate sciences such as modern astronomy and studies of the Earth's resources. As 'Abduh notes, "God has sent down two books: one created, which is nature, and one revealed, which is the Qur'an. The latter leads us to investigate the former by means of the intelligence which was given to us. He who obeys, will become blessed; he who turns away, goes toward destruction."[63]

Like Qutb, 'Abduh argues that Islamic law is part of the divine universal law that is also embedded in physical and biological phenomena. But while Qutb emphasizes the dark mystery that constitutes the core of the divine will, 'Abduh argues that the inherent rationality of such laws makes reason not only an appropriate but a necessary means by which human beings may know (most of) them.[64] Indeed, reason is the human faculty that enables us to distinguish between true and false beliefs, and by which we may obtain awareness, if not full understanding, of the divine truths necessary for living and living well.

> Religion is a general sense for investigating the means to happiness that are obscure to reason. Reason is the ultimate authority in the recognition of this sense and the uses for which it was given; it also [establishes the necessity of] obedience to the beliefs and rules of conduct that religion reveals. How can reason be denied its due in this matter, for it is reason that examines the evidence for this sense in order to arrive at its knowledge and that it is given by God?[65]

Moreover, the Islamic exhortation to exercise reason encourages a healthy skepticism toward, rather than an unquestioning obedience to, the authority of tradition. Adopting Afghani's evolutionary view of knowledge, 'Abduh avers that simple precedence in time is insufficient to establish precedence in knowledge or ability. Thus the exhortation to reason about the world precludes the uncritical acceptance of dogma (*taqlid*, or blind imitation) on the authority of tradition, or the submission to logical contradictions against the clear weight of sense-evidence.[66]

In arguments like these, 'Abduh most clearly defines reason in terms of what it is not: reason is posited as the opposite of imagination without evidence, tradition without proof, suspension of intellectual reflection, and adherence to unexamined dogma and credulous superstition.[67]

> Islam reproaches leaders of religions for simply following in the footsteps of their forebears, and for their adherence to the plans of their ancestors. . . . Thus it liberates the power of reason from its fetters, releasing it from enslavement to blind imitation of tradition. Islam has restored reason to its kingdom, a kingdom in which it reigns with judiciousness and wisdom, deferring to God alone and conforming to His sacred law. There are no limits to the possible pursuits within its domain, and no end to the extent of the explorations possible under its banner.[68]

Reason for 'Abduh thus means the exercise of critical judgment on the basis of logical and empirical proof. Importantly, though this understanding of reason is clearly indebted to Afghani, and by extension to the Islamic philosophers and their Greek masters, it is also more than slightly reminiscent of the ways in which reason came to be defined in modern European thought in opposition to the authority of the clergy, the pull of habit and tradition, and the suspension of critical judgment they were thought to presuppose. Indeed, in 'Abduh's later life, European political, social, historical, and educational thought came to exercise an increasing influence on his thinking; he displays a particular affinity for, among others, his friend Herbert Spencer, whom he cites when arguing that spiritual and material progress are dialectically intertwined, and that such interaction is the motor for civilizational advancement.[69] As Hourani argues:

> His intellectual problems were those of Islamic thought but they were also those of nineteenth century Europe, in particular the great debates about science and religion. . . . Islam seemed to him to be a middle path between the two extremes: a religion fully consistent with the claims of the human intellect and the discoveries of modern science, but safeguarding the divine transcendence. . . . Islam indeed was the religion of human nature, the answer to the problems of the modern world.[70]

In 'Abduh's understanding of reason we thus see a complex interaction of Western and Islamic influences. Like the *philosophes* discussed in chapter 2, 'Abduh defines reason in opposition to blind authority to all inherited truths; yet unlike the *philosophes* and like Afghani, he does not oppose reason to faith in divine truths.[71]

Afghani's commitment to Islam as a source of political solidarity at times diminishes the theological dimension of Islamic faith. By contrast, 'Abduh was particularly attentive to the costs and dangers that unchecked reason posed for those religious truths that are beyond human comprehension. His anxieties in this regard place him closer to Qutb than to Afghani.[72] As a result, 'Abduh insists upon the relevance and role of reason in the "true Islam" but also carefully delineates its limits. In every passage where 'Abduh celebrates the rationalism of Islam, he concludes with a crucial, if vague, qualification: the imperatives of reason must be in conformity with Islamic law, its exercise guided by the aim of maintaining rather than undermining faith. This repeated qualification implicitly suggests, first, that 'Abduh is intent on granting to religion the ultimate power to determine truth, and, second, that there is a constant danger that reason will overreach itself, and in so doing transgress the principles of faith and destroy the purchase of Islamic truth. Therefore, while 'Abduh exhorts believers to exercise their critical faculties in accordance with Qur'anic injunctions, he also admonishes rationalists to attend to the limits of rational inquiry. Toward the latter end, 'Abduh establishes levels of knowing, or kinds of truths: those that are accessible to human understanding, those that are entirely inaccessible, and those that require confirmation by an authority other than reason. For example, reason can lead to belief in the existence of God, an understanding of some of his attributes, awareness of the afterlife, distinctions between good and evil, and the authority of prophecy. Reason can thus lead human beings to accept the authority of revelation whose truths are therefore consistent with the products of rational inquiry. Such revelation—disclosed by the Prophet whose authority has been established by reason—provides the means to accept truths that reason cannot reach. But 'Abduh cautions repeatedly that reason cannot penetrate such unknowable concepts as God's essence and the essences of nature and human nature, which are, by definition, beyond human comprehension. In language reminiscent of Qutb, 'Abduh argues that pursuit of the unknowable is not only fruitless but transgressive of the precepts of faith:

> As for speculation about the essence of the Creator, on the one hand, it is an attempt to probe that which is forbidden to human reason; on the other hand, the pursuit of His essence is beyond the grasp of human faculties. These pursuits are foolish and dangerous, foolish because they are a search for that which is unattainable, dangerous because it amounts to a strike against faith in that it is an attempt to define that which cannot be defined, and an attempt to limit that which has no limits.[73]

The authority of the truths contained in the Qur'an and the traditions is thus established by way of both reason and revelation. Reason confirms some truths directly and others indirectly, by way of the Prophet's authority; other truths flow from the authority of God whose existence—but not essence—can be established rationally. Indeed, 'Abduh attempts to illustrate the ways reason confirms revealed truth through what he takes to be rational proofs of God's existence, the Prophet's authority, the divine origin of the Qur'an. Yet these proofs often abruptly abort in the middle with the statement that the belief under discussion should now be sufficiently "self-evident." For example, in attempting to establish that prophets are the recipients of divine knowledge, 'Abduh avers that at some point we must simply assume that they are among yet not *of* men. He concludes with a tautological argument that the authority of the prophets derives from the prophets' authority. "[The prophets' status among people] is unique and extraordinary," he claims. "This stature is what distinguishes them and establishes proof of their message; it is a sign of the perfection of their experiences and their testimony."[74] Earlier in the *Theology of Unity*, 'Abduh concludes his "proof" for the existence of God with an admonishment to cease all further investigation with regard to the relationship between God and human will:

> Further discussion of the balance between what has already been proven about the compass of God's knowledge and will, and what is self-evident about human freedom of choice entails an attempt to penetrate the secret of destiny which is forbidden, and involves the pursuit of that which is beyond human reason. Ex-

tremists of all sects, especially Muslims and Christians, explored this subject deeply, but after long discussions they are still at the point where they started. All that they accomplished was to divide and disperse. Some of them declared the authority of the individual over all his actions and the autonomy of that authority; this is an obvious conceit. Some of them embraced predestination, while others disavowed it. All such pursuits involve the destruction of sacred law, obliteration of God's commandments, and abolition of the judgments of intuitive reason, which is the pillar of faith.[75]

These proofs are an attempt to substantiate, by example and argument, the collaborative balance between the authority of reason and that of revealed truth. Yet they paradoxically illustrate the limits of 'Abduh's argument, for they reveal his resistance to engaging the actual complexities of the argument and their implications and, in so doing, suggest either that such a balance is illusory, or that 'Abduh is simply not diligent or rigorous enough a thinker to establish it on firm foundations. While scholars such as Sharabi doubt 'Abduh's mental agility, Badawi suggests that 'Abduh avoids pushing the arguments out of a pragmatic concern to avoid conclusions that would divide rather than unite Muslims. Although on more than one occasion 'Abduh accuses some Muslims of accepting rational proof only to the degree that it affirms the principles of their faith, his own writing makes it difficult to avoid the conclusion that the purported unity of reason and revealed truth has devolved into a subordination of reason to the affirmation of fairly orthodox articles of faith.[76] Indeed, while he affirms the right of reason to examine rules of conduct and belief in revealed law, he also hastens to assure his Muslim readers that the ultimate arbiter of morality and belief is religion based on revealed truth: "The religious force is the most powerful element to morality, both public and private. Its authority over human souls eclipses that of reason, which is distinctive to human nature."[77]

It seems plausible that 'Abduh's insistence on the primacy of revealed law in these moments derives from his conviction, à la Afghani, that most human beings are either deficient in or incapable of fully exercising their reason. While the elite may, after long reflection, be persuaded by rational argumentation, in this view the limited intelligence of most people requires the deployment of myths and examples designed to speak to emotion, fear, and tradition.[78] Thus some truths cannot be known by reason at all, but other limits upon reason are related to the defects in human nature. While the imperatives of reason and the appeal to the authority of tradition and the persuasion of sentiment correspond to different dimensions of human perception,[79] they are not in conflict but are simply two ways of knowing the same set of truths. Herein lies the necessity of Islamic revelation: although it is congruent with reason, revelation can persuade without appeal to reason and provide the authority and rhetoric necessary to bring those not given to reflection to right belief. Islamic revelation thus leads the reasonable to affirm the inaccessible and the unreflective to believe the necessary: "It confirms reason and lends certainty to its conclusions when reason is right, and corrects and supplements it where it has been misguided. It also enumerates certain special duties which cannot be determined by reason, such as ritual exercises. Only revelation can give man any certainty as to the substance of his beliefs and principles."[80] Furthermore, as reason can never really know the essence of the afterlife or its characteristics, it is revelation, not reason, that provides the knowledge of the punishments and rewards of the afterlife. Contemplation of such possibilities provides the impetus not only to acknowledge but to adhere to the precepts of divine law. As Kerr aptly puts it, 'Abduh believes that "reason can tell men *what* they should or should not do, and revelation tells them the most compelling reason *why* they should or should not do it"[81] (emphasis in the original).

Like Afghani, then, 'Abduh insists that as rationality and reason are both creations of God they are in absolute harmony. Nadav Safran contends that this insistence is itself "an act of faith,"[82] one that buttresses 'Abduh's confidence that the divine text can be adjusted to conform to the dictates of reason without danger. Indeed, unlike Afghani, 'Abduh addresses the issue directly, suggesting that such adjustment by way of reasoned reinterpretation is the necessary means by which to arrive at the "true" meaning of the passage in question. "If there comes something that seems contradictory, it is necessary for reason to believe that the apparent meaning is not the meaning intended. It has the freedom after that to engage in interpretation guided by the rest of the text, or to entrust it to God and His omniscience."[83] Similarly, 'Abduh contends that "If anything appears in the doctrine that would compromise the supremacy of the divine by equating God with other creatures, it is necessary to dismiss this apparent sense, either by referring it to God for knowledge of its real meaning with the faith that the apparent meaning is not intended, or by interpretation based on a reasonable approximation."[84] 'Abduh's argument here reflects, in Kerr's words, the assumption that "a rational explanation exists although man has not discovered it."[85]

Yet in this critical moment 'Abduh's tenuous balance between reason and revelation is inadvertently tipped in favor of reason. By encouraging rational reinterpretation of revealed law when necessary, 'Abduh unintentionally grants reason an extraordinarily wide scope; reason now operates to *define* as well as *elaborate* the meaning of scripture. If such reinterpretation simultaneously involves the creation, reflection, and clarification of scriptural meaning, 'Abduh's careful admonishments to limit reason by the letter and spirit of revealed law are insufficient bulwarks against the ascendence of reason as the arbiter rather than servant of the meaning of revealed truth. Indeed, reason assumes a particularly prominent role when it comes to matters relating to political life, for 'Abduh regards religious precepts and the prophetic mission as general principles or "underlying conditions" that serve primarily to effect, as Kerr puts it, the proper "moral orientation" in politics and social relations.[86] Here 'Abduh endorses the frequently made argument that religious authority is complete with regard to duties of worship (*'ibadat*), while human judgment substantially determines the realm of social relations (*mu'amalat*). Thus while reason may be required to reinterpret revealed law where it is explicit, reason is also necessary when revealed law is silent or unclear on particulars. Consequently, 'Abduh encourages *ijtihad* (independent interpretation) provided it is always exercised with a view to harmony with Islamic law and is undertaken only by those with the requisite knowledge and intellectual acuity. *Ijtihad* is thus the means by which general Islamic truths are realized and renewed in each historical age, and such renewal is an absolute necessity to meet the challenge of the modern world.

Despite the political activism that marked the earlier stage of his life, 'Abduh's later work tends to resign such explicitly political matters to God's will, instead taking up the prior task of developing the methods by which such arguments can be made.[87] This reticence may be informed by his journey from radical-in-exile to appointment later in life as Grand Mufti of Egypt. For after six years of exile, 'Abduh was pardoned by the Khedive and returned to Egypt in 1888 with the help of influential British supporters. Upon his return he was appointed to the bench of one of the "Native Tribunals," a court that administered a jurisprudence based on the French code.[88] Again with the help of British influence, in 1889 he was appointed Grand Mufti of Egypt—the highest institutional religious authority in Egypt—an office he would hold until his death in 1905. In assuming this position, 'Abduh became the most influential authority in Egypt on matters of religious law, his *fatwas* (legal opinions) "authoritative and final."[89]

It may be, as Kedourie argues, that 'Abduh's tenure as Grand Mufti was devoid of innovation and marked by a traditionalism peculiar given the heterodoxy of his early religious beliefs and the radicalism of his political commitments, both of which he had at one time shared with Afghani:

> The rebel of the eighteen-seventies, the subversive journalist of the eighteen-eighties, was thus indebted for his exalted position to the despotism of the Khedivial Government which the British occupant was endeavouring to tincture with some benevolence. It remains to add that successive annual reports . . . record with unfailing regularity the absolute failure to effect any substantial reform in the religious courts. 'Abduh's appointment thus added one more link to the long chain by which the Muslim Institution was shackled into utter subservience to the Ruling Institution.[90]

Or it may be, as other scholars contend, that 'Abduh's career did not signify a betrayal of his earlier political commitments because he had always regarded politics with suspicion: "['Abduh] shows a certain aversion to politics which helps to explain his lack of enthusiasm for comprehensive doctrines in that field. He speaks of politics as if of the inevitably distasteful manifestation of the weaknesses of human nature. Politics is apparently synonymous with partisanship, rivalry, self-seeking, and *ʿasabiyya* [solidarity] (in the strictly pejorative sense)."[91] Or again, ʿAbduh's religious rulings may have been, as Adams argues, characterized by real innovation and "a spirit of liberality and a freedom from bondage to tradition and a desire to render the religion of Islam entirely adaptable to the requirements of modern civilization."[92] Whatever the case, ʿAbduh's own political proposals were often fragmentary, and his reluctance to address systematically the relationship between religious and political authority means that the few arguments he did make are vulnerable to interpretations ultimately inconsistent with his insistence that there is "at most a coincidence of religious and rational dictates, and not a delegation by religion to reason of the authority to make political judgments."[93] ʿAbduh at one time advocates representative government rather than an Islamic state. At another time, he argues that the traditional theory of the Islamic Caliphate is consistent with secular civil law in the West.[94] Indeed, ʿAbduh is quite overt in his attempt to reinterpret Islamic concepts in terms of Western ideas and vice-versa. As Hourani points out, ʿAbduh follows an earlier generation of Muslim intellectuals in linking *maslaha* (reform in the interests of the community) to utilitarianism, *shura* (the principle of consultation) to parliamentary democracy, and *ijmaʿ* (consensus) to public opinion.[95] Unlike Afghani, then, ʿAbduh is less concerned to square his rationalist Islam with a repudiation of the West than to show that qualified acceptance of Western models of modernity and reason need not entail Westernization or a repudiation of Islam.

These claims are, in other hands, open to interpretations inimical to ʿAbduh's premise that all political principles ultimately derive from revealed law. Here we can see the ways in which ʿAbduh, not unlike Afghani, paves the way for the supremacy of reason at the expense of the authority of revealed truth. This is so despite ʿAbduh's own explicit intentions. Thinkers who succeeded ʿAbduh, such as his student Rashid Rida, at times strove to remain true to his intent; but others used their methods to reach conclusions ʿAbduh would not have endorsed: that science, rather than Islam, is the measure of real civilization, that Islam is peripheral to political and social matters, and that the territorial unit of nation takes precedence over Islamic identity.[96] In the work of a younger generation of Egyptian intellectuals, ʿAbduh's delicate if not entirely persuasive balance between the authority of reason and revealed truth is transformed into a battering ram for all things modern.

THROUGH THE BACK DOOR: RATIONALISM AND ISLAMIC MODERNISM

There are significant differences between Afghani's and ʿAbduh's projects, and a full account of the relationship between them is beyond the focus of my argument. In just one example, it seems that Afghani's focus on Islam is more often in the form of a defense of culture than a preoccupation with divine truths. 'Abduh's modernism is, at least in intent, simultaneously an attempt to defend Islam and to confirm the truth, relevance, and ultimately supremacy of revealed law. As Hourani argues, 'Abduh's "own writings were controlled by a deep knowledge of the traditional sciences of Islam, and— what was more important—by a vivid sense of responsibility to it."[97] Yet despite differences in temperament, and at times in politics and moral orientation, both Afghani's and 'Abduh's attempts to revive Islam and preserve it from Western encroachment entail a portrayal of the true Islam as "the rational religion" in opposition to a "degraded Islam" manifest in much of Islamic history and current Islamic practice. The inherent rationality of Islam is expressed in the way the Qur'an and traditions either contain or prefigure modern knowledge and encourage an exercise of human reason unfettered by uncritical acceptance of received truth. The argument that Islam properly understood, is *rational* in these ways enables Afghani and 'Abduh to argue that Islam is largely constitutive of modern truths (and, for 'Abduh, their final judge), while at the same time problematizing the equation of rationalism and the West, modernity and Westernization.

In the previous discussion I have followed Keddie in emphasizing the ways in which such an understanding of rationalism is indebted to Islamic philosophy and, by extension, to the classical philosophy from which Islamic philosophers liberally borrowed. But the "rationalism" of Afghani and 'Abduh is also influenced by the modern rationalism of the European Enlightenment: the continuing debates regarding the relationship between reason and revelation and church and state, the definition of rationalism in opposition to inherited religious and philosophical truths, the insistence that free exercise of reason and the authority of science it facilitates are constitutive of both progress and modernity. This engagement with the theories and dilemmas characteristic of modern European political thought leads Gibb to conclude that the work of Islamic "modernists" can be understood as an attempt to "interpret Islam in terms of liberal humanitarian ideas and values: in this first stage they contended that Islam was not opposed to these ideas; but they soon went on to claim that Islam was the embodiment of them in their highest and most perfect form."[98] While it is perhaps an overstatement to read liberalism into the efforts of modernists such as 'Abduh, what is certainly the case is that both Afghani's and 'Abduh's revivalism neither entails the embrace of all things Western that characterizes a later generation of intellectuals, nor advocates a revitalization of a "pure" and original Islam in a modern context. Like the work of Qutb, 'Abduh's and Afghani's projects are an amalgamation of multiple cultural influences, an intricate and dense fabric spun not only from the threads of Western and European influence—from the Greek-inspired rationalism of Islamic philosophy to the reason of the Enlightenment [99]—but also from the

Islams, orthodox and heterodox, that comprise their indigenous cultural traditions.

Afghani's and 'Abduh's conclusions regarding the compatibility, or, more accurately, *identity*, of Islam and reason are especially interesting in light of Qutb's critique of modernity and of rationalism in particular. Like Afghani and 'Abduh, Qutb acknowledges that the Qur'an encourages the exercise of reason, and argues that it both allows and prefigures the development of modern technologies. But central to Qutb's political thought is the argument that proper recognition of divine authority requires using reason to see the substantial limits of human insight into the most important secrets of the universe. Reason thus reaches its limits when confronted with questions of moral judgment, human purpose, and the divine plan for all creatures and things in the world. While 'Abduh, too, is attentive to the limits of human capacities to know the world, ultimately he affirms the role of reason in interpretation of scripture and thus as a guide to meaning and morality as well as to the material world. Granting reason such wide scope is inimical to Qutb's insistence that unchecked reason will destroy both the substance of and authority behind revealed truths. Thus while Afghani and 'Abduh accept both the objectivity and truth of modern knowledge, Qutb seeks to unmask such claims as vehicles for the erosion of divine authority and expression and acceleration of Western influence. From Qutb's point of view, then, 'Abduh's and Afghani's arguments regarding rationalism exemplify the *jahiliyya* from within.

Yet despite Qutb's explicit repudiation of both the West and Muslims who accommodate it, Qutb's political thought is also an amalgamation of Western and Islamic ideas; his very indictment of modern *jahiliyya* and his version of a purified Islamic worldview betray the pervasive influence of Western paradigms of modernity.[100] Qutb, Afghani, and 'Abduh are similarly engaged with and influenced by Western frameworks and ideas, even as they seek to critique, redefine, or provide an indigenous antidote to such influence. The stream of thought represented by Afghani and 'Abduh is thus the predecessor of twentieth-century Islamist political thought in more than a merely chronological sense: both kinds of thought claim to revive what is "authentically" Islamic in the shadow of Western power, and both reveal in different ways the dubiousness of notions of cultural authenticity in an increasingly syncretic world. This suggests yet a further point. Given such syncretism, Qutb's quarrel with Islamic modernism is no more a purely Islamic debate than Qutb's Islam is "authentic," in the sense of being entirely without Western influence.

Finally, this analysis shows how Qutb's critique of Islamic modernism profoundly echoes his critique of rationalism adumbrated in the previous chapter. Indeed, inasmuch as Qutb's complaint about Islamic modernism turns on the limits modern rationalism, this analysis reveals the ways in

which Qutb's indictment of post-Enlightenment rationalism is simultaneously a repudiation of modernist Islamic political thought. Indeed, given the
ways in which the rationalism of Islamic modernism relies upon arguments
of medieval Islamic philosophers and, by extension, the Greek philosophers
who influenced them, this comparison across time underscores the nature
and extent of Qutb's engagement with centuries-old disputes about the relationship between Islam and rationalisms. Just this one contrast demonstrates that, despite Qutb's claim to be in possession of the one true understanding of what it means to be a Muslim in the modern world, there are
and always have been voices who reject the particular oppositions that
define Qutb's fundamentalist thought. For a variety of reasons, these are
voices who find no inherent incompatibility between Islam and parliamentary democracy, reason and scripture, cultural authenticity and rationalism.
This lends force to the contention that, even or especially within the paradigm of "Islamic revival," there are other ways of perceiving the same challenges posed by European hegemony and modernity, and perhaps most importantly, other ways of meeting those challenges. This particular strand of
Islamic thought does not exhaust the diversity of Islamic responses to the
processes and ideas constitutive of "modernity." Yet just these two voices
are perhaps sufficient to challenge arguments that portray the current
strength of Islamic fundamentalism in the Middle East as the inevitable
return of an Islamic "essence," or as the "natural" reaction of archaism
against modernity.

CODA: KHOMEINI AND SHIʿITE FUNDAMENTALISM

The preceding analysis is of Sunni modernist and fundamentalist assessments of the relationship between rationalist and revealed truth: Qutb and
ʿAbduh were Egyptian Sunni Muslims, and Afghani deliberately obscured
his Shiʿite origins in Iran to speak more effectively to Sunni Muslim audiences. But while most of the Islamic fundamentalist movements in the contemporary Middle East are Sunni, perhaps the most notorious example of
Islamic fundamentalism to Westerners is the Islamic revolution in Shiʿite
Iran. A responsible treatment of both Sunni and Shiʿite fundamentalist
thought would require a thorough discussion of the break between Sunnism
and Shiʿism that is beyond the focus of this book.[101] Yet even a brief look at
the work of perhaps the best known Shiʿite thinker of the Iranian Revolution, Ayatollah Ruhollah Khomeini (1902–1989), suggests that Qutb's critique of modern, rationalist forms of sovereignty is neither idiosyncratic nor
particular to Sunni Islam.

Afghani's traditional Shiʿite education exposed him to Islamic philosophy
and a mysticism deemed heretical in Sunni Islam, influences that would
prove significant for his subsequent arguments about rationalism and poli-

tics. 'Abduh and Qutb were profoundly influenced early on by Sufi mysticism, although their arguments about the role of human reason in comprehending the truths necessary for living differ significantly from each other. Thus it is interesting to note Khomeini's early and extensive involvement with an Islamic mysticism—and *irfan* in particular—that tends to privilege human intuition and cognition over reason and rational sciences: "It has been said that 'knowledge is the thickest of veils,' for pursuit of knowledge causes man to be preoccupied with rational and general concepts and hinders him from embarking on the path. The more knowledge increases, the thicker the veil becomes, and the scholar may come to imagine that the knowledge he has achieved rationally represents everything. For man is arrogant."[102] Much as the later Qutb harbored the conviction that human reason is inadequate to grasp the truths of faith, Khomeini argues that, just as the "body itself is a mystery, the shade or reflection of a higher mystery . . . the shadow cast by the unity of the Divine Essence," the truths of revealed law can only be grasped—and even then incompletely—by intuition and faith.[103] Knowledge of the rational sciences may serve as a means to approach real knowledge, but mystical gnosis and direct vision are "cognitive instruments that by far surpass all rational sciences, which are only able to provide an approximate and inexact picture of Reality."[104] Indeed, as Akhavi points outs, Khomeini argues that the nobility of man is not related to his rational powers but rather is "limited to the realm of intuitive understanding of the world." The influence of such mysticism on Khomeini reveals itself in a view of knowledge where "ultimately reason betrays man . . . rationality obscures the search for God."[105]

I have noted that Qutb's insistence on the limits of human reason and the omniscience of Allah expresses itself in a focus on divine sovereignty as the vehicle for redemption, a focus Afghani and 'Abduh do not share for various reasons.[106] In a famous treatise on the nature of Islamic government, Khomeini similarly insists that God's will is (at least penultimately) expressed in the human endeavor to realize the just community on Earth. And also like Qutb, Khomeini argues that the legitimacy of sovereignty revolves around Allah's exclusive right of legislation, and therefore that justice is defined by the rule of revealed law. It is thus the source of legislation that distinguishes Islamic government—which for Khomeini as for Qutb is synonymous with just government—from constitutional monarchies, republics, and the "unbelieving" governments of the United States, Britain, and the Soviet Union, that is, governments that "execute anti-human laws and policies for the sake of their own interests."[107] In a passage that could easily have been written by Qutb, Khomeini argues that "in Islam the legislative power and competence to establish laws belongs exclusively to God almighty. The Sacred Legislator of Islam is the sole legislative power. No one has the right to legislate and no law may be executed except the law of the Divine Legislator."[108]

Like Qutb, Khomeini concludes that as the source of all law is divine, government is therefore limited to the "administration of a country, and the implementation of the sacred laws of the *shari'a*."[109] Such law applies equally to individual and society, leader and led, although the ruler is distinguished by superior knowledge of the ordinances and provisions of Islamic law and by great personal justice, that is, superiority and excellence in beliefs and morals.[110] As in Qutb's argument about Islamic sovereignty, Khomeini's understanding of Islamic government recalls the Platonic Philosopher-King.[111] Indeed, Plato had been "studied in Muslim *madrasahs* for a thousand years or more, and whose concept of the philosopher-king has been translated through time into the Islamic mystical concept of the 'perfect man.' It was this Islamized philosopher-king who was the supreme figure of authority in Khomeini's theory of Islamic government."[112]

Yet in a crucial departure from Qutb's repudiation of theocracy and suspicion of the *'ulama'*, Khomeini maintains that the rule of Islamic law must be under the guardianship of those most knowledgeable in matters of divine law, the *fuqaha* (jurists), a difference at least in part reflective of divergent perspectives on the role of the *'ulama'* in Sunnism and Shi'ism. For Khomeini, the rule of the jurists is necessary to preserve the lives, properties, and rights of the people against the vices of profligate monarchs and tyrants; to defend the community from being forced to submit to the political, economic, and cultural power of the "unbelieving" and "barbaric" imperialist West; to rectify the false reading of Islam as a religion concerned with private conscience rather than worldly affairs; and to strive to fulfill God's command to actualize Islamic justice on Earth. Unlike Qutb, then, Khomeini writes explicitly about an Islamic state and insists that law alone without institutions and executors is not enough. Yet like Qutb, Khomeini says that the very meaning and worth of government and the officials who administer it is entirely dependent upon fulfilling their proper function: establishing and maintaining Islamic justice and the rule of divine law. In this way, essentially selfish and arrogant human beings are made moral. "It is obvious then, how much care Islam devotes to government and the political and economic relations of society, with the goal of creating conditions conducive to the production of morally upright and virtuous human beings," Khomeini writes.[113] Thus in another passage reminiscent of Qutb, Khomeini underscores how inadequate modern advances are to the task of preserving and nurturing humanity:

> For the solution of social problems and the relief of human misery require foundations in faith and morals; merely acquiring material power and wealth, conquering nature and space, have no effect in this regard. They must be supplemented by, and balanced with, the faith, the conviction, and the morality of Islam in order to truly serve humanity instead of endangering it. This conviction, this morality,

these laws that are needed, *we* already possess. So as soon as someone goes some-
where or invents something, we should not hurry to abandon our religion and its
laws, which regulate the life of man and provide for his well-being in this world
and the hereafter.[114]

These commonalities between Qutb and Khomeini must be placed in the
context of a shared experience of foreign power and influence whereby the
process of modernization and certain forms of modern sovereignty were experienced first as Western imports, then as impositions by often Westernized Muslim elites. Moreover, Emmanuel Sivan notes that although Sunni
fundamentalist ideas appear little influenced by Iranian-Shi'ite thought, and
conversely that Shi'ite thought has been equally insulated from Sunni Islamist ideas, the notable exception to this apparently mutual disregard is the
impact of Qutb's and Mawdudi's work on Iranian fundamentalist thought.[115]
Haddad concurs when she notes that Qutb influenced 'Ali Shari'ati, another
thinker central to the Iranian Revolution, and Hamid Algar suggests that
Qutb's *Social Justice in Islam* in particular enjoyed considerable popularity
in Iran.[116] Indeed, since the 1970s the works of Qutb and many other Sunni
thinkers have been translated into Persian by an Iranian radical group committed to Shi'ism, the Fidāiyan-i-Islam (Devotees of Islam) and Devotee
supporters.[117] Said Amir Arjomand goes so far as to argue that Qutb and
Mawdudi were crucial in the development of an Iranian-Shi'ite ideology:[118]

> [Shi'ite clerics] did have the advantage of institutional autonomy and of indepen-
> dence in the exercise of religious authority, something the Sunni Islamic ideo-
> logues . . . could only dream of. But it was exceedingly slow in creating a consistent
> ideology in order to defend itself against the state. In fact, the Islamic *ideology* was
> developed elsewhere, by publicists and journalists like Mawdudi in Indo-Pakistan
> and Qutb in Egypt. Its essence consisted in presenting the secular state as an
> earthly idol claiming the majesty that is God's alone. When Khomeini finally rose
> against the Shah, he imported the Islamic ideology from Pakistan and Egypt as a
> free good.[119]

Emphasizing these parallels between Qutb's and Khomeini's fundamentalist thought does not erase crucial distinctions or undermine nuanced accounts of the diversity of "Islamic fundamentalisms." Nor do these commonalities and connections negate the significant doctrinal, juridical, and even
regional[120] differences and discontinuities between and within Sunni and
Shi'ite fundamentalism, and the diversity of historical, political, social, and
cultural conditions under which they developed. It is important to note, as
Arjomand does, that Khomeini's theocracy was in no way an application of
Qutb's or Mawdudi's radicalism; rather it represents an extension of the
already formidable authority of the jurists in Shi'ite theology.[121] This requires, in turn, attending to the dispute about the successor to the Prophet

Muhammad at the heart of the Sunni/Shiʻite divide, the divergence of Sunni and Shiʻite attitudes toward legitimacy and state power, toward the role of *ijtihad*, and the different historical and institutional relationships between the jurists in Iran and the *ʻulama'* in a country such as Egypt.[122]

Yet I suggested in the introduction that despite the tremendous variety of contexts and histories in which Islam has flourished, there are unifying patterns at least to Islamic fundamentalists' constructions of "tradition" out of the Qur'an and the life of the Prophet, and that, moreover, Qutb's worldview lends crucial insight into them. Delineating such patterns and themes, I argued, does not presuppose the revival of an essential Islamic tradition, but rather refers to the ways in which the global ascendance of Western social political, and economic norms has presented a common set of dilemmas and problems to prevailing understandings of "Islamic tradition," an interaction that has produced a particular "remake of things traditional, one among other possible remakes of things traditional, themselves impossible to apprehend as substances and in an unmediated way."[123] Just so, I want to suggest that this brief discussion of Qutb and Khomeini highlights particular continuities and unifying patterns that have interesting implications for my larger argument regarding Qutb's critique of modernity, and of rationalism in particular. Qutb shares with Khomeini, for example, a critique of all forms of modern, secular authority as corrupt and of obedience to such authority as idolatry; a focus on sovereignty as the means by which to fulfill God's will on Earth; advocacy of the definition of legitimate rule in terms of the authority of divine law over public and private domains; a suspicion of rationalist modes of understanding; and an insistence on the limits of human capacity to know and thus rule the world without the aid of revealed law.[124] Although this hardly exhausts the entire list of commonalities and differences, these few parallels suggest a rough convergence of Islamic fundamentalist ideas around a rejection of modern forms of sovereignty and of human claims to knowledge that sustain them, and an insistence that, by contrast, God's knowledge of the deepest meanings of human existence justifies divine rule over not only the moral but the political life.

Thus I argue that Qutb's most radical and influential text is not an idiosyncrasy explicable by reference to the interaction of the peculiarities of one man's life, Egyptian political and economic history, Sunni Islamic traditions or something loosely gathered under the umbrella of "Arab political culture." The echoes between Qutb's and Khomeini's rejection of modern forms of sovereignty and emphasis upon the limits of human reason mean that Qutb's fundamentalist project shares with other Islamists—Sunni and Shiʻite, Arab and non-Arab—a critique of a vision of modernity that embodies and expresses the supremacy of rationalist ways of knowing and mastering the world.[125] Consequently, I would like to suggest that convergence of these Islamic fundamentalist ideas means that Sunni and Shiʻite variants of fundamentalist thought can be understood, at least in part, as engaged in a common critique of rationalist epistemology, and in a project to "reenchant" a modern world defined by disenchantment. What this means is that my reading of Qutb's text may speak to the study of Islamic fundamentalist ideas in general. As I will argue in the following chapter, this reading may speak to Western critiques of modernity as well.

CHAPTER FIVE

Inside the Looking Glass: Views within the West

> [T]he relationship to the world that modern science fostered and shaped appears to have exhausted its potential. The relationship is missing something. It fails to connect with the most intrinsic nature of reality and with natural human experience. It produces a state of schizophrenia: man as an observer is becoming completely alienated from himself as a being. Classical modern science described only the surface of things, a single dimension of reality. And the more dogmatically science treated it as the only dimension, as the very essence of reality, the more misleading it became. We may know immeasurably more about the universe than our ancestors did, and yet it increasingly seems they knew something more essential about it than we do, something that escapes us.
>
> —Vaclav Havel, 1994

THE EXTENT to which modern Islamic thinkers from Afghani to 'Abduh to Qutb are engaged with the problems and dilemmas of Western political thought suggests that, in a colonial and postcolonial world in particular, questions that define political theory have ceased to be, if they ever solely were, Western. This points to an understanding of political theory as a field attentive to broad questions about living together rather than answers located in a specific set of canonical texts. Such a broadened understanding of political theory, I have argued, actually entails a reclamation of a comparative dimension to "theory" presupposed by its earliest meanings. The terms and questions of political theory may therefore illuminate non-Western worlds of thought all too often considered beyond its jurisdiction. My analysis of Qutb's work in terms of political theory, for example, foregrounds the centrality of divine sovereignty, limited human knowledge, and the primacy of the community in the Sunni fundamentalist *Weltanschauung*, features most often neglected by the dominant social scientific explanations of Islamic fundamentalism.

But while comparative political theory reclaims a displaced dimension of theory, it is also transformative, for it provides a perspective from which to see parallels and comparisons that narrower conceptions of political theory occlude. In this chapter, I take Qutb's critique of post-Enlightenment rationalism as a point of departure for a specific comparison with critiques of modernity in contemporary Western political thought. As I suggested in chapter 2, attentiveness to the costs and contradictions of modernity has characterized Western modernization from its inception: Marx analyzed alienation, Durkheim posited a condition of anomie, and Weber charted the course of Occidental disenchantment. Even earlier, writers such as Justus Möser and M. de Bonald decried the moral decay and civic unrest that had accompanied such modern processes as specialization, commercialization, and industrialization.[1] But Qutb's pessimistic vision finds its more recent counterpart in Western perspectives where modernity is a crisis defined by a degeneration of common meanings. In this chapter, I focus on Hannah Arendt's analysis of modern authority, Alasdair MacIntyre's, Charles Taylor's, and Richard John Neuhaus's discussion of modern moral discourse, and Robert Bellah's and Daniel Bell's arguments regarding the decline of modern community. Despite differences in politics and theoretical sensibilities, these voices see in modernity a crisis due to a rupture with tradition, the dual rejection of theology and teleology inaugurated by Enlightenment rationalism, and the subsequent diminishment of meaning—in authority, morality, and community—that that rejection is said to entail.

This is not the only fruitful comparison possible between Qutb and aspects of Western political thought. Qutb's critique of rationalism could be, for example, situated among the discussions on reason and revelation in Augustine and Aquinas, and aspects of his thought might be usefully compared with that of fascist thinkers. This comparison, however, places Qutb in the company of other critics with whom he shares certain quite contemporary anxieties about the costs and limits of rationalism in modern life and, in so doing, takes him seriously rather than dismissing him prima facie as fascistic. The sheer abundance and diversity of voices that today emphasize what is lost in the modern, rationalized world make any one account of this perspective incomplete.[2] Thus these few voices may be taken to illustrate, in a necessarily limited fashion, the lineaments of Western ambivalences and indictments of modern rationalism.[3] A crucial implication of this particular analysis, however, is the possibility and richness of many comparisons between Western and Islamic thought, and across cultures generally.

Placing *Signposts along the Road* in the context of Western reassessments and critiques of modern rationalism lends additional force to the suggestion that there is a transcultural problematic of modernity. This problematic does not simply arise out of perennial questions derived from ahistorical, transcendent needs and human dilemmas, but rather emerges because the history of colonialism and imperialism and the imperatives of globalization ensure that Western paradigms will continue to frame the sensibilities of non-Western, indigenous critics. Such a problematic suggests that while Qutb is engaged in Islamic debates both past and present, his fundamentalist thought is not a self-enclosed world of meaning to which others cannot gain access, nor is it a self-referential argument with implications only for the world in which he lived and worked. On the contrary, Qutb's perspective may illuminate the workings of rationalist discourse itself. In *Orientalism*, Said argues that the Orientalist discourse says more about its "authors" than about its stated subject, the Orient that is the Other to our Self. Just so, my analysis of Qutb's political thought can perhaps be understood as reverse Orientalism: in Qutb's critique we can see how the Other constructs what we regard as the Self.

Here, then, the question arises: do we see ourselves in this critique of the "Self"? To what extent does Qutb's critique capture aspects of Western rationalism and modernity we recognize? Might it illuminate our own understanding and experiences of modernity, or lend insight into aspects of our world we may be unable or reluctant to see? For many observers of contemporary politics, these questions extend an undeserved interpretive charity to a thinker who, were he alive, would be most unlikely to respond in kind. To still others, these are easy questions with obvious answers: Qutb should be dismissed as a pedant whose inconsistencies, ignorance, maddening vagueness, and frequent descents into polemic fail to demonstrate the rigor of true theory. Finally, as Qutb's argument rests on an absolute faith in the existence and authority of God, an authority unseen, undemonstrable, and at times counterfactual, his arguments may seem unworthy of sober consideration at all. For some, then, the question of "what Qutb might tell us" can be easily resolved. The standards of basic morality and scholarship demand the conclusion that his work is substandard, misguided logically, intellectually, and ethically, a threat to be overcome rather than a perspective from which we might learn.

But a crucial argument of this work is that these verdicts on Qutb's perspective are overdetermined. It is all too easy to dismiss Qutb and thinkers like him as reactionary, fanatical, simplistic, and just plain wrong. The endeavor to understand where and why Qutb's political thought poses a distinct challenge to concepts and principles we value is in this way short-circuited. As *Signposts* is somewhat of a manifesto for the Sunni fundamentalist movement, such conclusions miss the opportunity to engage a perspective that apparently captures a more widespread and popular sense of political and moral discontent. Indeed, much like the communist manifesto of Marx and Engels, it contains strategies that demand to be taken seriously politically and seeks to create an audience not yet in existence; its validity thus depends, in part, upon the effect that it has on the world. Hence, as I have suggested, Qutb's project is located in a tradition of political theory in which the text is "not an invitation to other men to pronounce upon the logical or factual merits of the words," but an attempt to transform the world.[4]

Moreover, in teaching us about other views of the world, the study of non-Western political thinkers such as Qutb also counteracts the tendency of political theorists to see the world through only Western eyes. More particularly, the juxtaposition of such thought with Western political theory can tell us about the extent to which concepts we value do or do not make sense in a different cultural context and concomitantly, the extent to which the experiences and sensibilities that underlie such concepts are reflected in other traditions. Yet, at the same time, such an endeavor may enlarge, transform, and challenge these very assumptions, commitments, and sensibilities. What we learn is surely determined by the questions we ask, but if the process of inquiry into unfamiliar realms is understood in terms of dialogue that is ongoing and transformative—a "hermeneutic mediation" between participants—the very endeavor may subtly shift the terms and focus of the questions themselves. Just so, in seeking to understand Qutb and hear his perspective on modernity, it becomes less helpful to censure his work and more urgent to investigate the extent to which he may be engaged in a discussion about the nature and costs of modernity that we recognize, if not endorse. To focus such an inquiry, the question I propose to address in the following discussion is this: How might Qutb's critique of rationalism and diagnosis of modernity echo not only past but contemporary Western voices on the problems endemic to the modern condition? Or alternatively, in what ways do contemporary Western critiques of the modern condition share Qutb's experience and analysis of modernity?

This inquiry can be regarded as the third piece of a tripartite exploration. If chapter 2 showed how the discourse of the Western "Self" constructs the "Other," and Qutb provided a window on how the "Other" constructs the "Self," this chapter is, in part, a glance at how the West has reevaluated its "modern Self," how disparate voices have united in interrogating the premises and assumptions that have framed Western intellectual thought since the Enlightenment. Such reevaluation, I argue, shares Qutb's critical conclusion that modernity must be primarily understood as a condition of schizophrenia, a disease into which humanity has been thrown by the simultaneous eclipse of transcendent authority and the rise of modern rationalism. These commonalities suggest that Qutb should be regarded not as a wild-eyed, alien fanatic but rather as a critic whose anxieties mirror worries within our own theoretical tradition, and that such echoes defy accounts that regard either vision as culturally or politically idiosyncratic. Indeed, in the end, this mirroring may call the very boundaries of "Islam" and "the West," "Self" and "Other" into question. For I have suggested that Qutb's fundamentalist "Other" is already a culturally syncretic perspective, a complex and eclectic amalgamation of Western ideas and reinterpreted Islamic traditions. In this chapter I suggest that "the West" is itself riven with disagreements and characterized by concerns and ambivalences not unlike Qutb's. In the very process of viewing modernity "from both sides," then, the boundaries between the sides themselves may begin to blur, the oppositions built upon them to unravel.

In making this argument, I am not attempting to elide the political and intellectual divisions among and between these Western critics and Qutb. Nor am I endorsing a dark vision of modernity they largely share.[5] Indeed, there is reason to be suspicious of any one-sidedly pessimistic assessment of modernity and rationalism. Yet as in my analysis of Qutb, here I am less interested in evaluating these arguments about modernity than in teasing out the perspectives expressed in and presupposed by them.[6] Such perspectives suggest that many contemporary Western critiques of modernity are themselves animated by concerns about the eclipse of ends, the hegemony of rationalism, the loss of worldly meaning, and the impoverishment of contemporary understandings and experiences of politics. In this light, Qutb's project can be usefully understood as part of a transcultural problematic in which modernity is a condition of decay—whether called *jahiliyya*, emotivism, radical subjectivism, or the rise of the therapeutic. Qutb's work in *Signposts along the Road*—his critique of modernity and rationalism in particular, his insistence on the urgency and nature of redemption—thus becomes one interlocutor among a chorus of voices attempting to capture the causes and character of the leaching of meaning from modern life, one attempt among many to "reenchant" the modern world. We need not agree with either Qutb or the Western critics to recognize these echoes and the anxieties they express, and see, moreover, that there is a pragmatic imperative to acknowledge and understand them.[7] Yet it may also be that these perspectives teach us not only about the *extent* of the critique of modernity but also something about modernity itself. These voices may, despite their flaws, capture an aspect of the limits and costs of modernity by suggesting that the rationalist foundations of modern political and moral life have failed to sustain us in some crucial ways.

THE CRISIS OF AUTHORITY

Hannah Arendt originally cast the title of the essay now known as "What Is Authority?" in the past tense: "What *Was* Authority?" The earlier title reflects her conclusion that what had served as genuine political authority from classical time forward has become a historical artifact in the contemporary world.[8] That is, in Arendt's somewhat unorthodox approach, political authority is not so much a concept as an event, a phenomenon that existed once but whose historical specificity meant that the demise of particular beliefs and political structures entailed its eclipse. *Political* authority is thus historically, structurally, and substantively distinctive. According to Arendt, the prototype of political authority was born in the Platonic tension between philosophy and politics or, more specifically, in the hostility of the polis toward philosophy and the philosopher's mistrust of the polis in classical Greek thought. In this context, the end of real political authority was to compel obedience without use of violence, and by means more effective than persuasion through reason, which works only upon the few. Political authority thus emerged in the search for "a relationship in which the compelling element lies in the relationship itself and is prior to the actual issuance of commands."[9] As she suggests, one of the earliest and most enduring formulations of authority is Plato's Philosopher-King, a ruler whose legitimate domination of the realm of human affairs depends upon the transformation of philosophic truths into a set of transcendent measurements and rules.

ut of the tension between philosophy and politics in Greek political thought, then, real authority, as distinguished from prepolitical authority or mere power, came to require standards of truth or rightness that transcend but refer to the immediate political realm. Although the relationships of master to slave, parent to child, teacher to student have been commonly invoked as prototypes for political authority, Arendt argues that such examples are drawn either from the distinctively private sphere or from the sphere of "making," or fabrication, in which men confront nature, a confrontation that incorporates an element of violence incompatible with genuine political authority. Furthermore, such instances of authority presuppose a relationship of inequality inconsistent with an Aristotelian ideal of political life where "[t]he polis is a community of equals for the sake of a life which is potentially the best."[10] The nature of properly *political* authority is thus distinct from prepolitical relationships of tutelage. Political authority is also distinct from power, coercion, and violence,[11] and it does not entail persuasion that, in its Greek formulation, assumed not only a basic equality among men but also an equal capacity to be subject to the calling of reason. Authority is not expressed in the form of a command, but nevertheless, like self-evident truths, obligates like a command. For Arendt, it is akin to the binding power of the Greek auspices where the gods cast judgment on decisions made by men without actually directing them. Here the gods have "authority among, rather than power over, men."[12]

In Arendt's narrative, political authority was first realized fully in the nexus of religion, politics, and tradition expressed in the founding of Rome, an experience that both incorporated and institutionalized Greek transcendent standards and measurements. The founding of the city was considered an unrepeatable, sacred event that endowed the Roman ancestors with an unquestionable authority that outlived them. Authority thus "had its roots in the past, but this past was no less present in the actual life of the city than the power and strength of the living."[13] Likewise, for Arendt religion meant to be tied to the past, and piety entailed participation in the ongoing effort to lay foundations for eternity; in the city the gods found their permanent

home. "As long as this tradition was uninterrupted, authority was inviolate."[14] With the Christianization of the Roman Empire, the continuity of
such authority was assured by virtue of an amalgamation of Greek transcendent measurements, the Roman sacredness of foundation, and the punitive
notion of an afterlife.

Crucial to Arendt's narrative is the claim that over time the original experience of the founding has been forgotten, and the belief in "future states"
has disappeared through secularization. "The outstanding political characteristic of our modern secular world," she writes in "Religion and Politics,"
"seems to be that more and more people are losing the belief in reward and
punishment after death."[15] As the Arendtian conception of authority both
requires common reference points for meaning and is a reference point that
solidifies the world, she contends that the loss of such "authentic and indisputable experiences common to us all" signals the loss of permanence, dura-
bility, and meaning. Arendt thus suggests that political authority has van-
ished from the modern world because the self-evident experiences and
truths that had formed a common world have lost their commonality. The
formal language used to describe institutions of leadership hides a void; such
language is but a remnant of a world where authority was grounded in a
firmament that made such notions as obligation, duty, and legitimacy robust
and stable. At moments Arendt suggests that this is a moment of great opportunity; in others, she implies that this void, hidden but not entirely obscured, at once reflects and makes real the fragility of ties among human
beings, the vulnerability of the modern project to guide social interaction
rationally.

Although it is not clear that there ever was an inclusive "we" united by
such shared meanings, Arendt argues that it is the demise of such purportedly stable and shared meanings that is constitutive of modern political life.
History has become unmoored, the groundwork of the world has been lost,
and the world has begun to shift, "to change and transform itself with ever-
increasing rapidity from one shape into another."[16] The modern condition is
characterized by a crisis of authority, a vacuum where shared meanings used
to be. Building upon Arendt, John Schaar contends that the modern state is
one in which personal and visible leadership has been replaced by "impersonal, anonymous, and automatic mechanisms of control" concerned with
efficiency rather than responsibility and accountability.[17] This development
has made it "impossible for men to relate to one another on the basis of
shared commitments to transcendent and demanding purposes and values."[18] So entrapped are we in the discourse of objectivity and rationality
that our methods of study cannot help us see the ways in which bureaucratic
authority, language, and epistemology have failed to provide for our "needs
for understanding and counsel on the basic, inescapable questions of human
existence."[19] The very language through which we study life embodies and

thus reinscribes the abstraction of the empirical from the context that endows facts with meaning.

> Reality is that which is tangible, discrete, external, quantifiable, and capable of being precisely conveyed to others. Everything that is left over—and some might think that this is half of life—becomes curiously unreal or epiphenomenal. If it persists in its intrusions on the "real" world, then it must be treated as trouble; and those who act from motives embedded in the unreal world are treated as deviant cases, in need of repair or reproof.[20]

In this way, the crisis of authority is also a crisis of meaning, because the foundations that endowed authority with legitimacy also gave meaning to the experience of community and of human existence itself. For the absence of foundations—past or future—that transcend the realm of human power and existence signals the absence of a shared world, which signals a crisis related to but beyond that of political authority: for what is left, Arendt writes, is "a society of men who, without a common world which would at once relate and separate them, either live in desperate lonely separation or are pressed together in a mass."[21] Indeed, in *The Human Condition* she argues that the gradual ascendancy of scientific thought has facilitated the rise of an inherently apolitical laboring society that, in turn, has locked us into a pattern of inaction that is steadily foreclosing the possibility of regeneration, even as it develops.[22]

Although Arendt views authority as an invention of classical philosophy—and sees philosophy as antipolitical—the dominant theme of her essay is that history is in these ways a process of decay and modernity an expression of loss. Yet Arendt's analysis of modernity is not reducible to a nostalgic yearning for an ancient past, nor does it issue in unrelieved pessimism. For Arendt, belief in transcendence was forged in a particular historical epoch and served to hold that world together. We must not, she cautions, "allow ourselves to be misled by such generalities as the disenchantment of the world or the alienation of man, generalities that often involve a romanticized notion of the past."[23] She is ambivalent about the possibility or even the desirability of such belief now. As she argues in "The Crisis in Education," "wherever the crisis has occurred in the modern world, one cannot simply go on nor yet simply turn back. Such a reversal will never bring us anywhere except to the same situation out of which the crisis has just arisen."[24] Indeed, she claims that there are great potentialities as well as dangers in the erosion of a common and fixed world of meaning, and at the end of "What Is Authority?" she holds out the possibility that revolutions can renew the thread of tradition.[25] As Dana Villa argues, Arendt's "'faith in action' does not rest on the futile desire to resurrect the *agora* in contemporary society; rather it reflects a continuing wonder at the fact that political action persists in the various 'defeated causes' our political historians relegate to the dustbin of history. . . . For some, this state of affairs may be a source of untempered regret; for Hannah Arendt, however, it signifies both loss *and* hope."[26]

Lest we be condemned to live forever in such a meaningless and increasingly fragile world, then, Arendt cautiously entertains the possibility of overcoming the alienation of the modern condition, of redeeming modernity by reclaiming a certain kind of politics. More specifically, in *The Human Condition* she argues that the threat to political life is averted and the human condition redeemed by the possibilities of meaningful political action. For political action to carry such existential weight it must be distinguished from the purely instrumentalized understandings of action so common in modern political discourse. The primary mode of political action for Arendt is speech. Speech requires a community of distinct and equal citizens for meaning, it does not express interests or life processes, and above all it is not instrumental to some goal beyond itself. Its object is politics—the founding of a constitution or state, or the defense of both from internal or external attack. Freedom and worldliness are not the results but the embodiment of and precondition to political action: "The *raison d'être* of politics is freedom, and its field of experience is action."[27]

For Arendt, then, the "life of action, of political action, is thus the one vindication of life."[28] For it is only in action that we stand apart from the dreary preoccupation with the life cycle and escape from the laboring condition to which we are otherwise condemned. Of course, her model of political action is drawn from ancient Athens, and as such it is understood in terms of a public sphere no longer possible in a modern age characterized by "the rise of the social" and what Villa describes as "the profound and irrevocable consequences of the public realm's loss of reality.[29] Yet political action is the sole activity in which humans become distinct from nature. As such, political action is what gives meaning and coherence to human existence; indeed, it is the only possible response to Silenus's question of what makes life worth living. Arendt in no way claims to "cure" the modern condition. Indeed, the irrevocable nature of the loss and the "autonomy of process" behind such modern mechanisms of foreclosure seem to suggest that even these possibilities of agency are slim.

Without overstating the case, let me suggest that there are certain parallels between Arendt's critique of modern authority and Qutb's critique of *jahiliyya*. For Qutb as for Arendt, legitimate political authority was and is predicated on the existence of standards that transcend yet refer to human affairs. Indeed, while Arendt is critical of Greek philosophy, the prototype for her understanding of authority, Plato's Philosopher-King, evokes Qutb's argument that the only legitimate authority is divine authority expressed in the supremacy of Islamic law. Legislation is thus beyond human power, and as justice flows from adherence to Islamic law alone, government officials are more aptly characterized as "selfless instruments of timeless truths" than legislators or leaders.[30] There is a convergence around the assumption that the demise—or, from Qutb's perspective, the repudiation—of the traditions, or frameworks, that sustain such standards signals the disappearance of legitimate authority itself. A host of illegitimate claimants to power—from bureaucratic experts to totalitarian demagogues to agents of satanic corruption—march into this void. The apparent barrenness of modern authority testifies to a common narrative of historical loss. That is, embedded in this shared account of authority is a shared experience of modernity itself. Modernity is constituted, in part, by a crisis of authority produced by the absence, or rejection, of foundations that transcend the world of human affairs. Arendt suggests that it is a feature of this condition that it is increasingly difficult to perceive, let alone realize alternatives to it; similarly, in describing *jahiliyya* as a kind of myopia, Qutb implies that it is a disease whose strength lies in part in the way it colors our very tools of perceptions, and thus obscures its own nature.

Such critical echoes do not, of course, eclipse substantial differences between the thinkers. Qutb objects to the conditions actuating the "modern condition" because they express the failure of human power per se; his central complaint about modern sovereignty is that it is constructed without reference to, and in explicit opposition to, the authority of the transcendent divinity. This story of the relationship between human will and transcendent foundations determines the course of history— decline—and concomitantly dictates the nature of the cure. The solution to these modern crises for Qutb depends upon an act of recognition rather than of re-creation. The authority that accrues to "those who know" is underwritten by a truth whose force is guaranteed by no less than God. In this sense Qutb exemplifies the literal meaning of the word "fundamentalism": a return to and excavation of indisputable foundations that are taken to exist in a realm beyond human power and interpretation.

By contrast, Arendt traces the demise of foundations through a series of related but uncoordinated historical and philosophical developments that eroded not a metaphysical truth, but the human capacity to believe in such truth. This pushes both her historical narrative and her restorative project in a decidedly sociological rather than theological direction. Arendt's distance from Qutb's metaphysics does not preclude her from valuing the solidity transcendence has given certain kinds of authority, particularly that of the Roman republic. But the demise of legitimate authority and the common meanings presupposed by it does not evoke a search for new foundations. Rather, authority and the future of the human condition require the reconstitution of a public space where "meaning" is woven from shared narratives enacted through political action. For Arendt it is political action—defined as public speech and deeds among equals—and not transcendent truth that can provide an answer to Silenus's question of what makes life worth living.

Thus while Qutb's project is essentially foundational, Arendt's is antifoundational. It is antifoundational not in the postmodern sense of the radical impossibility of foundations, but rather in the sense that her project of renewal
does not rely on the reconstitution of such foundations; she locates belief in
transcendence in shared meanings and communal practices that no longer
exist.

These differences, however, only make the similarities more striking. For
Qutb as for Arendt, the loss of foundations that create a common world of
meaning is a source of political decay and human alienation. It expresses the
crisis of modernity because "inescapable" questions of human existence do
not lose their urgency when the answers decay. A significant dimension of
the modern crisis is thus a crisis of meaning.[31] Such a common diagnosis
calls forth redemptive projects that, despite radical differences, are at times
strikingly similar in intent. Arendt and Qutb are driven by an understanding
that human flourishing depends significantly on the possibility, in her terms,
of being at home in the world, that is, of overcoming the alienation endemic
to the modern condition (or in Qutb's terms, of triumphing over the alienation endemic to *jahiliyya*) and finding meaning in human existence. Moreover, Arendt's project, like Qutb's, radically challenges the conventions of
modern politics. In the same way that Qutb draws selectively from a political
ideal embodied in the ancient city of Medina, Arendt looks to ancient
Athens for her inspiration. Importantly, neither project is an expression of
mere nostalgia. They are both essentially modern projects, addressed to a
specifically modern malaise, using tools selectively drawn from the politics
of a past and, in Qutb's case, golden age. Furthermore, in arguing that action
can overcome existential alienation, Arendt, like Qutb, accords action redemptive yet worldly significance. For political action is transformative: it
simultaneously presupposes and actualizes the possibility of a radically different, that is, humanly meaningful, public space.

THE DECAY OF MORALITY

Where Arendt finds in modernity a crisis of authority, there are others who
find decay in the form of moral chaos and impotence. Both link modernity
with loss and thus suggest a counterhistory to Enlightenment portrayals of
modernity as an expression and fulfillment of progress. Among the heralds
of moral loss, Alasdair MacIntyre argues that modernity signals a descent
into what he calls an emotivist culture. Emotivism, according to MacIntyre,
is the doctrine that all evaluative judgments are nothing but expressions of
preference, attitude, or feeling.[32] It rests on the claim that since all rational
justifications for objective morality have failed, right and wrong can no
longer refer to criteria beyond the individual.[33] Emotivism thus represents
the triumph of bureaucratic individualism, a worldview in which both col-

lectivist and individualist doctrines ultimately share the conclusion that reason can no longer adjudicate between rival values and rationality is solely about means. This is what MacIntyre means when he suggests that the contemporary vision of the world is primarily Weberian. Without appeal to impersonal and unassailable criteria, modern moral debate is chaotic, defined by incommensurability and interminability. Countering claims for moral progress, he avers that the prevalence of emotivism not only indicates that "morality is not what it once was, but also and more importantly that what once was morality has to some large degree disappeared— and that this marks a degeneration, a grave cultural loss."[34]

In counterpoint to Arendt's crisis of authority, MacIntyre argues that the modern crisis of meaning is a function of moral decay, and that such decay originates in the incoherence of the Enlightenment's intellectual project. But like Arendt's description of authority hollowed out by the demise of transcendent foundations, MacIntyre locates the source of contemporary moral impotence in Enlightenment rejections of transcendent foundations and a doomed attempt to ground morality rationally. For the rationalist rejection of such foundations entails the separation of fact from value, a rupture that disables the very project of rationalist morality. Within the older theological and teleological frameworks, the project of ethics was defined by the attempt to move from the "is" to the "ought," from "man-as-he-happens-to-be" to "man-as-he-could-be-if-he-realized-his-essential-nature."[35] But in the attempt to ground morality in the imperatives of reason, Enlightenment theorists could no longer address the ends of moral action.

> The explanation of action is increasingly held to be a matter of laying bare the physiological and physical mechanisms which underlie action; and, when Kant recognizes that there is a deep incompatibility between any account of action which recognizes the role of moral imperatives in governing action and any such mechanical type of explanation, he is compelled to the conclusion that actions obeying and embodying moral imperatives must be from the standpoint of science inexplicable and unintelligible.[36]

In referring to individual conscience rather than shared values, morality in its current form has been emptied of all that it once entailed. Thus MacIntyre writes: "once the notion of essential human purposes or functions disappears from morality, it begins to appear implausible to treat moral judgments as factual statements."[37] Of course, the presence of foundations or traditions that provide common standards to adjudicate between points of view does not end serious debates over interpretation. As centuries of scriptural commentary show, real and often interminable debates over meaning and interpretation raged prior to the development of emotivism. But MacIntyre argues that modern life is distinguished by the fact that the dominant debates about rights and justice take ends to be incommensurable and thus unsettlable in the public realm in any final way. Thus "[r]ules become the primary concept of the moral life" in the public sphere, and morality per se becomes the purview of the private sphere; ends are a matter of individual conscience alone.[38] Paradoxically perhaps, such essentially modern rules are intertwined with a "set of fragmented survivals" from these earlier traditions. Their continuing if merely residual power in moral discourse is demonstrated by the inconsistency of maintaining modern individualist notions of rights and utility along with classical notions of virtue.[39] The "deontological character of moral judgments is the ghost of conceptions of divine law which are quite alien to the metaphysics of modernity and . . . the teleological character is similarly the ghost of conceptions of human nature and activity which are equally not at home in the modern world."[40]

If the modern moral debate is characterized by inconsistency and indeterminacy, such moral impoverishment has its counterpart in an atomistic vision of social life, one where fellow citizens stand in relation to one another as strangers, as though shipwrecked together on an uninhabited island.[41] Unable to relate to one another via shared ends, MacIntyre argues that social interaction is mediated by rules and procedures constructed to adjudicate between the demands of strangers. Liberalism appears as the political expression of the historical and intellectual rejection of public morality in favor of privatized notions of the good. But the liberal tradition does not exhaust the extent of the problem, although its currency among contemporary moral philosophers provides MacIntyre with the most frequent occasion for complaint. Rather, he argues that the Enlightenment project is a repudiation of an entire moral tradition of which "Aristotle's thought was the intellectual core. . . . [N]o doctrine vindicated itself in so wide a variety of contexts as did Aristotelianism . . .when modernity made its assaults on an older world its most perceptive exponents understood that it was Aristotelianism that had to be overthrown."[42] If the problem at hand is a moral impoverishment stemming from precisely this move, then all post-Enlightenment political theories in the Western tradition are implicated—Marxist, conservative, and liberal alike. In other words, if the rejection of the transcendent—theological and teleological—in human affairs is the ultimate culprit in the process of moral decay, the entire modern Western moral tradition is itself "exhausted."

As a result, we now live in a world where rationality is primarily about means, not ends. Bureaucratic authority is culmination of this split between fact and value, for it justifies its own power by appeal to its own effectiveness and expertise rather than to its ends. But MacIntyre argues that bureaucratic efficiency is itself a myth; the lawlike predictions that constitute expertise are themselves a fantasy belied by the vicissitudes of life. Mastery and expertise are the illusions that mask the incoherence of the rationalist project.[43] Indeed, MacIntyre concludes that the contemporary cult of expertise "disguises and conceals rather than illuminates and it depends for its power on its success at disguise and concealment."[44] Echoing Qutb's language regarding the myopia of modern *jahiliyya*, MacIntyre suggests that the modern moral crisis is like a disease that contaminates our very powers of perception and imagination. Essential to the modern predicament is our ignorance that the barbarians now hold the reins of power.[45]

However, MacIntyre insists that Nietzsche's nihilism is the logical culmination of modern moral philosophy *only if* Enlightenment rejections of Aristotelian teleology were correct. Not only was this rejection misguided, MacIntyre argues, a return to and restatement of the Aristotelian tradition can restore "intelligibility and rationality to our moral and social attitudes and commitments."[46] Herein lies his redemptive project: this Aristotelian tradition enables us to relearn that the authority of laws and virtues can be firmly grounded in a conception of the good that is itself meaningful only within the context of certain practices and traditions. In opposition to the individualist account of the world, then, goods "can only be discovered by entering into those relationships which constitute communities whose central bond is a shared vision of and understanding of goods."[47] Although this formulation is somewhat tautological, MacIntyre suggests that this tradition of the virtues shows us the ways in which local forms of community both presuppose—and resurrect—a vital moral life and sustain it through the "new dark ages which are already upon us."

For MacIntyre, the demise of purportedly unassailable prior standards of truth is tied to the incoherence of current moral debate and the increasing role of therapeutic notions of self-realization as a refuge from moral meaninglessness. Similarly, in the *Ethics of Authenticity*, Charles Taylor argues that the Enlightenment's simultaneous rejection of an established social hierarchy and transcendent moral criteria destroyed a universally recognizable hierarchy of ends, thereby facilitating the emergence and eventual dominance of moral subjectivism and the atomistic pursuit of self-realization. Thus what MacIntyre calls emotivism, Taylor refers to as the ethic of authenticity. This ethic is a debased form of individualism that centers the notion of fulfillment on the self without regard for demands that transcend the self. Without impersonal criteria by which to decide moral debates, therefore, all social relations are transformed into instrumental interactions by which each uses another to pursue one's own ends. By contrast, an "appeal to impersonal criteria of validity of which each rational agent must be his or her own judge" treats all others as ends. In an emotivist culture—or one guided by a debased ethic of authenticity—there are no such criteria and all social relations become manipulative.[48]

For MacIntyre, the disease of emotivism requires the retrieval and reassembly of fragments of earlier moral traditions which lie behind the moral chaos, and which continue to speak to our current malaise. Taylor, however, argues that the ethic of authenticity was originally actuated by a laudable concern for increased individual responsibility and the insistence, against utilitarian theory, that morality had a voice within, that "human beings are endowed with a moral sense, an intuitive feeling for what is right and wrong."[49] For Taylor, the "massive subjective turn" that is constitutive of modern culture came when heeding the inner voice ceased to be a means to acting rightly and became intrinsically significant. Self-fulfillment, in other words, became a matter of being a true human being, and the pursuit of self-realization became the modern project par excellence. According to Taylor, such tendencies have been both expressed and further fortified by those in the Nietzschean tradition who posit a linkage of self-discovery and artistic creation against the constraints of morality, thereby exalting the notion of an agent with radical freedom and untrammeled power to create value. The atomism and radical anthropomorphism that characterize modern culture thus find their roots in precisely this linkage of self-fulfillment, self-creation, and the good life: "Being true to myself means being true to my own originality, and that is something only I can articulate and discover. In articulating it, I am also defining myself. I am realizing a potentiality that is properly my own. This is the background understanding to the modern ideal of authenticity, including its most degraded, absurd, or trivialized forms. It is what gives sense to the idea of 'doing your own thing.'"[50] While material and structural processes such as industrialization and bureaucratization have contributed to the entrenchment and fortification of contemporary atomism and subjectivism, Taylor contends that the slide toward the self-centered modes of the ideal of self-fulfillment is also derived from tendencies within the ethic of authenticity itself.

The Ethics of Authenticity assumes a tone of relative optimism that belies the striking similarities to MacIntyre's pessimistic vision of modernity. Importantly, Taylor argues that the massive subjectivism characteristic of modern culture is neither irreversible nor without moral content. More specifically, he suggests that there is a nondebased ethic of authenticity that is worthy of revival; by contrast, there is no nondebased form of emotivism for MacIntyre. As a mediator between unalloyed narratives of decline and progress, Taylor is perhaps closest to Arendt, for whom the modern crisis has opened the doors to both great dangers and radical possibilities. For Taylor, the task is to avoid condemnation[51] or celebration, and to recall the moral impulse behind the now debased ethic of authenticity. Taylor's redemptive project is thus one of retrieval, to "identify and articulate the higher ideal behind the more or less debased practices, and then criticize these practices from the standpoint of their own motivating ideal."[52]

Importantly, retrieval for Taylor is not an expression of nostalgia. He does not yearn for the return to an older civilization before subjectivism. As he makes clear elsewhere, ideals are themselves set in and nourished by our particular historical and cultural situation.[53] In the case of authenticity, then, retrieval requires a recognition that human life is dialogical, not monological. Values are formed only against what Taylor calls a background of intelligibility, a shared horizon that make the conditions of significance possible. This suggests that, while the end of self-fulfillment may be expressed subjectively, self-fulfillment actually requires investments in things that have "significance independent of us or our desires."[54] Given the loss of a publicly acknowledged social and moral order, the only defense against the slide to subjectivism and atomism is the recognition that the identity of the autonomous individual is sustained by certain social practices—such as deliberation about public action—and that self-fulfillment both presupposes and requires noninstrumental ties to other human beings.[55]

The urgency of redemption takes on an altogether higher pitch in Richard John Neuhaus's analysis of religion and American politics in *The Naked Public Square*. For in Neuhaus's narrative, the banishment of religion from the public sphere results not only in moral chaos and meaninglessness, but in a vacuum that invites the invasion of the state as religion and the hegemony of secular humanism. Neuhaus thus argues that the rejection of such foundational public-religious morality poses a threat to the democratic project itself because the eclipse of transcendence in public life enables the slide from liberalism to totalitarianism.[56] For secular humanism has, in the name of neutrality, cleansed the public space of all contending moralities and, in the process, has stripped American democracy of its only weapon against either the overwhelming ambitions of the modern state or of the crusades of the New Christian Right.

> Such a religious evacuation of the public square cannot be sustained, either in concept or in practice. When religion in any traditional or recognizable form is excluded from the public square, it does not mean that the public square is in fact naked. . . . When recognizable religion is excluded, the vacuum will be filled by *ersatz* religion, by religion bootlegged into public space under other names. . . . [T]ranscendence abhors a vacuum.[57]

Neuhaus's central premise is that the democratic experiment is simultaneously a religious and political enterprise. It is religious because democracy was born in the collaborative tension between Protestant ethics and associational life, on the one hand, and the politics of the nation-state, on the other. It is also religious because politics inescapably concerns itself with moral questions of right and wrong, good and bad. And it is religious because, Neuhaus insists, the American people remain deeply invested in religion and are animated by religious values despite the dominant discourse of secularism. Given the prevalence of religious values in American culture, proponents of secular humanism are undemocratic insofar as they refuse to give public voice to religion.[58] Religion, when banished from the public realm, can neither be the source of a rich associational life nor serve as sustenance for a "public framework of moral reference" that can check the ever-increasing ambitions of the modern state to dominate political life.[59] For "once religion is reduced to nothing more than privatized conscience, the public square has only two actors in it—the state and the individual."[60]

Furthermore, the triumph of secular humanism and the successful privatization of morality disguise an underlying alienation from the public realm caused by the disjunction between public and private selves. Much like Qutb, Neuhaus argues that the modern self is fractured between two different worlds, and finds its home in neither the world of unrelieved privacy nor the public world where we must "abandon our deepest convictions." The citizen of Neuhaus's impoverished liberal democracy is a "cipher" who, like Michael Sandel's "unencumbered self," must "check our deepest beliefs at the door" in order to gain entry to the public arena.[61] "Most particularly, identities tarred by the brush of religion must be left behind or disguised. In the public theater we are all to don the masks of anonymity."[62]

Indeed, Neuhaus makes the controversial suggestion that, in purging all religion from the public realm, secular humanism has in fact become a collaborator in the resurgence of antidemocratic fundamentalist movements intent on forcibly clothing the naked square with their own meanings. American fundamentalism and other religious revival movements are thus primarily interpreted as protests against the meaninglessness of the naked public square (although for Neuhaus, the danger of antidemocratic fundamentalism movements is most vividly embodied in the Iranian Revolution of 1979). Such examples serve to articulate the tension between liberalism and democracy: liberalism, Neuhaus implies, insists on purchasing tolerance and equality at the expense of democracy. Consequently, the very survival of an increasingly fragile democratic project may depend on a rejection of the liberal discourse of pluralism, interests, and private morality in favor of a revitalization of the biblical tradition already present within Americans' democratic heritage.

Neuhaus portrays America as, on the one hand, on the brink of totalitarianism from within, the inevitable danger of the public square stripped of the religious content that endows it with meaning. But on the other hand, the public square can never be empty. As American democracy is rich in Christian tradition, its politics couches an essentially moral debate in the more permissible discourse of interests. Thus he contends that, despite its pretensions to neutrality, secular humanism generates a "religion of relativity" that is camouflaged in the discourse of interests and pluralism. For Neuhaus we must both recognize our poverty and return to our richness. The revitalization of politics does not, therefore, entail creating a new world but recognizing and embracing the world that already is and who we already are. The choice then is not between neutrality and morality: "The question is not *whether* the questions of positive freedom will be addressed. The question is *by whom*—by what reasonings, what traditions, what institutions, what authorities—they will be addressed."[63]

Despite radically different political positions, MacIntyre, Taylor, and Neuhaus concur that the modern paean to diversity, pluralism, and tolerance masks a danger: the diminished possibility of moral meaning in the context of shared and, therefore what they deem democratic, ends.[64] Thus MacIntyre argues that the radical detachment of the modern self from all social particularity and its subsequent capacity to assume any moral standpoint is not the essence of moral agency, as some would have it, but the absence of such agency.[65] Likewise, the interminable controversies between analytical and moral philosophers of relatively like minds only serve to confirm the doomed nature of the contemporary rationalist project to establish principles on which moral agents agree.[66] For MacIntyre, the possibility of generating a common context in which genuine moral arguments are exchanged is thwarted at every turn by a worldview that hastens the forces of atomism and egoism. In this perspective, the much touted separation between individual conscience and public rules purchases not the freedom, dignity, and well-being of democratic citizens, but isolation, chaos, mass consumption, and a diminishment of democratic freedom.

In this common narrative these modern pathologies are understood to be linked to the Enlightenment rejection of a shared public order and the transcendent principles that were thought to have sustained it. Such a rejection is understood to have doomed the rationalist moral project from its inception, ensuring that the purview of reason become means rather than ends; that the public realm would likewise concern itself with rational administration and leave morality to the private realm; that, without reference to impersonal criteria transcending human affairs, even private moral debate would become inconclusive and slide into what Taylor calls soft relativism, a relativism that assumes that "vigorous defence of any moral ideal is somehow off limits," yet is itself actuated by the moral ideal of authenticity.[67] While attentive to the material and structural processes that have contributed to modern malaise, these theorists view contemporary crisis as the logical conclusion of Enlightenment rationalism, a phenomenon, to borrow the language of Horkheimer and Adorno, "deduced from the nature of the dominant *ratio* itself."[68] As Thomas Spragens puts it, Enlightenment reason was built on the incoherence of maintaining inherited moral absolutes while inaugurating the inexorable drive of scientific rationalism to undermine all that cannot be intelligible through reason.[69] This fundamental contradiction reaches its end in the erosion of the very liberal values—equality, liberty, justice—that animated the Enlightenment project in the first place. In this view, then, the disenchantment of the world culminates in a narrowing expressed in "the dark side of individualism," a "centering on the self, which both flattens and narrows our lives, makes them poorer in meaning, and less concerned with others or society."[70]

Qutb shares with these Western theorists an insistence that the rationalist rejection of transcendent foundations has plunged the moral project into radical subjectivism and thus into moral incoherence. Indeed, I have argued that Qutb's investment in divine sovereignty is formulated precisely in opposition to modern rationalist understandings of knowledge and the marginalization of revealed truth they entail. This means that, first, these critics share with each other, and with Arendt, an understanding of modernity as defined in part by a crisis that is ultimately a crisis of meaning. Second, this modern crisis is understood to be an expression of the bankruptcy of the Enlightenment aspiration to ground morality rationally. The failure characterizes all post-Enlightenment political theories, individualist and collectivist alike: this is what MacIntyre means when he speaks of the exhaustion of the Western moral tradition, and what Qutb intends by subsuming all modern theories of sovereignty in the word *jahiliyya*.

Such substantive similarities are underscored by certain rhetorical echoes. In Qutb's work, as in MacIntyre's, Taylor's, and Neuhaus's, the extent of the moral chaos is consistently expressed in the language of pathology— "degeneration," "impotence," "malaise," "schizophrenia," and "disease"—so extensive it has clouded our very ability to perceive our own sickness and thus to imagine alternative worlds. In another evocative parallel, however, this image of atrophy and pathology is shot through with a language of power and domination. The rationalist rejection of the transcendent is seen as diminishing the public relevance and purchase of moral truths only to dominate the moral as well as the political realm; the decay of meaning both presages and facilitates the hegemony of a rationalist cosmology that endows efficiency and technique with supreme value. The implication is that the moral incoherence endemic to radical subjectivism is like a sickness that gains strength through its parasitic hold on the victim.

Thus Qutb and Neuhaus explicitly argue that secularism, far from expressing a principle of neutrality, has served as the Trojan horse of ersatz religion, corruption and totalitarianism. Neutrality is understood as a myth, a lie that Qutb, as well as Neuhaus and MacIntyre, wants to unmask. For claims to neutrality camouflage secularism—or, alternatively, relativist, or subjectivist, domination. Once revealed, it will again be possible to see the ways in which moral and political life are intimately connected. The question becomes, in Neuhaus's language, not *whether* morality guides public life, but *which* morality is the "right" morality. Of course, while Qutb, Taylor, MacIntyre, and Neuhaus share this question, their answers diverge radically. Qutb calls for the establishment of Islamic sovereignty, Taylor for the retrieval of the original ethic actuating individualism, MacIntyre for a kind of Thomist cosmology, and Neuhaus for a recognition of latent Christian traditions. Yet unlike other critiques of rationalist domination in critical and postmodern theories, these critics clearly do not see such unmasking as proof of the radical impossibility of metanarratives capable of sustaining common meaning. On the contrary, the contemporary moral chaos—now seen to be linked to an essentially modern alienation from the world—testifies to the essentially religious idea that (in Taylor's relatively mild language) "we may still need to see ourselves as part of a larger order that can make claims on us."[71]

THE DECLINE OF COMMUNITY

There is yet another dimension to what Taylor refers to as the "flattening and narrowing" of modern life. This dimension, often expressed as the decline of community, reflects the way in which social life is understood to be impoverished, and political freedom diminished, by the same forces of disenchantment that have emptied formerly robust, shared constructions of political authority and moral discourse. In *Habits of the Heart*, Robert Bellah and others argue that the cosmology of individualism has grown "cancerous," a threat not only to the ties that bind society together, but to freedom itself.[72] Despite a rich diversity of traditions latent within contemporary American culture, Bellah suggests that modernity is predominantly defined by the hegemony of individualism in both private and public life. Whereas the private sphere is defined by pursuit of self-fulfillment (Taylor's debased ethic of authenticity), the economic calculus of utilitarian individualism prevails in the public realm. In this way, formerly participatory democratic communities are fractured into atomistic and isolated constellations or "lifestyle enclaves"—groups that cohere around similar patterns of consumption, appearance, and leisure activities rather than shared histories and traditions.[73] What Bellah alternatively calls the "permissive therapeutic culture," "the culture of manager and therapist," "the culture of separation," and "the culture of radical individualism" both augurs and reflects the diminishment of political freedom seen as inherent in the bureaucratization of public life. The ascendancy of this culture represents the fulfillment of de Tocqueville's prophetic warning against the danger of American individualism facilitating a slide into administrative despotism, and a diminishment of democratic freedom.[74]

> Over this kind of men stands an immense, protective power which is alone responsible for securing their enjoyment and watching over their fate. . . . It likes to see the citizens enjoy themselves, provided that they think of nothing but enjoyment. . . . It does not break men's will, but softens, bends, and guides it . . . it is not at all tyrannical but it hinders, restrains, enervates, stifles, and stultifies so much

that in the end each nation is no more than a flock of timid and hardworking animals with the government as its shepherd.[75]

In this view, the decline of community is simultaneously an expression of and corollary to a crisis of meaning: the disintegration of political community into such "pseudo-communities" is a reflection and reinforcement of the atrophy of moral discourse and the rise of a therapeutic language to express and justify all life choices. Disconnected from communities wider than "life-style enclaves" and estranged from the "second language" that can transcend the morally truncated discourse of radical individualism, Bellah argues that many Americans either retreat into a private life or, when they emerge into the community, do so for the therapeutic goal of "self-fulfillment" or at the behest of "value priorities" that appear arbitrary without the generational, historical, and religious context that makes meaning intersubjective. While the therapeutic discourse strains to express the necessity of relationships and fulfillment through commitments beyond the self, Bellah implies that, insofar as it is primarily concerned with individual well-being, this discourse is constrained by the parameters of its own premises. Thus, for Bellah, the bleakness of middle American cultural and political life is a product of its submersion in particularly anemic forms of modern individualism that obstruct access to older, richer traditions of community. In modern culture, Bellah avers, "our poverty is as absolute as that of the poorest of nations."[76] We have achieved tremendous material and technological prosperity, "[y]et we seem to be hovering on the very brink of disaster, not only from international conflict but from the internal incoherence of our own society."[77] In a passage eerily reminiscent of Qutb's opening salvo in *Signposts*, Bellah writes:

There is a widespread feeling that the promise of the modern era is slipping away from us. A movement of enlightenment and liberation that was to have freed us from superstition and tyranny has led in the twentieth century to a world in which ideological fanaticism and political oppression have reached extremes unknown in previous history. Science, which was to have unlocked the bounties of nature, has given us the power to destroy all life on the earth. Progress, modernity's master idea, seems less compelling when it appears that it may be progress into the abyss.[78]

Along with Arendt, MacIntyre, and Neuhaus, Bellah sees the resources for redemption in the lessons and languages of older biblical and republican traditions drowned out by the cacophony of individual voices pursuing "their own thing." In an echo of Taylor's argument about the debasement of the ethic of authenticity, Bellah argues that the pursuit of self-fulfillment has been abstracted from the traditions that produced it, traditions that "placed individual autonomy in a context of moral and religious obligation that in some contexts justified obedience as well as freedom."[79] If modernity is a "culture of separation," its failure primarily a function of the insistence on placing the individual good ahead of the common good, then integration requires reviving the biblical and republican traditions that posit communities guided by explicitly moral and shared ends, divine or civic. That is, Bellah argues that the revitalization not only of civic virtue but of meaning itself requires a recognition of shared ends broader than the minimalist consensus required for tolerance and procedural justice. In Bellah's world such a move does not entail a return to traditions that had depended upon gross social and political inequalities, but rather demands an eclectic revival of communitarian principles and participatory democratic ideals. For Bellah, real communities, or "communities of memory," embody the principles of social interdependence, collective participation, and shared practices, and as such they can sustain a greater integration of the public and private good than an individualist cosmology. In such communities, individuals do not merely use one another in pursuit of private ends; on the contrary, the private good becomes contingent upon the public good to which it contributes. According to Bellah, the vitality of such communities both militates against the slide into administrative despotism and provides resources for meaning. Only in this way can we "reverse the slide toward the abyss."[80]

While Bellah concentrates on the tension between democratic principles and the hegemony of individualism in both private and public spheres, Daniel Bell delineates what he sees as the contradictions between the rise of individualistic modes of cultural meaning—what Bell sometimes refers to as the ideology of modernism—and the principles that actuate the modern capitalist economy. In *The Cultural Contradictions of Capitalism*, Bell argues that modernity is characterized by a disjunction between a social structure defined by bureaucracy, hierarchy, and specialization and the pursuit of fulfillment of the whole individual (Bellah's expressive individualism) that defines contemporary culture.[81] Bell endorses Weber's argument that at the inception of capitalism such economic imperatives were conjoined with the Puritan's conception of the calling. The modernist supplanting of religion with what Bell calls the "idolatry of the self," however, has separated bourgeois society from the Protestant ethic that both framed and restrained the pursuit of capital.[82] It is Bell's contention that this break and consequent contradictions between society and ethics become the source of the cultural crises of modernity: the rise of alienation, the impoverishment of meaning, and the demise of civic virtue.

Like Bellah, Bell argues that these modern crises are expressed along two interrelated dimensions, that of meaning and that of community. In the first dimension, rationalization and disenchantment have inaugurated an age radically discontinuous with the metanarratives that formerly endowed life with meaning. Modern justifications of contemporary life fail precisely because they presuppose the impossibility of such metanarratives. Thus Bell argues that the secularization of modern Western culture has stripped bourgeois society of the transcendent, shared meanings that provided the moral and cultural justifications of capitalism. The bourgeois idea has in this way lost its anchor, which was "rooted in experience yet provided some transtemporal conception of reality."[83] Without Western religion, the "religions of restraint," what is left is mere hedonism. "The real problem of *modernity* is the problem of belief. To use an unfashionable term, it is a spiritual crisis, since the new anchorages have proved illusory and the old ones have become submerged. It is a situation which brings us back to nihilism; lacking a past or a future, there is only a void" (emphasis in the original).[84]

According to Bell, herein lies a central contradiction of the modern condition: historically, religion has been the repository of shared meanings through which individuals could relate themselves to the past, to the world, and to others. Unlike the principle of unending progress animating economic development, Bell avers, culture is the realm in which perennial questions derived from the universality of human mortality recur. Culture, Bell writes elsewhere, encompasses "the modalities of response by sentient men to the core questions that confront all human groups in the consciousness of existence: how one meets death, the meaning of tragedy, the nature of obligation, the character of love."[85] Thus, the imperatives of rationalization in modern society have come to work against those of culture, for while rationalism entails institutional secularization and the cultural eclipse of theology, culture is the realm of symbols that both embodies a definition of life and expresses the ceaseless search for meaning. The rejection of transcendent meanings through secularization means that fundamental questions of human existence now go unaddressed but for the resurgence of cults that, as Neuhaus also assures us, will clothe the naked public square in new and terrible meanings. Thus, Bell contends, "where religions fail, cults appear."[86] Moreover, just as Durkheim argues that the sacred is the repository of shared cultural sentiments that solidify otherwise fragile social ties, Bell argues that the decline of religion signals the eclipse of the sacred, which, in turn, weakens the ties that hold communities together. For the rules that bind social relations are justified and given permanence only by reference to a shared but ultimately transcendent moral order. "To say, then, that 'God is dead'" is, Bell warns, to say that "the social bonds have snapped and that society is dead."[87]

As Bell sees it, Western political thought has shown that nature is an inadequate foundation on which to ground morality, and history proved to have no telos other than the continual expansion of instrumental rationality. Religion is thus the only viable foundation for the meaning that remains, and as such it is for Bell the answer to the institutional and cultural decay inherent in the advance of rationalization. Religion alone can assuage the despair of a fruitless search for a "transcendent response to the self" and thus fulfill the "primordial need" for meaning and interconnectedness.[88] Given the intimate connection between the way a culture endows society with meaning and the foundations of social life, in resurrecting the continuity of moral meanings, Bell suggests that religion simultaneously allays the crisis of belief and solidifies the ties that bind a community together.

The rise of what Bellah calls expressive individualism, or Bell's idolatry of the self, at once presupposes and reinforces a narrative of modernity as radical discontinuity: the notion of life as a work of art, of self-fulfillment as becoming one's own person, both presupposes and expresses a dramatic break with older traditions where the meaning of individual life had been derived from a shared moral and social context. In place of priest and king, Bellah avers, we now have managers and therapists whose authority and success are determined by reference to expertise, efficiency, and successful "problem solving." The modern paradox, however, is that self-fulfillment so understood has proven doubly inadequate: it neither enables individuals to understand their own existence nor allows them to relate to one another in morally meaningful ways. Individualism thus understood has replaced transcendent meaning with pursuits that can have no justification beyond themselves.

In the dissolution of community we find the third and last interlocking piece of the narrative of modern decay. In this story, as in the prior stories, disenchantment is a prelude not to progress and liberation but to alienation and despair. Such alienation at once expresses and hastens the turn inward that is endemic to the individualist cosmology, thus reducing the space for political action and inviting the expansion of bureaucratic and non-democratic authority. Although it is the case that the emphasis on individual autonomy emerged in the fight against oppressive social hierarchies and restrictive traditions, critics such as Bellah and Bell imply that principles of autonomy and tolerance have been bought at too high a price. For when social ties become extrinsic to self-fulfillment, the very stability of the community in general, and the democratic project in particular, is undermined. In Taylor's language, the individual is abstracted from a "background of intelligibility," thereby reducing the resources necessary endow human relations, and political relations, with meanings not reducible to rational self-interest or the subjective pursuit of "one's own thing." In such a world, politics becomes the purview of bureaucratic experts and utopian demagogues, political concepts lose their moral force, individual preferences come to determine both the meaning and the form of social relations, and ideas such as obligation and duty are residual fragments from a lost world. The crisis of authority, the decay of morality, and the decline of the community are but three heads of the same hydra.

These analyses are specifically concerned with the decline of *democratic* communities, but they at times imply that the rise of individualism has eroded the very possibility of social ties per se, that is, any ties beyond those that are merely instrumental. This means that, aside from parallels already noted—the theme of modernity as disease; of the modern crisis as a crisis of meaning; of the rationalist failure to provide the conditions for meaningful authority or coherent morality; and of the necessity of recognizing foundations that transcend yet refer to the real of human affairs—Bellah and Bell offer a critique of individualism that mirrors, paradoxically, Qutb's quite explicitly antidemocratic critique of modernity. For while Bellah and Bell argue that the pursuit of self-fulfillment is an expression of and a catalyst for the decay of community life, Qutb regards individualism and the assumptions about worth and meaning it presupposes as inimical to the metaphysical truths that make possible living and living well. Although Qutb would, I think, endorse Bell's attack on the "idolatry of the self," he does not, of course, use the terminology of individualism. Yet both perspectives, in different languages, concur that communities cannot cohere in either the political or moral sense around consumption styles or mutual self-interest. And in both perspectives the antidote to the impoverishment of community entails a reversal of individualism's hierarchy of ends; private ends must be evaluated in light of the extent to which they contribute to public goods. Such shared ends presuppose a larger moral order, whether derived from God's law or embodied in common practices and shared beliefs. Such an order thus serves as the foundation for new connections between individuals and counters the very conditions under which modern despotism and fragmentation flourish.

[M]aterial and political gains have not been matched by the attainment of a loftier wisdom or a more profound culture. The spiritual panorama of the West is desolating: cheap tastes, triviality, shallowness, rebirth of superstition, degradation of eroticism, pleasure enrolled in the service of the communications media.[89]

The voices that have shaped this narrative of modern decay represent radically different political sensibilities. While Taylor calls for a reactivation of the moral traditions behind modern individualism, MacIntyre insists that individualism and its modern liberal justifications are at variance with the richer and ultimately more substantial tradition of Aristotelian virtues. This rejection of the individualist cosmology is echoed in Arendt's conclusion that only political action in a shared public space can answer Silenus's question of what makes life worth living. Bell agrees with MacIntyre and Bellah that modern individualism poses a grave threat to the life of a community, but he locates redemption in the resurrection of the sacred rather than in the tradition of civic republicanism. Similarly, while Bellah insists that only democratic participation in communities of memory inhibits the slide toward administrative despotism, Neuhaus prophesies that only the return of religion to the public domain can save the democratic project from theological fanatics and bureaucratic encroachment.

Yet the construction of modernity in these voices reflects a common vision of history that opposes itself to precisely the modernist aspiration to "rest human prospects on the expansion of productive efforts, relying on a continuous flow of technological innovations to make life better for a higher and higher proportion of humanity" and to foster "an acceptance of efficiency and instrumental rationality as sufficient to minister to the totality of needs in organized societal life."[90] Indeed, contrary to Enlightenment aspirations of opening up the world to new forms of knowledge, experience, and politics, in these perspectives, the organizing principle of modernity is not enlargement but foreclosure. Arendt contends that the rise of the laboring society has almost closed the space for political action. Taylor argues that the debased ethic of authenticity leads to an atomism and radical anthropomorphism that has "narrowed and flattened" modern culture. MacIntyre believes that the possibility of substantive moral debate is itself undermined by modern moral discourse. Neuhaus worries that the modern myth of secularization increases our vulnerability to totalitarianism, and Bellah argues that the course of modern individualism leads inexorably into the maw of administrative despotism. Modernity is not a teleological ascent from the darkness of superstition to the freedom of enlightenment. On the contrary, the defining feature of modern history seems to be the relatively rapid decay of precisely these ideals through the inexorable advance of atomism, disintegration, meaninglessness, and even the return of chaos and the irrational.

Of course, mapping the advance of reason onto a narrative of decline risks diminishing the ways in which an increasing emphasis on reason in matters political underwrites powerful arguments for equality, tolerance and universal suffrage. Visions of a glorious age sinking into the depths of barbarism and radical isolation, no less than accounts of a dankly shadowed past giving way to a brightly illuminated future, distort the complex of achievement and loss that defines Western "rationalization." Both optimistic and pessimistic narratives in some way press the complexity and contradictions of history and cultural experience into the service of a coherent story. Moreover, such narratives of decay often assume the existence of a group—a "we"—that previously shared a world of common meanings and experiences eroded by forces of modernization. Indeed, it is against this set of common meanings shared by an ill-defined yet supposedly inclusive collectivity that the ills of modernity are brought into stark relief, and in terms of which the possibility of redemption is formulated. Arendt's ancient Athens is acknowledged as the cradle of democracy, of traditions of political theory that provided the resources for critique and self-critique, and of institutions that extended citizenship to the poor; yet it was also the site of political conventions and institutions that at one and the same time narrowed the "we" to a minority— exclusive of women, slaves, and resident aliens. Similarly, Neuhaus assumes a common Christian identity both past and present; the very preservation of democracy requires recognizing who "we" are, which is to say, Christian democrats. In another example, MacIntyre opposes the interminable and unresolvable moral debates of the emotivist culture to a prior world in which such debates reached real conclusions by virtue of shared standards of truth. Yet the liveliness of political and moral philosophy and religious commentary has for centuries testified to the formidable disagreements that have characterized worlds said to embody more moral coherence than our own.

Even Bellah's more empirically based analysis draws broad conclusions about the past and present based on a "we" almost entirely defined in terms of a white, middle-class American experience. In Bellah's analysis, the alienation so disruptive of democratic practices is tied to pursuit of "one's own thing," a pursuit that presumes and requires a certain amount of leisure and income, as does participation in the therapeutic subculture and discourse.[91] If the pluralism of contemporary American life renders such a "we" at the very least suspect, requiring rigorous and explicit definition, must we not also regard with some caution a "we" constituted by shared, stable meanings that existed in some distant past community?[92] "But where and when was there ever such a stable, tradition-rooted *Gemeinschaft* community?" Daniel Bell asks. "What period of history, what place, what generation has escaped the incursions of marauders, the ravages of plagues, civil wars, famine, plunders, soil exhaustion and enclosures, forced migrations and driven voyages, the upheavals which have destroyed families, mixed the races by rape and pillage, and sacked the villages and cities by fire, sword, shot and shell?"[93]

As in my analysis of Qutb, here I am less interested in judging these narratives of decay "right" or "wrong" than in illuminating common experiences of Western modernity and the perspective presupposed and expressed by them.[94] Thus it is particularly appropriate at this point to return to Weber. For while Weber's tone at times implied that rational-legal authority is for the mature, adult stage of the race,[95] he also worried that rationalization posed a significant threat to human autonomy and spontaneity. Of the final stage of cultural development, Weber suggested this epitaph: "Specialists without spirit, sensualists without heart; this nullity imagines that it has attained a level of civilization never before achieved."[96] The voices here echo Weber's ambivalence about rationalization and his anxiety that the achievements of rationalization may have been bought at too high a price, that rationalism has been the midwife not of maturity but crisis. Indeed, the vision of moral, political, and social decay represented in this chapter at times suggests that Weber's vision does not extend far enough. For in their most explicit registers, many of these perspectives reflect not Weber's wary appreciation of rationalism but rather his bleak cautionary note regarding the iron cage, his worry that modern reason would eventually, like Mars, devour its own progeny. It is, as Thomas Spragens calls it, "the irony of liberal reason": the very ideals that "liberal reason" had initially served are themselves destroyed in the inexorable purge of value from fact.[97] In this view, then, what passes for morality in the modern world is nothing more than an expression of subjective will, and thus there is no guarantee that instrumental rationality serves morality at all. On the contrary, as Horkheimer and Adorno argue, the evils of the twentieth century suggest it is in the nature of rationality that enlightenment returns to myth, that modernity is in fact merely one stage in the dialectic that oscillates between civilization and savagery, reason and tyranny.

MODERN ANXIETIES AND METAPHYSICAL URGES

On the basis of this discussion, I want to argue that the Western critiques of modernity adumbrated here resemble Qutb's critique of rationalism elaborated in the previous chapter. Like the voices represented in this chapter, Qutb regards modernity as decay, and rationalism as its axial principle and underlying cosmology. Crucial to this cosmology is the use of reason as the embodiment of and justification for human beings' mastery over nature and claim to absolute knowledge. In the name of such mastery, both Qutb and Western critics of rationalism argue, the common and "unassailable" meanings grounded in foundations that transcend the realm of worldly affairs are banished from the public realm, moral discourse comes to center on the self rather than shared, universal ends, and all aspects of social life are corrupted by the unending pursuit of selfish pleasures and consumption shaped and abetted by the imperatives of the marketplace.

Beneath a diversity of political sensibilities and metaphysical presuppositions there is also a common suggestion that modern decay and crisis require a kind of redemption, and that redemption turns on a reconfiguration of the relationship of individual to common ends. In opposition to the insistence that, when a conflict arises, individual goods "trump" common goods, many of these critics argue for the necessity of a politics where community needs are prior to those of the individual, and individual goods are constituted by, rather than opposed to, those of the community. By uniting these visions in this way, I am not suggesting, for example, that MacIntyre and Qutb share a political perspective. Rather I maintain that their differences exist against a backdrop of shared convictions about the origins of modern moral decay, the excesses of individualism, the limits of modern rationalism, and the necessity of recognizing shared ends. This suggests that even Qutb's advocacy of a community in which politics, culture, and economy alike are determined by the ends of the community is not at all unfamiliar to the West; indeed, there are many Western voices driven by similar aims.

Such commonalities should not, of course, obscure significant political and theoretical differences. In contrast to Qutb's indictment of democratic sovereignty, for instance, many of the voices represented in this chapter are largely intent on rescuing the foundations that justify shared *democratic* ends. Such foundations may be said to reside in tradition, divine law or the resurrection of teleology, but in these narratives all such foundations function to sustain a viable conception of democratic freedom, a freedom not merely to be left alone but to act and participate in the name of shared democratic ends. Moreover, Qutb's attempt to locate foundations in divine omniscience is in direct contrast to the ways in which many of these Western theorists attempt to find in common world *practices* that at once presuppose and express shared meanings located within, yet ultimately "transcendent" of, the flow of everyday life. For Arendt and Taylor, for example, shared meanings are both the precondition to and expression of common political practices; they intentionally define such commonality in opposition to a metaphysical account of truth justifying absolutist authority.[98]

Yet it is my contention that these quite significant differences only make the resonances more remarkable. In particular, this discussion suggests that there is a shared paradigm of modernity at work here, one that bears out my earlier contention that Qutb's project is not confined to a local critique of Nasser's Egypt, nor to Middle Eastern politics and culture. These parallels thus suggest that an explanation of Islamic fundamentalism cannot only consist in an elaboration of context-specific economic, cultural and historical conditions, but must also be situated within an extensive and ongoing critique of modernity and the processes that define it. The attempt to acknowledge and to incorporate this wider context in the task of interpretation must be distinguished from an insistence on interpreting non-Western cultural phenomena with categories derived from peculiarly Western experience. Rather, this aspiration reflects the fact that, in a postcolonial world, the context is no longer peculiarly Western—although it may be Western in origin—but has come to frame the projects of non-Western as well as Western critics of modernity. This is not the case because, as I've said, Europe and the Americas are "the only true subjects of history," while all others are condemned to be only "perpetual consumers of modernity,"[99] or mere extensions of Western power. Rather it reflects the growing awareness that, as Featherstone argues, "the West is both a particular in itself and also constitutes the universal point of reference in relation to which others recognise themselves as particularities.[100]

Such parallels return us to my earlier suggestion that Qutb and the views he represents must not be dismissed. I have suggested that Qutb must be heard in part because he provides a window into the world of Islamic fundamentalism and, by extension, insight into the prevalence and purchase of what I have called foundationalist political practices; this means that we dismiss Qutb and those like him at our own political peril. Moreover, the sheer power and persistence of political actors intent on repudiating rationalist ways of defining and organizing the world—actors for whom the "eclipse of ends" Taylor describes as the conclusion to the logic of rationalization is not just a philosophical hypothesis but an existential disaster—suggests that it is politically imperative to entertain the possibility that there are crucial limits to rationalist ways of understanding and organizing the world. Indeed, I have argued that fundamentalism is itself evidence of the ways in which such a project has already failed significantly—in the West and elsewhere—to link individuals together in morally and politically meaningful ways. In such a light, fundamentalism appears to be less a cultural and political aberration than an extreme attempt to "reenchant" the modern world.[101]

There may never have been an "enchanted" past in which there was a "we" that unproblematically partook of shared meanings that undergirded a stable, coherent political world. Yet Arendt is right to argue that human beings are shaped by the conditions of "life itself, natality and mortality, worldliness, plurality and the earth,"[102] and, crucially, are distinguished from other creatures by consciousness of these very conditions. At the same time, the conditions of mortal and worldly existence can never fully explain or define what human beings are or human nature is "for the simple reason that they never condition us absolutely."[103] Human beings are left, then, with questions of meaning, about our nature, our significance, our place within the world, questions of purposes and ultimate ends in terms of which scientistic and rationalist cosmologies are radically inadequate: "The perplexity is that the modes of human cognition applicable to things with 'natural' qualities, including ourselves to the limited extent that we are specimens of the most highly developed species of organic life, fail us when we raise the question: And *who* are we?"[104]

This argument suggests that Nietzsche may have captured a crucial aspect of the human condition when he observed a "metaphysical urge" in every culture to construct myths that give meaning to life and its struggles.[105] Such an observation is not, however, the same as arguing that societies everywhere require belief in metaphysical foundations to cohere. On the contrary, Taylor's discussion of the essentially dialogical character of human life, for example, suggests that the standards and commitments that endow life with meaning, that make judgments, values, and indeed choice itself possible, are only intelligible in terms of everyday coexistence with others. If "we become full human agents, capable of understanding ourselves, and hence of defining an identity, through our acquisition of rich human languages of expression," languages that include "not only the words we speak but also other modes of expression whereby we define ourselves, including the 'languages' of art, of gesture, of love," then meaning cannot depend on unassailable standards that transcend human existence and power. Rather, meaning is derived from the practices that constitute everyday social existence.[106] In Taylor's argument, common endeavors, practices, and communicative interactions to some degree presuppose, and provide an occasion to elaborate, shared commitments and goods irreducible to self-interest. Importantly, such an argument need not rest upon a valorized conception of "the community"; shared commitments and ends do not inhere in communities per se, but rather are made possible by them insofar as the conditions of coexistence enable its members to carve out mutually meaningful purposes. Communicative practices and interactions, located in and not beyond the world of everyday human affairs, may in this way serve as the basis of an overarching framework in which moral claims, political relations, and human struggles are endowed with larger meaning.

Taylor's argument alone challenges Qutb's insistence that the pathologies of the modern condition can only be cured, and human existence redeemed, by way of acknowledging the absolute sovereignty of a transcendent divinity. Yet at the same time this discussion suggests that Qutb is instructive because he provides another perspective on a modern condition we both recognize and to some degree share. This does not mean we cannot disagree or challenge such perspectives. Yet the temptation to see only the chasm that separates Qutb from our tradition misses the opportunity to develop a richer sense of the ways in which modernity in general, and rationalism in particular, has been experienced and defined in terms of loss. This means that Qutb's critique must be attended to because our own intellectual traditions insist that we worry, along with Qutb, about the rise of rationalism, the loss of meaning, and the possible erosion of much of what we hold dear by forces we no longer control. They insist together that we temper our celebration of modernity and the progress it represents with the distinct possibility that the ideal of human mastery through the rationalization of the world is somewhat illusory. They insist we see how, in the name of freedom from religion and superstition, rationalism has, like Freud's return of the repressed, called forth the very forces of nihilism and irrationality it sought to control.[107] They thus suggest that such mastery is a particularly modern myth that has at one and the same time presaged great achievement and masked just how little we control, how much is threatened, and how we may again need "foundations" that can justify common ends and ground intersubjective human meaning.

CHAPTER SIX

Conclusion: Cultural Syncretism and Multiple Modernities

LET ME briefly summarize the argument threading through the preceding four chapters. In chapter 2, I demonstrated that rationalist discursive practices continue to define contemporary Western social scientific analyses of the phenomenon of Islamic resurgence. I did so to illustrate the ways in which rationalist discourse explains the appeal of fundamentalist ideas by reference to their function as conduits for processes and tensions in the material and structural realm. In deriving meaning from function, these explanations serve not to make fundamentalist ideas rational—in the literal sense, meaning intelligible—but to divorce explanations of Islamic fundamentalism from the fundamentalists' own understandings of the world. This abstraction of meaning from function, I argued, has given a certain shape to our understanding of Islamic fundamentalism. While these analyses aim simply to reflect empirical aspects of the phenomenon (e.g., class origins, age, professional orientations, ideological goals), facts are used to sustain causal interpretations, which, taken together, suggested that the growing appeal of fundamentalism is explicable as a mechanical response to structural pressures and, as such, owes little to its inherent power as an ethico-political vision of the modern world.

In contrast, it is precisely this vision that I place at the center of an account of Islamic fundamentalism. My analysis of Qutb's political theory provides an exploration of one particularly influential ethico-political vision within modern Sunni Islamic fundamentalism. This vision, I suggested in chapter 3, challenges modern political sovereignty and offers a moral indictment of post-Enlightenment political theories such as Marxism, liberalism, and socialism, which assume the exclusion of religious authority from the political realm. I argued that the insistence of Qutb's Islamic fundamentalist thought on divine sovereignty is a rebuttal of and antidote to rationalist discourse itself, that is, the Western discourse that has posited reason as the source of truth, knowledge, and authority. In chapter 4, I extended this reading by illustrating the ways in which Qutb's critique of post-Enlightenment rationalism engages him not only in a repudiation of modern, Western assumptions and arguments about the bases of political life, but in a rejection of a prior generation of Muslim modernists who sought to render Islam as the religion of reason and, thereby, as compatible with an originally Western paradigm of modernity.

This reading of Qutb's fundamentalist political theory is intended, in part, to speak to prior interpretations regarding the content and import of Qutb's political analysis. It has not necessarily done so, however, by replacing them: "A study is an advance if it is more incisive—whatever that may mean—than those that preceded it; but it less stands on their shoulders than, challenged and challenging, runs by their side."[1] Specifically, I have argued that my interpretation challenges accounts that emphasize the purely local dimensions of Qutb's critique, that is, accounts that identify Qutb as, first and last, a critic of Nasserist socialism and Egyptian corruption. My reading suggests instead that Qutb's critique of Nasser and the Egyptian government is one expression of a broader theoretical analysis of rationalist epistemology and the political theories it justifies. I have argued that we miss a central dimension of Islamic fundamentalist thought if we fail to situate it within this theoretical context. This reading is also intended to augment and refine the view, advanced by scholars such as Sivan, that Qutb and fundamentalists like him are responding to something called modernity. As I suggested in chapter 3, Qutb is not a critic of modernity per se—for he views modern technologies and scientific achievements as desirable—but an opponent of post-Enlightenment rationalism. As such, Qutb's work must be understood as a "dialectical response" to rationalism and Westernization, as a dynamic critique rather than a scripturalist reflex.[2]

This argument suggests that, despite the apparent alienness of Qutb's ethico-political worldview, and his profound engagement with specifically Islamic debates about reason, interpretation, and revealed law, he is also participating in a conversation that we, as Western students of politics, not only recognize, but in which we participate. This implication led, in chapter 5, to an exploration of the ways in which Qutb's concerns are shared by several Western political theorists who criticize modernity and rationalism from relatively diverse political and moral perspectives. Understanding Qutb in the context of a "company of critics" that includes Charles Taylor, Alasdair MacIntyre, Robert Bellah, Hannah Arendt, Richard John Neuhaus, and Daniel Bell is suggested by Qutb's own critique of the "failures of modernity." I insisted that we do not need to endorse any of the perspectives examined to acknowledge and learn from the resonances among them. Such resonances suggest that Qutb's perspective is neither unfamiliar nor pathological but is rather one interlocutor among a chorus of voices attempting to capture the causes and character of what I have called the leaching of meaning from modern life.

This reading of Qutb's political thought, in turn, enables me to make three methodological points. The first is the possibility and, by extension, the necessity of engaging the content of Islamic fundamentalist ideas on their own terms, or at least on as close to their own terms as is possible for an interpreter whose position is exterior to the worldview of the subject. To do so I have offered what I have likened to a "thick" description of Qutb's Islamist ideas, a reading of one particularly influential account of the meaning and purpose of Sunni fundamentalism. As I argued in the introductory chapter, the concept of a "thick description" and the semiotic approach to culture in which it is located is—despite differences between action and text—useful here because it not only presumes the possibility of intelligibly rendering the world of the Other, but also demonstrates that interpretive accounts are central to the endeavor. Using Geertz's language, then, this reading of Qutb's political thought is intended to render a deeper, richer, fuller account of Islamist ideas than those available in social scientific explanations of Islamic fundamentalism I explored in chapter 2. My "thick" description aims not only to make such ideas intelligible, but to do so in a way that makes participants' self-understandings central to the very standard of intelligibility. This must be distinguished from the attempt simply to replace a primarily functionalist account with a purely interpretive one, for I have insisted that meaning and function are mutually determinative. Yet the substance and methodology of such a "thick" description bypass the reflex to categorize and dismiss fundamentalism as irrational. Resisting such reflexes is necessary to engage and understand fundamentalist ideas and learn about the increasing purchase of such ways of seeing the modern world. Put slightly differently, such understanding enables us to grasp another way of looking at the world, but in so doing also helps disaggregate the "fundamentalist challenge" so that we may understand what, specifically, fundamentalists are challenging.

These observations occasion my second methodological point: interpretive accounts not only make fundamentalist ideas intelligible but also contribute to current social science explanations of the increasing power of Islamic fundamentalism by making them causally adequate. As I argued in chapter 2, rationalist explanations of Islamic fundamentalism are particularly problematic because they tend to occlude by assumption and argument ideas central to the appeal of fundamentalist ways of seeing the world. Such interpretive meanings are crucial if we are to grasp the particular attraction of fundamentalist ideas, and not just the general relationship, for example, between unemployment and rebellion. The limitations of such mechanistic explanations indicate that Islamic fundamentalism cannot be fully understood in the terms currently employed by social scientists, precisely because the terms and categories of social science are constitutively unable to adequately capture a central dimension of fundamentalism. This is not to say that if scholars were better, smarter, or just more careful, this dimension of fundamentalism would come into focus. It is to argue that rationalist social scientific analyses are defined by discursive practices that tend to obscure precisely the theoretical and transcultural aspects of fundamentalist thought that are central to its meaning.

I have thus criticized current social science accounts of fundamentalism on both methodological and substantive grounds and, in so doing, have attempted to problematize not only the interpretations but the analytic tools that generate these interpretations. Given the particular deficiencies of these analyses of Islamic fundamentalism, I have argued that a dialogic model of interpretation is particularly useful. This model insures that the process of explicating meanings and advancing causal explanations begins with the terms and categories used by the participants themselves. I have shown that a dialogic approach does not entail relinquishing standards of objectivity, but rather the rejection of positivist standards of objectivity in favor of a view of understanding as a reciprocal, transformative, and, perhaps above all, ongoing process. This process is not, of course, innocent of distortion and power but at least remains permanently open to the ways in which the radical inequalities of a postcolonial world increasingly marked by globalization are implicated in cross-cultural dialogue.

In sum, I conclude that the emphasis on material conditions in social science analyses of fundamentalism is the backdrop that explains the emergence of a particular class acutely aware of, and frustrated by, real and perceived failures of state-initiated policies associated with nationalist, liberal, and socialist ideals. Such conditions thus explain the receptivity of a particular class to revolutionary challenges to current conditions without showing why such ideas should take a specifically Islamic form. Analysis of Qutb's highly influential *Signposts*, however, suggests that Islamic ideas are compelling to this class as well as others in part because they are particularly powerful indictments not only of such failures and the corruption attendant upon them, but also of modern modes of sovereignty imitative of Western political theories and the rationalist cosmology that underlies and justifies them. I do not claim that this particular interpretation is the final and authoritative truth of Qutb's thought, freed from the distortionary power of language, history, and human interests, but rather that it offers a richer, more compelling understanding of it: as it draws on fundamentalists' own ideas about the movement's meaning and purpose, I submit that this interpretive account is one in which the subject would recognize himself and his politico-moral project.[3]

This reading does not presume, however, that there is no perspective adequately distant from the participants from which to critique their account of their own experience; on the contrary, compelling interpretations are simultaneously aware of their own conditionality and open to the distinct possibility that participants have themselves misunderstood their own experiences. Thus "there is a difference between *starting* with the actors' point of view and ending with it. . . . The actor may be right, but the assumption that the actor is automatically right *is* dogmatic."[4] As Qutb disagrees strenuously not only with Western advocates of post-Enlightenment sovereignty but also, as I argued in chapter 4, with Muslim modernists and other Islamic fundamentalists, so too can an interpreter challenge his own account of events without either claiming the epistemologically privileged position of neutral social scientist or allowing the authority of participants to silence critique. This means, among other things, that while I emphasize the centrality of Qutb's worldview to understanding Sunni Islamic ideas, I do not relinquish the right or responsibility to contest his insistence that his Islamic worldview is free of the "corruption" of Western influences; to challenge his assurances that his organicist model of solidarity leads to a toleration of diversity; or to question whether the freedom to choose any religion after *jahiliyya* has been destroyed is freedom in any meaningful sense of the word.

As Qutb's text is itself animated by questions about the nature of legitimate sovereignty, the relationship between the moral and the political life and the individual and the community, the particular form of the hermeneutic insight I offer is shaped by the terms of political theory. This is not because political theory comprises a corpus of universal wisdom whose essential truths transcend the specificities of culture, language, and history. Rather it presumes that political theory is best defined in terms of certain questions rather than particular answers. Such a presumption militates against the tendency to see Qutb as locked in a culturally bounded box of meaning and, in so doing, resists the tendency to assign "cultural differences to some sacrosanct spot safe from our critical faculties." It thus avoids cultural relativism "which begins by urging us to respect the other [and] ends by denying other cultures and other human beings the serious consideration they deserve . . . presum[ing] a common human condition may help us get beyond the impasse to which respect-for-The-Other leads and to achieve the more blessed state of learning-from-one-another."[5]

What then can we learn from Qutb's political thought? I want to suggest that Qutb's preoccupations with questions about the moral foundations of political communities challenges narrower, ethnocentric definitions of political theory, and a reading of political theory as a distinctively secular enterprise. This argument occasions my third and final methodological point: that the questions and categories of political theory are useful heuristic tools through which non-Western thinkers concerned with the moral foundations of political life may best be heard. So understood, political theory is an enterprise that need not be and, in fact, does not make sense as a purely Western enterprise. Theory once was and should again be inherently comparative, because it is through comparisons that we make sense of ourselves, learn about others, and subsequently approach a level of general knowledge about the political world. This enlarges the domain of political theory to include a range of human, and not merely Western, thought, practice, and experience.

Indeed, reclaiming this comparative understanding of political theory is transformative, for it provides a perspective from which to see the ways in which disparate cultures can speak to one another about the nature and value of politics even if they have serious disagreements. I have explored one such "conversation" by arguing that we can see in both Islamic and Western critiques of modernity an ongoing and transcultural discussion about how and if a body politic can be constructed without the transcendent foundations that were thought to have previously sustained it. For Western attempts to find in communicative practices a resurrected realm of the sacred, or the tradition of Aristotelian virtues, reveal similar concerns with the limits of "rationalist modernity" and constitute parallel searches for an overarching framework in which moral claims, political relations, and human struggles are endowed with larger meaning. This reveals the scope and substance of the anxiety about rationalist modernity *within* "the West," yet such cross-cultural resonances may also yield a clue about modernity itself. As Kepel suggests in regard to fundamentalism, "[l]ike the workers' movements of yesteryear, today's religious movements have a singular capacity to reveal the ills of society, for which they have their own diagnosis."[6] It is my contention that the resonances in this one cross-cultural comparison in political thought delineate the extent and substance of the concern that rationalist ways of understanding and organizing the world fail to give meaning to life and its struggles. This suggests that as political theory provides distinctive ways of interrogating and reflecting upon the premises of political life, it is a particularly illuminating lens with which to open up the world of political ideas and moral principles that inform and guide much of the practices currently considered beyond its jurisdiction.

These arguments show that the academic boundaries commonly demarcated by the terms "comparative politics" and "political theory" arbitrarily carve up the study of politics into territories. They are arbitrary because comparisons not only provide information about other ways of living and organizing politics, they also provide information about what we take to be our own political world. For to see what is distinctive about our own values, institutions, and practices, we must also know other people, other institutions, other histories and cultures. Making heretofore implicit assumptions about political life explicit helps avoid seeing our own cultural conventions as universal truths, thereby making possible a certain kind of distance toward what we know, or what we think we know, whether that body of knowledge is defined as "American politics" or "political theory."[7] Such distance may call political shibboleths into question. But it may also deepen our understanding and commitment to practices and institutions with which we are familiar.

By way of conclusion, let me return to the larger themes of the introduction and speculate about the broader implications of my reading of Islamic fundamentalist political thought for what what I have called "foundationalist political practices," that is, practices driven by foundationalist certainties and the attempt to remake political, cultural, and economic power in accordance with them. One clear implication is that interpretive accounts are necessary not just to understand Islamic fundamentalist ideas but to grasp fundamentalism, in general, as a political phenomenon resistant to rationalist analysis. This is because the reflex to dismiss fundamentalism as irrational or pathological is not merely a product of the prejudices (in the Gadamerian sense) and fears operative in the relationship between the West and Islam. As I have argued, it is also a function of the way a post-Enlightenment, predominantly rationalist tradition of scholarship countenances religio-political practices in the modern world. I have argued that Qutb's political thought is an expression of the growing presence of actors for whom the advances of a rationalization inaugurated by Enlightenment reason have exacted costs that are not a footnote to progress but the defining disaster. This reading of Islamic fundamentalist ideas as one of many attempts to "reenchant" the world may be usefully placed within the larger context of fundamentalist resurgence in the twentieth century, a context that includes, for example, the increasingly powerful political purchase of Christian fundamentalist ideas in American political practice and discourse. For despite important differences, such a repudiation of rationalism can be heard from Christian fundamentalists who argue that the Enlightenment's vilification of religion has culminated in the moral impoverishment of secular humanism, a cosmology that underlies and ultimately unites both socialist and individualist ways of understanding and organizing the world. Thus Pat Robertson writes:

> In this decade the believers will stand firmly astride the failed and crumbling ruin of the secular colossus. . . . Today it is clear that secular humanism has failed. Like communism, to which it has been allied from the beginning, it is a bankrupt system without moral guidelines or reliable safeguards to protect the people from its own corruptions. It has degenerated into carnality, sensuality, lawlessness and disease, and it has left millions of men and women all over the world adrift, without purpose, and emotionally crippled. Nature abhors a vacuum, and secularism has left a spiritual vacuum in the hearts of all those who once turned to it for freedom and hope. To survive, the humanists will either have to decamp or change their ways, and this is the decade in which one of those two will most certainly come to pass.[8]

This supports Kepel's contention that Islamic, Christian, and Jewish fundamentalisms are all "at one in rejecting a secularism that they trace back to the philosophy of the Enlightenment. They regard the vainglorious emancipation of reason from faith as the prime cause of all the ills of the twentieth century."[9] Modernity, as Lawrence argues, thus "becomes and remains the enveloping context" for the study of fundamentalism,[10] but not, of course, because a fundamentalist is a modernist, that is, one who is "somehow at home in the maelstrom, making its rhythms one's own, moving within its currents in search of the forms of reality, of beauty, of freedom, of justice, that its fervid and perilous flow allows."[11] Rather the argument here is that while these fundamentalisms emerge in a modern context, they share a repudiation of many of modernity's central epistemological premises, Enlightenment rationalist epistemology in particular.[12] The sense in which these fundamentalist worldviews are defined in terms of and in opposition to modernity thus reveals a common historical and theoretical context; as Lawrence aptly puts it, "Because modernity is global, so is fundamentalism."[13] This bears out my contention that Qutb's engagement with post-Enlightenment rationalism reveals the extent to which a modernity originally defined in terms of Western experience is no longer a Western experience alone. And, like the arguments of the previous chapter, it also contests the image of a unified "West" whose history and current identity is coterminous with rationalist modernity.

Such "historical simultaneity"[14] provides the context for commonalities in, for example, the socioeconomic backgrounds of Christian and Islamic fundamentalists. Just as the most prominent Islamic activists are children of rural migrants to the city, often beneficiaries of an expanded higher education system inaugurated by modernizing elites, and schooled predominantly in the natural sciences, Christian fundamentalists are often urban children of rural parents, graduates of higher education, and disproportionately trained in the applied sciences.[15] These commonalities, in turn, underlie common paradoxes. For example, fundamentalists reject rationalism but not necessarily the technological and scientific fruits of modernity.[16] In fact, my analysis of Islamic fundamentalism shows how modern technology and science are actually used to advance a critique of the very epistemological and methodological ideas that produced them. Indeed, as Lawrence and Kepel argue, variants of scripturally based fundamentalism share an insistence on driving a wedge between such pursuits and the cosmology of which they are a product. In addition, this aim is expressed in a common repudiation of the generation of modernists that preceded and shaped them.[17] Thus, in various kinds of fundamentalism, rationalization has come full circle: the "radical challenge to the foundations of secular modernism is uttered by its own children."[18]

There are of course significant differences between Christian and Islamic fundamentalism. The critique of modernity offered by Qutb, for example, is bound up with the ways in which modernity was experienced in concert with domination and colonization by Western powers. Such a paradigm of modernity, although adopted by secular Middle Eastern leaders and Westernized intellectuals, was at least initially experienced as a foreign imposition. By contrast, Christian fundamentalists are very much part of "the

West"; indeed, Christianity has contributed substantially to the very idea of separating temporal and religious authority. Moreover, while many fundamentalists share a critique of secular modernity, they differ radically on the solution and on its method of implementation. For example, Islamic fundamentalists oppose regimes they conclude are fundamentally corrupt and concentrate on action designed to overthrow the status quo either by word or by sword. Christian fundamentalists in the United States do not generally seek the overthrow of the government but aim for increasing power in politics to legislate from beliefs they argue are fundamentally harmonious with what America "really is." Thus American fundamentalists selectively criticize the liberal democratic state not for illegitimacy but for what they view as a secularism bound up with the rhetorical, juridical, and political denigration of religion, and, more specifically, of Christianity, in public life.

Nevertheless, this very brief discussion of fundamentalist political thought brings commonalities into view that are not reducible to analyses of the social, economic, and political causes and effects of various fundamentalisms.[19] In particular, I want to highlight the ways in which different fundamentalisms cohere around the insistence that a secular, rationalist cosmology has failed to provide the moral basis not just of politics, but of life itself. It is not that fundamentalists fight against a secular ethic, which "according to them does not exist, but consider that in the final analysis the modernism produced by reason without God has not succeeded in creating values."[20] Such opposition is expressed in a variety of ways—from a preoccupation with women's sexual behavior, to crusades against movies, dance, and theater, to a vilification of intellectuals and the academy.[21] These convergences suggest that fundamentalist movements are, among other things, attempts to "reenchant" a world defined by a disenchantment or, alternatively, to unmask disenchantment as a modern myth propagated by the godless and whose time has now come to an end. In their view, the failure of modernity lies in the dominance of a rationalist cosmology in which human comprehension defines both the parameters of what is knowable and what is necessary for living well. At the heart of the modern condition, then, is not pursuit of truth but myopic arrogance. The world and its occupants have never really been bereft of meaning as an expression of divine will, but they are estranged from knowledge of the truths that make meaning and purpose possible.

Given these arguments, what can we conclude about the relationship of Islamic fundamentalism and fundamentalism more generally to "modernity"? Is it the last gasp of premodernism? As fundamentalism is in large measure determined by a modern context, it makes little sense to understand it as "premodern" in either a chronological or a substantive sense. Might we more logically conclude, along with Lawrence, Sivan, and others, that in rejecting the central epistemological premises of modernity fundamentalism is, with all the appropriate caveats, essentially antimodern? And by extension, must we therefore concede the corollary to this conclusion, that is, that what we see here is a contest "between two incommensurate ways of viewing the world, one which locates values in timeless scriptures, inviolate laws, and unchanging mores, the other which sees in the expansion of scientific knowledge a technological transformation of society that pluralizes options both for learning and for living"?[22]

This question of incommensurability returns us to the arguments of the introductory chapter. There I illustrated how such conceptions of fundamental incommensurability underlie narratives in which religio-political movements are, along with other "particularisms," positioned as archaic reactions to modernity, destined either to wither away in the face of liberalization, rationalization, and democratization, or to assume the mantle of nemesis to an otherwise democratic, rights-based, peace-loving consortium of nations and cultures. Importantly, I suggested not that such assessments were wrong but that the assumptions that generate them overdetermine the oppositional reading of the relationship between "The West and the Rest."[23] Unlike these post–Cold War prognoses, Lawrence draws his conclusions about incommensurability in part from close attention to the work and words of fundamentalists themselves; his is not an analysis beholden to methodological assumptions that marginalize the importance of actors' self-understandings to explanation. Yet Lawrence concludes that understanding specifically where and why fundamentalists reject modernity reveals that, while they cannot be seen as archaic ("[w]ithout modernity there are no fundamentalists"), we cannot avoid the conclusion that they represent a perspective fundamentally incommensurate with "our" own.[24]

But could the arguments advanced here suggest a different conclusion? Could they sustain the claim that fundamentalism is not an irreducible "Other," but is perhaps recognizable as a postmodern critique of modernity? Given the diverse and at times contradictory understandings of postmodernism, to begin to answer this requires an elaboration of what it could possibly mean to call fundamentalism a postmodern phenomenon. It could be argued, for example, that both fundamentalism and postmodernism of quite different stripes are reactions to modernity, and critical of the legacy of the Enlightenment in particular. Both emphasize the schizophrenic dimension of contemporary life, describing a world marked by disjunction and discontinuity, "a landscape in the manner of Bosch, composed of an infinitude of fragments, pieces."[25] Malcolm Bull extends this comparison by suggesting that fundamentalism and postmodernism share a globalized frame of reference and an exaggerated sense of crisis; an ambiguous—some might say symbiotic—relationship to modernity in that neither pretends that modernity never existed, and neither seeks a simple return to the past; a selective reappropriation of the past; a mixing of high and low cultures; and a dismissal of the need for any justificatory metadiscourse.[26] The argument that

Qutb's political thought is an attempt to "reenchant" the world seems to lend force to Akbar Ahmed's suggestion that the fragmentation of social and political ideas characteristic of postmodernism is to some degree causally linked to ethnic and religious revival: "fundamentalism is the attempt to resolve how to live in a world of radical doubt."[27] Similarly, Falk suggests they are united by "the feeling that modernism does not provide any longer the basis for human meaning and species survival." Thus fundamentalism in particular can be understood as a zealously antimodern type of postmodernism.[28]

Yet while fundamentalism may be regarded as postmodern in the historical sense of being literally "after modernity," and while it is indeed part of an increasingly common rebuttal to the ideas and assumptions taken as constitutive of modernity, it is not, I think, useful to understand it as postmodern inasmuch as postmodernism is associated, at the very least, with a radical suspicion of foundationalism and of all notions of truth. This is so despite the fact that the critique of the Enlightenment at the center of postmodernism has issued in, on the one hand, the insistence that the crucial "lesson in paganism" is "the need to be godless in things political"[29] and, on the other, a reassessment of religiosity and spirituality as experiences forced into the shadows of obscurity by the ascent of modern rationalism.[30] As I have argued, central to Islamic fundamentalism and to fundamentalism generally is an antihermeneutic embrace of absolute foundations. As Bassam Tibi rightly argues, "The fundamentalist yearning for the absolute introduces a concept of absolutism in human knowledge, definitely not a postmodern idea."[31]

Interestingly enough, in his analysis Tibi goes on to reject the postmodern argument in favor of one similar to Lawrence's incommensurability claim. Islamic fundamentalists, according to Tibi, represent a specifically Islamic form of knowledge that is fundamentally incompatible with modern knowledge. He concludes that the Islamist attempt to decouple modern sciences from modern secular knowledge will result in a

> fall back into an era of "flat-earthism" if the politics of the Islamization of knowledge becomes the authoritative source for determining the relationship between the contemporary culture of the Middle East and the place of sciences as an expression of modern secular knowledge in it. At the turn of the twentieth century, we are living in an age of the global confrontation between secular cultural modernity and religious culture. The challenge of Islamic fundamentalism has a most prominent place in this confrontation.[32]

We thus return again to the paradigm of incommensurability and the opposition between "modern secular knowledge" and "Islamic knowledge," an opposition that rests on the distinction between fundamentalists' yearning for meaning and unwillingness to live in a world of radical doubt and the Western ability to cope with a world in which human beings create their own knowledge and employ such knowledge to impose a way of being at home in the world. This suggests that, as W. Montgomery Watt puts it,

> when Muslims think of knowledge, they think primarily of what may be called "knowledge for living," whereas when a Westerner thinks of knowledge, it is mainly of "knowledge for power," that is, such knowledge as enables one to control natural and material objects and human individuals and societies. It is in respect of knowledge for living, consisting of religious and moral values, that Islam claims finality and self-sufficiency. . . . Muslims show surprisingly little interest in other forms of knowledge, even those which would be useful to them for practical purposes.[33]

These arguments are reinforced by the fact that fundamentalists themselves see the world in this way, that is, as a Manichaean clash between good and evil, Islam and the West. Indeed, as I have noted, Qutb's own tendency to read into history a battle between the forces of light and darkness—where Islam becomes the light penetrating Western darkness—mirrors the post–Cold War narratives in which the West is stalked by an old foe in a new "green" guise. Yet Islamic constructions of such a global standoff need to be regarded with no less skepticism than those of Huntington and other social scientists: attentiveness to Islamist self-understandings should not entail the abandonment of a perspective from which to argue that participants have themselves constructed a view of the world rather than merely reflected it. My analysis of Qutb's political thought suggests that, despite his insistence on the "purity" and "authenticity" of his version of Islam, Qutb's project is deeply engaged with and also shaped by the very categories and ideas he explicitly rejects. While Qutb accuses a prior generation of Muslim modernists of too readily accommodating Western ideas, he and others like him have learned the modern lessons of the relationship of knowledge and power quite thoroughly and, furthermore, have incorporated, albeit unconsciously, many of the ideas and assumptions of what modernity is and should be. Islamic fundamentalist political thought thus betrays a Western influence inconsistent with the stated attempt to cleanse an Islamic concept of foreign corruption; at the very least, then, such syncretism makes these arguments of incommensurability implausible.

To be sure, Islamic fundamentalists' own understandings include a challenge to what they take to be Western, rationalist epistemological assumptions about the world. But then again, this challenge is also posed from within the West itself, and not only by fundamentalists. As I have argued with regard to both Western scholarly critiques of modernity and Christian fundamentalism, the West is itself riven with disagreements and ambivalences about modernity and rationalism. Such disagreements *within* Western culture belie characterizations of a coherent "West" that is better able than the rest of the world to cope with doubt, with a human-centered universe, and with radical uncertainty. While many if not most of the ideas and assumptions constitutive of a rationalist, secular humanist vision of modernity originated in the West, the opposition between this vision *as* the West versus an Islamic East simply does not easily map onto, for example, the sociological religiosity of American culture, the growth of religious revivalism in American politics, and the critiques of rationalism among scholars in the Western academy. Nor does it capture the diversity of reactions to "Western modernity" among Islamic thinkers, the selective embrace of the fruits of modern progress among Islamic fundamentalists, and the interpenetration of Islamic and "modern Western" language and ideas suggested in the analysis of Qutb's political thought in particular.

Such complications cut across the categories and oppositions that underlie both Western and fundamentalist conclusions of incommensurability. Yet my argument here does not therefore entail an embrace of the reverse claim, that is, that all cultures and peoples by virtue of a common humanity are fundamentally commensurable and that ultimately "we are all the same underneath." Rather I take it that "human nature" is in large measure a culturally and historically embedded construct, yet human beings qua humans nevertheless confront the conditions of "life itself, natality and mortality, worldliness, plurality, and the Earth." Such conditions may, at critical junctures, pose common problems; in particular, in a postcolonial world recently characterized by accelerated globalization, the ways in which these conditions are defined, analyzed, and confronted takes place within an increasingly common problematic of "modernity."

Given these arguments, it becomes clear that fundamentalist critiques and movements and sensibilities are not premodern, although they certainly draw upon and reinterpret ideals located in a "Golden Past." Nor are they antimodern, although they cohere around a repudiation of many central epistemological assumptions constitutive of post-Enlightenment modernity. Like postmodernism, fundamentalists' paradoxical relationship to modernity represents an attempt to move beyond modernity in a way that is simultaneously parasitic upon it. Yet at the same time their antihermeneutic "foundationalism" is incompatible with the postmodern suspicion of foundations. It is the case that fundamentalists, along with postmodernists and western critics of modernity, emphasize the dark side of rationalism and insist we attend to what the post-Enlightenment vision of modernity has excluded and precluded. Contrary to postmodernists, however, voices such as Taylor and MacIntyre contend, along with Qutb, that there are or can be bases on which to reestablish "foundational" meanings necessary for living and living well; they thus seek an overarching moral unity to overcome the fragmentation of knowledge that characterizes the contemporary world.[34] The Western and Islamist critique of modernity explored here is thus perhaps best characterized as an attempt simultaneously to abolish, transcend, preserve, and transform modernity. To borrow from Shlomo Avineri (and Hegel), these perspectives represent a dialectical *aufhebung* of modernity rather than an a priori negation of it.[35] What this means is that the resistance to a world of radical doubt, and the "yearning for meaning" such resistance is said to produce, cannot be explained away as the inability of certain personalities, groups, or cultures to "cope" with the imperatives of modernity. Rather it reflects an increasingly vocal and transcultural preoccupation with limits of modern rationalism and the concomitant conviction that we "may still need to see ourselves as part of a larger order that can make claims on us."[36]

Notes

PREFACE

1. For example, the Associated Press recently reported that almost five million Americans say they were "too busy" to vote in the 1996 presidential election. "Polls Fall Victim to Lifestyles," *Boston Globe*, August 17, 1998.
2. By "A Mere Phantom."
3. This effect was dubbed "Pepper's Ghost." For a fuller discussion see Erik Barnouw, *The Magician and the Cinema*, 19–34.
4. Theodor Adorno, *In Search of Wagner*, 85.
5. Jonathan Crary, *Techniques of the Observer*, 132–33.

CHAPTER ONE
RE-MARKING TERRITORIES

1. For example: John Rawls, "Justice as Fairness." See also J. Donald Moon, *Constructing Community*.
2. In suggesting a shared postfoundationalist tendency in current political theory, I am not suggesting that there is anything approaching a consensus on the nature of, for example, the challenge of fundamentalism or the appropriate response (if any). For Rawls, worldviews (such as fundamentalism) actuated by ideals intended to govern all human life are impermissible to the extent that they do not "fall within the range permitted by the public conception of justice" (Rawls, *Political Liberalism*). By contrast, Foucault found in the Iranian Revolution (at least through early 1979) a quasi-Dionysian uprising against Western imperialism and rationalization, and thrilled to what he took to be an Iranian challenge to global hegemony, a challenge that revealed "an intensity of courage" (Foucault, "Is It Useless to Revolt?"). Foucault's brief love affair with the Iranian Revolution suggests interesting parallels between postmodernism and fundamentalism, which I take up in the concluding chapter.
3. Quoted by Sidney Blumenthal, "Christian Soldiers," 37.
4. In the following pages I seek to problematize categories such as "West" and "non-West," and the ways in which such categories are overlaid on generalized ahistorical oppositions between "us" and "them." To avoid the need to place all such references in quotation marks, here I want to specify that all future uses of "we," "us," and "our" in this text should be taken to refer to Western students of politics, and students of politics trained in Western methods of scholarship. "Non-Western" is—as I will argue—a misleading convention designed to, at the very least, acknowledge the "rest" of the world.
5. Francis Fukuyama, "The End of History?," 4, 18.
6. Ibid., 18.
7. Didier Bigo, "Grands Débats dans un Petit Monde," 22, n. 34. In his review of Hans Magnus Enzensberger's *Civil Wars: From L.A. to Bosnia*, Fukuyama argues

that this kind of conflict is inherently incoherent and goalless, and thus self-limiting. Fukuyama, "The New World Disorder," 12.

8. Fukuyama, *The End of History and the Last Man*, 45–46.

9. Of course, this and the "end of history" are not the only two modes of post-Cold War analysis: there is, for example, the neorealist emphasis on the "return of disorder" (see, for example, John J. Mearsheimer's "Back to the Future"), and more cyclical analyses of international relations, for example, Paul Kennedy's pre-1989 *The Rise and Fall of Great Powers*. However, Bigo suggests that these discourses fall roughly into two camps according to their pessimistic or optimistic assessment of social change: they all lead either to "an ethnocentric ideology of peace and democracy, or to an ideology of the 'threat from the South,' the clash of civilizations, and a view of the Other as a primeval threat." Bigo, "Grands Débats dans un Petit Monde," 11.

10. William Lind, "Defending Western Culture," 43–44.

11. Bigo, "Grands Débats dans un Petit Monde," 25.

12. Samuel Huntington, "The Clash of Civilizations?" See also Huntington, *The Clash of Civilizations and the Remaking of World Order*. In one of a series of responses to Huntington's article published in *Foreign Affairs*, Fouad Ajami notes that Huntington's conceptions of civilizations are oddly without fissures: he has "found his civilizations whole and intact, watertight under an eternal sky. Buried alive, as it were, during the years of the Cold War, these civilizations rose as soon as the stone was rolled off, dusted themselves off, and proceeded to claim the loyalty of their adherents" (Ajami, "The Summoning," 2). John Esposito provides a useful analysis of Huntington's thesis vis-à-vis Islamic fundamentalism in the concluding chapter to his *The Islamic Threat: Myth or Reality?*.

13. Huntington, "The Clash of Civilizations?," 31.

14. Huntington, "If Not Civilizations, What?," 192. The phrase is from Kishore Mahbubani, "The West and the Rest."

15. Huntington, "The Clash of Civilizations?," 40; Bigo, "Grands Débats," 42.

16. Bernard Lewis, "The Roots of Muslim Rage," *The Atlantic Monthly* 266 (September 1990), 60; quoted approvingly by Huntington in "The Clash of Civilizations?," 32.

17. Mark Juergensmeyer, *The New Cold War?*, 2. Bradford McGuinn writes that "fundamentalist forces are seeking to undermine America's position in the region. . . . The Islamization of Middle Eastern politics and the intensification of terrorism in America will evolve in tandem. . . . As the sole superpower, America will have to confront its challenges . . . resolutely and perhaps brutally" ("Why the Fundamentalists Are Winning," *New York Times*, 17). In *The New York Times Magazine*, Judith Miller argues that "[s]ome American officials and commentators have already designated militant Islam as the West's new enemy, to be contained much the way Communism was during the Cold War" ("The Islamic Wave," 42). In 1992 the Bush administration told the *New York Times* that they regarded the march of fundamentalism as the single most "worrisome" trend for policymakers (Barbara Crossette, "U.S. Official Calls Muslim Militants a Threat to Africa," *New York Times*, January 1, 1992, 3).

18. Morton B. Zuckerman, "Beware of Religious Stalinism"; see also Daniel Pipes, "Fundamental Questions about Islam."

19. Karla J. Cunningham, "Islamic Fundamentalism and the Domino Theory." Cunningham adduces convincing evidence that "domino logic is being utilized, albeit imperfectly, in order to organize U.S. foreign policy in the region" (15). A recent article in *The New Yorker* suggests that many observers and scholars see in Egypt an Islamist "revolution by stealth" that could spread like falling dominoes (Mary Anne Weaver, "Revolution by Stealth," 42).

20. Régis Debray, *Tous azimuts*, Paris: Odile Jacob/Foundation pour les études de défense nationale, 1990, 44–45, quoted by Bigo, "Grands Débats," 39.

21. Assistant Secretary of State Edward P. Djerejian states that while increasing cooperation between Islamic regimes and Islamist groups throughout the Middle East is a growing concern, he "detect[s] no monolithic international effort behind various Islamic movements." "We reject the notion that a renewed emphasis on traditional values in many parts of the Islamic world must lead inevitably to conflict with the West. We do not regard Islam as the next 'ism' replacing international communism" (Statement to the House Foreign Affairs Committee, July 27, 1993). Fred Halliday's *Islam and the Myth of Confrontation*, among others, similarly rejects the clash of civilizations thesis.

22. Charles Krauthammer rejects a theory of American decline by asserting that American power is at its pinnacle with the defeat of Communism ("The Unipolar Moment," 23). Similarly, Huntington writes, "[t]he West is now at an extraordinary peak of power in relation to other civilizations. Its superpower opponent has disappeared from the map. . . . Western military power is unrivaled. . . . It dominates international political and security institutions and with Japan international economic institutions" (Huntington, "The Clash of Civilizations?," 39).

23. Lind, "Defending Western Culture," 45. The Ottoman Turks' two-time siege of Vienna is again invoked by Huntington in his discussion of the 1,300-year-old fault line between Western and Islamic civilizations (Huntington, "The Clash of Civilizations?," 31).

24. See note 4 above.

25. In Gadamer's sense "prejudices" are not mistaken judgments but prejudgments. Indeed, Gadamer uses the word *Vorurteil*, which in German means both prejudice and prejudgment (*Vor* means "pre" or "before," and *Urteil* means "judgment"). Unlike the negative associations of "prejudice," for Gadamer such prejudgments do not inhibit but are in fact the precondition to knowledge; they are "biases of our openness to the world" (Hans-Georg Gadamer, "The Universality of the Hermeneutic Problem," in *Philosophical Hermeneutics*, 9).

26. For an account of Qutb's life and his earlier works, see Adnan A. Musallam, "The Formative Stages of Sayyid Qutb's Intellectual Career and His Emergence as an Islamic Da'iya: 1906–1952." For an account of his entire body of political thought, see Ahmad S. Moussalli, *Radical Islamic Fundamentalism*; Yvonne Haddad's "Sayyid Qutb"; and Haddad, "The Qur'anic Justification for an Islamic Revolution."

27. While (Shi'ite) Iran is perhaps the best-known example of Islamic fundamentalism to those in the West, many contemporary Islamic fundamentalist movements (e.g., in Jordan, Egypt, Saudi Arabia, Algeria, the Sudan, and the Occupied Territories) in the Middle East are Sunni.

28. Aziz al-Azmeh, *Islams and Modernities*, 1. In a review of this book, Akbar Ahmed argues that "although Muslims vary a great deal culturally and politically, and

are often at odds with each other, there is nonetheless a central unifying theme to their perception of Islam, one rooted in the Qur'an and the life of the Prophet. Globalization, the international communications networks, and developments in technology assist this process and are creating a greater awareness of unity than at any time in history" (Akbar Ahmed, "Review of *Islams and Modernities*," 736). Even John Esposito, who has insisted on the almost infinite variations of Islamic revival from context to context, acknowledges "recurrent themes" that make it possible to speak of a "revivalist worldview" (Esposito, *The Islamic Threat*, 14–19).

29. Bruce B. Lawrence, *Shattering the Myth*, 4.

30. And there are, of course, many such "locations" when it comes to Islam. Indeed, although I here analyze explanations of Middle Eastern Islamism and Qutb's fundamentalist political thought as the lens through which to explore the construction of "Islamic fundamentalism," many of the world's Muslims live outside the Middle East, including in Central Asia, India, Pakistan, China, Indonesia, and the United States.

31. Nicholas B. Dirks, ed., *Colonialism and Culture*, 8.

32. Part of this dynamic is captured by Michael Gilsenan: "The domination exercised in the Middle East, in particular by Britain, France and the United States, has deep repercussions. . . . Social and cultural institutions once part of the taken-for-granted everyday world are equally open to fiercely divergent interpretations. Many of the suppositions and predispositions that make up culture have come into conscious and often very critical self-conscious reflection. What Islam means for Muslims in the modern world is now an issue for debate and action. . . . What is Islamic government and in what forms and institutions must it be embodied? . . .The insistence on a self-conscious examination is born out of contest" (Gilsenan, *Recognizing Islam*, 14–15). Marshall Hodgson refers to this complex of processes as the "Great Western Transmutation" beginning in the late sixteenth century, where "great" signifies the extent of its reach (Hodgson, *The Venture of Islam*, 3: 176–222).

33. Abdellah Hammoudi, *Master and Disciple*, xx.

34. This makes sense when we consider how "Western political thought" is itself riven by various moral and political disagreements. This is an argument against what David Wong calls "incommensurability of translation," the stance where an attentiveness to the specificity of language leads to a sense that certain theories from different cultures simply cannot speak to each other in meaningful ways (Wong, "Three Kinds of Incommensurability").

35. Roland Robertson argues that as the term "globalization" gained popularity in the second half of the 1980s it took on a number of meanings, not all necessarily compatible or precise (Robertson, "Mapping the Global Condition," in *Global Culture*, 19–20). Pheng Cheah usefully captures "globalization" as a set of interrelated developments and processes over the last two decades that include the "accelerated pace of economic globalization—the intensification of international trade, fiscal and technology transfers, and labor migration, and the consolidation of a genuinely global mode of production through subcontracting— . . . the transnationalization of military command structures through NATO, and the rise of global hybrid cultures from modern mass migration, consumerism, and mass communications" (Cheah, "Introduction Part II: The Cosmpolitical—Today," *Cosmopolitics*, 20). Also significant have been the "increase in the numbers of international agencies and institutions . . . the

acceptance of unified global time, the development of global competitions and prizes, the development of standard notions of citizenship, rights, and conception of humankind" (Featherstone, *Global Culture*, 6). Thus, while "globalization" is often expressed primarily in economic terms, it also entrails the "extension of global cultural interrelatedness . . . linking together previously isolated pockets of relatively homogeneous culture which in turn produces more complex images of the other as well as generating identity-reinforcing reactions." (ibid.). Fred Dallmayr argues that globalization thus "involves to a large extent the spreading or dissemination of modern Western forms of life around the globe" (Dallmayr, *Alternative Visions*, 1).

36. Partha Chattergee, *The Nation and Its Fragments*, 5.

37. Ibid., 11.

38. Manfred Henningsen, "The New Politics of History," 425.

39. Stephen Salkever and Michael Nylan, "Teaching Comparative Political Philosophy," and "Comparative Political Philosophy and Liberal Education."

40. Herodotus, *The History*, book 1, Clio.

41. Sheldon S. Wolin, "Political Theory," 12: 319.

42. J. Peter Euben, "Creatures of a Day," 34; Wolin, "Political Theory," 319.

43. It could be argued that the connection between travel and wisdom has always been a feature of political theory. For example, Alexis de Tocqueville wrote of his project, "[l]et us not turn to America in order slavishly to copy the institutions she has fashioned for herself, but in order that we may better understand what suits us; let us look there for instruction rather than models" (Tocqueville, *Democracy in America*, preface) xiv. Yet Tocqueville's study illuminates not only his own world but that of American democracy—hence the inclusion of his work in syllabi on American political thought. An example of a different sort is Montesquieu's 1721 novel *The Persian Letters*. Here Montesquieu inverts classic travel literature to have two Persian characters who call themselves searchers after wisdom travel to Paris (p. 39). Yet *The Persian Letters* does not, of course, illuminate Persia.

44. Bernstein, "The Rage against Reason."

45. Francis Robinson, "Modern Islam and the Green Menace." Robinson notes, for example, that at least eighty Greek authors in fields including philosophy, medicine, math, physics, astronomy, geography, and the occult sciences were translated into Arabic during the 'Abbasid caliphate.

46. Dirks, *Colonialism and Culture*, 22–23.

47. Clifford Geertz, "Thick Description."

48. Ibid., 14.

49. Ibid., 24.

50. Hammoudi, *Master and Disciple*, xviii.

51. Charles Taylor, "Interpretation and the Sciences of Man," 2:42.

52. Those that employ a more interpretive approach to Middle Eastern politics and ideas include Leonard Binder's *Islamic Liberalism*, Emmanuel Sivan's *Radical Islam*, Fouad Ajami's *The Arab Predicament*, Eric Davis's "Ideology, Social Class and Islamic Radicalism in Modern Egypt," Abdulaziz Sachedina's "Activist Shi'ism in Iran, Iraq and Lebanon," and Ira M. Lapidus's cultural history, *A History of Islamic Societies*. Lapidus also emphasizes this approach in his "Islamic Political Movements: Patterns of Historical Change," in *Islam, Politics and Social Movements*, ed. Edmund Burke, III, and Ira M. Lapidus.

53. It is interesting to note that scholarly writing on Christian fundamentalism has so far exhibited a greater willingness to understand it from the "insider's point of view" than has the literature on Islamic fundamentalism (William Shepard, " 'Fundamentalism' Christian and Islamic," n. 4). For example, in his seminal book on the early fundamentalist movement in America, George Marsden insists that while tied to sociopolitical conditions, the emergence of American fundamentalism must be primarily understood as doctrinally driven, rather than epiphenomenal (Marsden, *Fundamentalism and American Culture*, 159).

54. In using this phrase I am intentionally evoking Gabriel Almond's attempt to "increase our understanding of the vulnerability of the free world to Communist penetration" in *The Appeals of Communism*, ix. This reference seems particularly apt given the ways the image of the "Green Peril" has replaced the "Red Menace."

55. The critique of Western colonialism and imperialism central to Islamic fundamentalist experiences of modernity is not, for obvious reasons, part of Christian fundamentalism. I will return to this topic in the concluding chapter.

56. Friedrich Nietzsche, *The Birth of Tragedy*, 139.

57. Derrida, *The Other Heading*, 77, 78–79. Emphasis in original.

58. For a powerfully argued case against the use of "fundamentalism" to describe Islamic revival, see Riffat Hassan's "The Burgeoning of Islamic Fundamentalism," 151–71.

59. Shepard, " 'Fundamentalism' Christian and Islamic," 368.

60. Esposito, *The Islamic Threat*, 7.

61. Gilles Kepel, *The Revenge of God*, and *Muslim Extremism in Egypt*; Sivan, *Radical Islam*. For a discussion of the various alternatives to fundamentalism, see Shepard, " 'Fundamentalism' Christian and Islamic," especially n. 15.

62. I do occasionally employ the often used "Islamism" to break the monotony, but with reservations aptly captured by an Algerian writer who objects: "Is David Koresh referred to as a Christianist?" Cited by Karima Bennoune, "Algerian Women Confront Fundamentalism," 37, n. 1. She goes on to suggest that the term "Islamist" is objectionable because it implies that they "capture some 'true' essence of Islam."

63. Voll, "Fundamentalism in the Sunni Arab World," 347.

64. According to Weber, the distinction between "this worldly" and "other worldly" orientations lies in requirements of salvation. In "world-rejecting asceticism," participation in worldly affairs may lead to alienation from God, so salvation requires withdrawal from the "world." In "inner-worldly asceticism," salvation is achieved through participation in the world, or more precisely "within the institutions of the world, but in opposition to them.... [T]he world is presented to the religious virtuoso as his responsibility" (Max Weber, *The Sociology of Religion*, 166).

65. Of course, as Martin Marty and R. Scott Appleby note, sacred texts do not play "the same constitutive role in South Asian and Far Eastern traditions as they do in the Abrahamic faiths." Yet it is all the more striking that in their study on comparative fundamentalism they find that at least four of the six South Asian or Far Eastern "fundamentalist-like movements . . . do in fact privilege a sacred text and presume to draw certain fundamentals—beliefs and behaviors—from it" (*Fundamentalism Observed*, 820). This is part of why the editors of "The Fundamentalism Project" find the term "fundamentalism" fruitful although not without controversy (they list several persuasive reasons for the comparative usefulness of the term on pp. viii–ix).

However, as Nikki Keddie rightly notes, this stretches the term too far by including movements that are often quite apolitical ("Comparative Method in the Study of 'Fundamentalism' ").

66. The understanding of the Qur'an as the eternal, literal and uncreated word of God has been central to "mainstream" Islam—although not without dissent—at least from the tenth century. This is why the *Encyclopaedia of Islam* suggests that the "closest analogue in Christian belief to the role of the Kur'ān in Muslim belief is not the Bible, but Christ" ("Al-Kur'ān," *The Encyclopaedia of Islam: New Edition*, 426–27). As a recent *Atlantic Monthly* writer put it, if "Christ is the Word of God made flesh, the Koran is the Word of God made text" (Toby Lester, "What Is the Koran?", 45).

67. Sivan, lecture in the Department of Near Eastern Studies, Princeton University, October 21, 1992; and Marty, "Explaining the Rise of Fundamentalism," A56.

68. Ira M. Lapidus, "Islamic Revival and Modernity," 444. Olivier Roy concurs when he argues that "[r]ather than a reaction against the modernization of Muslim societies, Islamism is a product of it" (*The Failure of Political Islam*, 50).

69. Indeed, it has often been noted that history is for Marx what God was to theologically minded philosophers. Samir Amin argues that there is a "fundamentalist state of mind" in movements where "a particular view of society is put forward, that is endowed with the virtues of being able to resolve once and for all the problems of society and humankind. To reject this view is to opt for evil against good. History is regarded as the locus of this confrontation." Amin provocatively suggests that such fundamentalist tendencies can be equally evident in Marxist movements, Khomeini's fundamentalism, and President Ronald Reagan's invocation of the American Constitution as the "revealed answer to all the problems of humankind today and for all time" (Amin, *Delinking*, 174–76). Esposito even suggests that the post-Enlightenment insistence upon the necessity and inevitability of secularism is itself a form of fundamentalism (*The Islamic Threat*, 232–35).

CHAPTER TWO
PROJECTIONS AND REFRACTIONS

1. This image is particularly characteristic of social science literature. By contrast, several noticeably more nuanced accounts of fundamentalism have recently appeared in the fields of comparative religion and/or history, for example, Bruce Lawrence, *Defenders of God* and *Shattering the Myth*; and Kepel, *The Revenge of God*. As I will argue in this chapter, there is a reason for these disciplinary differences.

2. Much of political science has, of course, moved beyond the crude modernization paradigm that had defined rationalization as the movement away from the patronage system, personalistic networks, and "vertical" affiliations based on clan, kin, or sect, toward an increasing emphasis on efficiency, promotions by merit, and "horizontal" affiliations—such as class—based on "objective" economic interests. Many now argue that patronage, for example, is *rational*, and in fact much of social science presumes that the political world can be explained rationally. The impulse to understand all action rationally rightly resists the tendency to regard many types of action as irrational, and thus inexplicable; yet often the attempt to regard all action as ra-

tional insists it be accessible through market logic and still generates an understanding of the fundamentalist as—what I will argue is—an irrational rational actor.

3. What I am calling the "modernization narrative" here does not refer to outdated and discredited versions of modernization theory. Rather it should be taken as referring to, in Ira Lapidus's words, "processes of centralization of state power and the development of commercialized or capitalist economies which entail the social and cultural changes we call modernity" ("Islamic Revival and Modernity," 444, n. 1).

4. Reinhard Bendix, "Tradition and Modernity Reconsidered," 345, 326.

5. Geoffrey Hawthorn, *Enlightenment and Despair*, 9.

6. Lawrence rightly insists on differentiating between "modernity" from "modernism," arguing that the former encompasses the processes associated with modernization, including but not limited to the "increasing bureaucratization and rationalization as well as technical capacity and global exchange," the latter signaling the "search for individual autonomy driven by a set of socially encoded values emphasizing change over continuity; quantity over quality; efficient production, power, and profit over sympathy for traditional values or vocations, in both the public and private spheres" (*Defenders of God*, 27). "Modernism" is thus the ideology of the "objective, structural givens" that constitute "modernity" (p. 2).

7. Richard Falk, "Religion and Politics," 379.

8. Although Said's approach draws substantially on the work of Foucault, Said's use of "authors" reveals a crucial disagreement between them over the significance of the author in the "otherwise anonymous collective body of texts constituting a discursive formation" (Edward Said, *Orientalism*, 23). Contrary to Foucault's beliefs that a discourse is primarily a body of anonymous knowledge and that specific texts and writers are ultimately of little importance, Said finds that Orientalism, as perhaps nowhere else, bears the imprint of a few seminal authors whose influence continues today. This chapter acknowledges the importance of individual authors, but primarily as representatives of the approaches to and explanations of Islamic fundamentalism characteristic of much of current social science.

9. Michel Foucault, *Power/Knowledge*, 82.

10. Said, *Orientalism*, 7.

11. Ibid., 20–21.

12. Sheldon S. Wolin, "The Politics of the Study of Revolution," 347.

13. Geertz, "Ideology as a Cultural System," 56–57.

14. Hannah Arendt, "Religion and Politics," 374. Arendt further comments that, in any previous period, the refusal to take participants at their own word, "as though it were a matter of course that what the sources themselves say can only prove misleading, would have seemed, to say the least, quite unscientific."

15. James Noble addresses the relationship between Marxism and functionalism in ways useful to this analysis of Islamic fundamentalism ("Marxian Functionalism," in *After Marx*, ed. Terence Ball and James Farr). Thus Kepel rightly eschews the use of the term "ideology" to describe Islamism; as al-Azmeh aptly puts it, Kepel treats Islamism "as neither mystification nor occlusion, but as revelation" (Kepel, *Muslim Extremism in Egypt*, 225; al-Azmeh, *Islams and Modernities*, 24). Religion and ideology, as Arendt notes, are two distinct phenomena: theology, for example, "treats man as a reasonable being that asks questions and whose reason needs reconciliation even

if he is expected to believe in that which is beyond reason," whereas ideology "treats man as though he were a falling stone, endowed with the gift of consciousness and therefore capable of observing, while he is falling, Newton's laws of gravitation"(Arendt, "Religion and Politics," 371).

16. Lawrence, *Defenders of God*, 8.

17. This janus-faced image of the fundamentalist illustrates the overlap of what Clifford Geertz calls "interest theory" and "strain theory." In the first, ideology is a mask and a weapon for the pursuit of power by groups whose motivations are derived primarily from social position. In the second, ideology is both the expression of and corrective to "sociopsychological disequilibrium." That is, in "strain theory," structural inconsistency is reflected in the individual as personal insecurity and psychological strain; ideology becomes a " 'symbolic outlet' for emotional disturbances generated by social disequilibrium" (Geertz, "Ideology as a Cultural System," 52–55).

18. Taylor, *The Ethics of Authenticity*, 20.

19. As John Esposito aptly argues, "The post-Enlightenment tendency to define religion as a system of belief restricted to personal or private life, rather than as a way of life, has seriously hampered our ability to understand the nature of Islam and many of the world's religions. It has artificially compartmentalized religion, doing violence to its nature, and reinforced a static, reified conception of religious traditions rather than revealing their inner dynamic nature. To that extent, a religion which does not seem to do so (a religion that mixes religion and politics) appears necessarily retrogressive, prone to religious extremism and fanaticism, and thus a potential threat" (*The Islamic Threat*, 233).

20. Taylor, "Interpretation and the Sciences of Man," 48–49.

21. The focus on how social scientific models explain fundamentalism in particular is pragmatic: it would be beyond the scope of this chapter to address fully the wealth of critical literature on modernization theory alone. Moreover, as this is an attempt to expose and explore the theoretical apparatuses behind each text's *explanation* of Islamic fundamentalism, I concentrate primarily on the causal explanations within each text, rather than the entire work.

22. Samuel Huntington, *Political Order in Changing Societies*, 34–35.

23. Cyril Edwin Black, *The Dynamics of Modernization*, 7.

24. Daniel Lerner, *The Passing of Traditional Society*, 45. Here Lerner has quoted von Grunebaum's definition of modernization (Gustave Edmund von Grunebaum, *Unity and Variety in Muslim Civilization*, 3).

25. Modernization theory in general, and Lerner in particular, have been widely criticized for ethnocentrism, overemphasis on domestic circumstances, essentializing, and just plain bad scholarship. Elbaki Hermassi offers a critique of modernization theory in the Middle East, and of Daniel Lerner in particular, in *Leadership and National Development in North Africa*, as does Reinhard Bendix in "Tradition and Modernity Reconsidered." For more recent criticisms not only of Lerner but of the paradigm of modernization, see, for example, Hisham Sharabi, "The Scholarly Point of View"; Bassam Tibi, *Islam and the Cultural Accommodation of Social Change*, 189–91; Binder, *Islamic Liberalism*; and Chatterjee, *The Nation and Its Fragments*.

26. Lerner, *The Passing of Traditional Society*, 402.

27. Ibid., 256. The Muslim Brotherhood, also referred to as the Muslim Brethren or *al-Ikhwan al-Muslimun* was founded in Egypt by Hasan al-Banna in 1928, and is usually considered the founding organization of the modern (Sunni) Islamic fundamentalist movement.

28. Ibid.

29. Karl Marx, "The Eighteenth Brumaire of Louis Bonaparte," 300.

30. Karl Marx, "On the Jewish Question," in *The Marx-Engels Reader*, 28. Emphasis in original.

31. Barrington Moore, Jr., *Social Origins of Dictatorship and Democracy*, 384.

32. Michael Fischer, "Islam and the Revolt of the Petit Bourgeoisie," 121.

33. Ibid., 115.

34. Ibid., 121. In Fischer's account of Iranian fundamentalism in two different texts published two years earlier, he places imagery, language, and ideas squarely at the center of interpretation, consciously eschewing rigidly functionalist and rationalist approaches. For example, in his discussion of Iranian clerics, Fischer is explicitly committed to an approach where culture and language are plumbed as "metaphorical representations of experience" whose "validity resides not in verifiable science-like propositions but in their aptness for capturing or expressing experience" (Michael Fischer, "Becoming Mollah," 103). In *Iran: From Religious Dispute to Revolution*, Fischer also places cultural symbols and messages at the center of the text. This approach sustains his conviction that the appeal of Iranian fundamentalism is not merely a matter of mechanistic pressures or utilitarian calculations but resides in a "configuration of cultural or symbolic forms . . . which tacitly resonate with deeply felt understandings about the world" (p. 101).

35. Ernest Gellner, *Muslim Society*. Sami Zubaida criticizes Gellner's model in "Is There a Muslim Society?"

36. Fischer, "Islam and the Revolt of the Petit Bourgeoisie," 112; and Pierre Bourdieu, "The Disenchantment of the World."

37. Fischer, 111.

38. Ibid., 113.

39. Khoury, "Islamic Revivalism and the Crisis of the Secular State," 215. This argument is also made by Alan Richards and John Waterbury in *A Political Economy of the Middle East*.

40. Talcott Parsons, *The Social System*, 29.

41. Derived from Durkheimian sociology, structural-functionalism is most closely associated with Talcott Parsons' integration of social Darwinism and evolutionary sociology such that social change is understood in terms of an "evolutionary adaptation of a social system to its environment, especially in terms of the structural differentiation of the parts of a system" (Bryan S. Turner, "Preface to the New Edition" of Parsons' *The Social System*, xxiv). While Parsons' particular version of structural-functionalism has been criticized for its conservative preoccupation with order and American triumphalism, by structural-functionalism here I mean loosely the analysis of a social practice as it relates to the functioning of a society as a whole, a definition that does not presuppose either a particular purpose to that function or a Parsonian teleology ("Functionalism," *Encyclopædia of the Social Sciences*, ed. Edwin R. A. Seligman, vol. 6; and Anthony Giddens, *Sociology*, 695–97).

42. Sivan, *Radical Islam*, 185–86. Sivan's emphasis on the cultural aspect of fundamentalist resistance is also articulated by Fouad Ajami. For Ajami, the appeal of Islamic fundamentalism is a function of its authenticity in the context of foreign weakness, domestic breakdown, and cultural seduction. Ajami states this position succinctly: power engenders resistance. "Caught in the midst of a massive historic crisis, buffeted by powerful outside forces that have made their world pivotal and exposed, the Arabs have fallen back on the symbols and weapons they know best: their religious identity" (*The Arab Predicament*, 141, 16, 198). Fundamentalism is again a vehicle, but here it is a vehicle for the fury and resistance to the dominance of the West as evinced by a legacy of colonialism and the continuing presence of "indirect" imperialism. Fundamentalism is understood as a psycho-cultural phenomenon: an indigenous reaffirmation of Self against the Western Other. It is at once a vehicle of anti-Westernism and an expression of identity and self-pride.

43. Nazih N. Ayubi, "The Political Revival of Islam." Ayubi develops and broadens this argument in *Political Islam*.

44. Ansari, "The Islamic Militants in Egyptian Politics," 141.

45. Saad Eddin Ibrahim, "Anatomy of Egypt's Militant Islamic Groups," 448.

46. Two cases in point: Mark Tessler's "The Origins of Popular Support for Islamist Movements"; and Olivier Roy's *The Failure of Political Islam*. For an example of newspaper coverage that reflects the currency of this explanation, see Youssef M. Ibrahim, "Palestinian Religious Militants: Why Their Ranks Are Growing."

47. Sivan, *Radical Islam*, 11.

48. Ansari, "The Islamic Militants in Egyptian Politics," 140–41.

49. Ibrahim, "Anatomy of Egypt's Militant Islamic Groups," 424.

50. Gary Becker, *The Economic Approach to Human Behavior*, 8, 14. For an expanded discussion of this, see my article, "When Worldviews Collide."

51. An early analysis of religious participation using this model can be found in Corry Azzi and Ronald Ehrenberg's "Household Allocation of Time and Church Attendance." Laurance R. Iannaccone applies rational choice theory to religious behavior in "Risk, Rationality, and Religious Portfolios." Iannaccone also analyzes the economic positions of Protestant fundamentalists in "Heirs to the Protestant Ethic?" Becker and Kevin M. Murphy refer to religious participation as behavior that, along with eating, watching television, drinking alcohol, smoking cigarettes, and snorting cocaine can be considered part of addictive behavior illuminated by a rational model ("A Theory of Rational Addiction"). Clyde Wilcox published a book explaining support for Christian fundamentalism in America using the model (*God's Warriors*).

52. The origin of rational actor theory is usually traced to the application of Adam Smith's classical economic theory of the market model to politics. But while Smith had insisted that the market metaphor did not apply to politics, in the 1880s the "marginalists" extended its scope to make it a more general model, removed from the political and sociological cultural context. The marginalists—the best-known British marginalist was Alfred Marshall—shifted the basis of economic theory from Ricardo's labor theory of value to one where the value of an item was based on its marginal utility. See Jaan W. Whitehead, "The Forgotten Limits"; and Henry William Spiegel, *The Growth of Economic Thought*. This set the groundwork for the beginning of modern rational actor theory, which, in its basic form, assumes that all

political behavior is intelligible by reference to certain universal aspects of human psychology (Whitehead, "The Forgotten Limits").

53. Becker, "The Economic Approach to Human Behavior," 110.

54. Kristen R. Monroe, "The Theory of Rational Action," 1:78. Here Monroe makes explicit many of the assumptions that underlie, for example, Becker's account of the economic approach in *The Economic Approach to Human Behavior*, 3–9. Of course, this original model has been subjected to criticism from a variety of quarters. Most notably, cognitive psychologists have argued that actors aim less at "maximizing utility" than at "satisficing"—seeking a minimum level of satisfaction. This modification—frequently referred to as "rational *choice* theory"—nevertheless shares with rational *actor* theory a model of decision-making as a function of a cost-benefit calculus where risks and rewards are weighed and evaluated in relation to an agent's goal (Herbert Simon, "Human Nature in Politics").

55. Kristen R. Monroe, "Rational Actor Theory and Fundamentalism."

56. Taylor, *The Ethics of Authenticity*, 21.

57. Amartya Sen, "Rational Fools," 322.

58. Wilcox, *God's Warriors*, 224.

59. Paul Diesing, *Reason in Society*, 63.

60. Azzi and Ehrenberg, "Household Allocation of Time and Church Attendance," 28; Iannaccone, "A Formal Model of Church and Sect," S245; Hechter, *Principles of Group Solidarity*, 13, 148–49.

61. Monroe, "Rational Actor Theory and Fundamentalism."

62. This echoes Marvin Harris's argument that messianic faiths often flourished as a consolation to people whose lives were filled with unhappiness and misery (*Cows, Pigs, Wars and Witches*).

63. Adam Smith, *An Inquiry into the Nature and Causes of the Wealth of Nations*, vol. 3, book 5, chap. 1, pp. 206, 205.

64. See Ken Binmore's *Playing Fair*. I am grateful to James W. Bailey for this point.

65. Monroe, "Rational Actor Theory and Fundamentalism," 23.

66. Steve Bruce, "Religion and Rational Choice," 201.

67. A complete account of this image is beyond the scope of this work; it would, of course, include Durkheim and the British anthropological tradition and would attend to, for example, the Durkheimian roots of structural-functionalism, and the role of classical economics in rational actor theory. Just an account of Enlightenment rationalism would require a discussion of, for example, the differences between English and French rationalism. For example English rationalism had a distinctively empiricist bent. Through the Calvinist and Lockean tradition, man was considered his own authority in intellectual as well as spiritual matters: truth was to be determined inductively from each man's experience in the world. By contrast, French rationalists developed a model Hawthorn calls "schematic rationalism": "the construction of systems, as thorough, as all-embracing and as monistic as the ecclesiastical and monarchical systems they challenged" (Hawthorn, *Enlightenment and Despair*, 12). In French Rationalism, then, the emphasis was less on experiential observations than on abstract axioms of reason as the source of truth and knowledge.

68. Ian Hacking, "The Archaeology of Foucault," 29.

69. In Book 9 of *The Republic*, Plato suggested that true freedom lies in obedience to reason, in opposition to the rule of the passions and appetites. Enlightenment reason, however, is not defined in the contrast between the rule of wisdom and of appetites. On the contrary, as Peter Gay points out, in the simultaneous elevation of reason and nature, Enlightenment theorists sought to rescue pride and sensuality from the degradation into which Christianity had cast natural passion (Peter Gay, *The Enlightenment*, 3:187–207). Thus, although Enlightenment thought insisted on the rationality of human psychology, it was tempered by a recognition, then a celebration, of the role of natural passion in human achievement. Rousseau's emphasis on sentiment is well known; Diderot also emphasizes the greatness of passion (*Pensees Philosophiques*, in *Oeuvres Completes*, 1:273); as does David Hume (*A Treatise of Human Nature*, 415). Adam Smith in *The Wealth of Nations* is careful to note that human self-interest originated in the desires, not in a conscious calculus. This aspect of Smith is emphasized in Whitehead, "The Forgotten Limits," and in Milton L. Myers, *The Soul of Economic Man*.

70. Of course, the reading of Enlightenment rationalism as a radical break from what came before needs to be balanced with a consideration of the continuities between medieval and Enlightenment political thought. In 1931 Carl Becker argued that the eighteenth and thirteenth centuries shared a preoccupation with the combination of rationality and Christian theology such that the Enlightenment looked much more like the Middle Ages than the twentieth century (*The Heavenly City of the Eighteenth Century Philosophers*). Robert Anchor describes the "hidden hand" doctrine in Adam Smith's laissez-faire economics as a revised version of the medieval belief that there is "a basic but unseen harmony under[lying] the apparent discord of the world" (*The Enlightenment Tradition*, 11). Or consider Carl Schmitt's argument that despite appearances, such concepts as Hobbes's absolute sovereign have infused modern politics with what can only be referred to as "secularized" Christian theology.

71. Marx, *Capital*, 12–13.

72. For example, some of Weber's influential interpreters have insisted on characterizing Weberian rationalization as a totalizing, unilinear progression from the traditional to the modern, whereby the modern is posited in absolute opposition to and superiority over the traditional. Talcott Parsons and Wolfgang Schluchter have, for example, imputed an evolutionary view of social development to Weber (Parsons, "Introduction" to *The Sociology of Religion*, lx–lxv, and Schluchter, *The Rise of Western Rationalism*). Yet, as Anthony Giddens notes, Weber always maintained an ambivalent stance toward rationalization, a mix of regard for its achievements and fear for the "human values of spontaneity and autonomy" (Giddens, *Capitalism and Social Theory*, 235).

73. Moreover, as Arendt notes, in other hands Weber's ideal types served to advance a larger process of functionalization. For example, while Weber intended the paradigmatic "charistmatic leader" to be Jesus, pupils of Karl Mannheim later applied this category to Hitler. "From the viewpoint of the social scientist," Arendt contends, "Hitler and Jesus were identical because they fulfilled the same social function . . . such a conclusion is possible only for people who refuse to listen to what either Jesus or Hitler said" ("Religion and Politics," 378).

74. Of course, Marx (and Weber) has a paradoxical relationship to the Enlightenment, a full analysis of which is beyond the scope of this chapter. However, it is important to point out that while Marx has been called a "child of the Enlightenment," his sympathies are most clearly with those who are the victims, not the victors, of the march of progress. So while dialectical materialism is in some ways the continuation of the philosophy of history inaugurated by Enlightenment rationalism, it also furnishes the grounds for a scathing critique of bourgeois domination that Enlightenment theorists are often interpreted as justifying. Likewise, while Weber also acknowledges the claims of reason and the fact of rationalization in history, his pessimism regarding the future is hardly consistent with much of Enlightenment optimism regarding the triumph of reason and the mastery of nature. In the end of Weber's narrative, it is not clear who has mastered whom, for the rules devised to control nature have come to dominate the human spirit as well. This is a far cry from Enlightenment paeans to the power of reason to liberate the greatness of the human spirit.

75. "The German Ideology," in *Marx-Engels Reader*, 150–55. Teleological accounts of history such as those found in both Marxist and Hegelian theories can and have been interpreted as instances of religious transference: a Christian deity, which both creates and controls human destiny, is tranformed into a quasi-secularized conception of history through which a necessarily progressive human destiny unfolds. The idea of history, much like that of the divinity, rested on a faith many have criticized as ultimately incompatible with the march of rational thought.

76. Condorcet, *Sketch for a Historical Picture of the Progress of the Human Mind*, 175.

77. Arendt, "Religion and Politics," 375.

78. Ibid., 374.

79. Stephen Kalberg takes issue with the translation of *entzauberung* as "disenchantment," a "far more general term that conjures up images of the romanticist's yearning for the *Gemeinschaft* and an earlier, simpler world," and argues that through it Weber meant the much more religiously specific concept of "de-magification" ("Max Weber's Types of Rationality," 1146, n. 2).

80. Michel Foucault, "Nietzsche, Genealogy, History," 142.

81. The crucial texts here are Martin Heidegger, *Being and Time*, and Hans-Georg Gadamer, *Truth and Method*. Fred Dallmayr argues that Jacques Derrida, particularly in his *The Other Heading: Reflections on Today's Europe*, is an important accomplice in developing a (deconstructive) "hermeneutics of difference" (Dallmayr, *Beyond Orientalism* and *Alternative Visions*). Hermeneutics' central proposition is that all interpreters are "situated," that is, located within particular traditions and defined by what Gadamer calls "prejudices," and that consequently the "understanding of the text is conditioned by the self-understanding of the interpretation" (David Couzens Hoy, *The Critical Circle*, p. viii). Interpretation is thus not a matter of a disinterested and unbiased observer finding objective knowledge about a particular subject: interpretation is defined by the hermeneutic circle, the dependence of any interpretation upon prior common understandings embedded in (in Gadamer's case) language and expression. Escaping the circle requires an illusory perspective outside of tradition. This is not the same thing as subjectivism, as I will show later.

82. Gadamer, *Truth and Method*, and *Philosophical Hermeneutics*. This insight is one that Foucault and Habermas share with Gadamer, although, as I will show later, Habermas diverges from Gadamer's model of interpretation as dialogic understanding in ways crucial for my argument.

83. Gadamer, *Truth and Method*, 452.

84. Thomas A. McCarthy, *The Critical Theory of Jürgen Habermas*, 174.

85. Gadamer, *Truth and Method*, 389. Gadamer's characterization of interpretation as a "fusion of horizons" has been criticized for seeming to presuppose a false consensualism. Yet Fred Dallmayr argues that in his neglected *Wer bin Ich und Wer bist Du?* Gadamer engages in a hermeneutic reading of Paul Celan's cycles of poems profoundly respectful of their Otherness (Dallmayr, *Beyond Orientalism*, 41–49).

86. Ibid., 269.

87. Dallmayr, *Beyond Orientalism*, xviii.

88. Gadamer, *Truth and Method*, 397.

89. Habermas, "A Review of Gadamer's *Truth and Method*," 335.

90. Ibid., 360. This is the crux of Habermas's rejection of Gadamer's idealist assumption that "linguistically articulated consciousness determined the material practice of life" (p. 361). See also Thomas A. McCarthy, "Rationality and Relativism."

91. Habermas, "A Review of Gadamer's *Truth and Method*," 360.

92. This is why Habermas argues that hermeneutics must be conjoined with critique of ideology and study of social systems.

93. Ibid.

94. Georg Henrik von Wright, *Explanation and Understanding*, 4.

95. Terence Ball, "The Ontological Presuppositions and Political Consequences of a Social Science."

96. Taylor, "Interpretation and the Sciences of Man," 26.

97. Daniel R. Sabia, Jr., and Jerald Wallulis, "The Idea of a Critical Social Science," 13; emphasis in the original.

98. Habermas makes this argument in the context of a consensus theory of truth that is problematic. The possibility of a universal truth is tied to the fact that the test of validity is not just the agreement of actual participants, but the *potential agreement* of all rational subjects willing to subject themselves to the "unforced force of the better argument." The claim of universality is itself dependent upon Habermas's theory of "universal pragmatics," the claim that there are "general and unavoidable—in this sense transcendental—conditions of possible understanding" in language ("What Is Universal Pragmatics?," 2). The structures of communicative interactions are knowable through a process of "rational reconstruction," the process of making explicit the structures and rules underlying all speech and action, of attaining explicit knowledge of the "anonymous rule systems" and of the "intuitive knowledge that is given with competence with respect to the rules in the form of 'know-how'" (Habermas, *Theory and Practice*, 22–23).

99. McCarthy, *Critical Theory of Jürgen Habermas*, 302.

100. Alfred Schutz, "The Problem of Rationality in the Social World," 85–86.

101. Part of Habermas's critique of Gadamer is also what he takes to be the conservatism of insisting upon the impossibility of a point from which to critique tradition, or to see how tradition functions in relation to processes such as labor or power. Of course, Gadamer has his own critique of Habermas's critique of him. See Gada-

mer, "On the Scope and Function of Hermeneutical Reflection," in *Philosophical Hermeneutics*.

102. For example, at times his reference to a perspective outside of tradition from which to view and critique distortion in language seems to replicate various aspects of the transcendentalism of positivist epistemologies he has so effectively criticized. But my interest in Habermas here is limited to the way his emphasis on distorted communication highlights the limits of hermeneutics for social inquiry (Habermas, *The Theory of Communicative Action*, esp. 1:332–33; *Legitimation Crisis*, esp. xiv–xviii, 110–14; *Knowledge and Human Interests*, esp. chaps. 10–12, and 310–17).

103. Thomas A. McCarthy, *Ideals and Illusions*, 45–46. Foucault's analyses of the way a discourse simultaneously organizes and subjugates knowledges in the name of "functionalist coherence or formal systemisation" also underscores the necessity of creating distance from our social practices (*Power/Knowledge*, 81). This is perhaps not surprising, for as McCarthy suggests, "neither genealogy nor critical theory wishes to leave to the participants and their traditions the final say about the significance of the practices they engage in" (*Ideals and Illusions*, 45–46). Indeed, despite significant differences, McCarthy suggests that in some crucial ways, Foucault's genealogy lies closer to Habermas's critical theory than to Gadamer's philosophical hermeneutics.

104. Arendt, *The Human Condition*, 57.

105. Cheah, "Given Culture," *Cosmpolitics*, 310.

106. Hodgson, *The Venture of Islam*, 3:428.

107. I take the meaning of "enframing" here from Timothy Mitchell's description of it as a "method of dividing up and containing" space. "Enfaming" thus usefully captures not only the ordering of architectural space but also the connection between colonialism and disciplinary discursive techniques (Mitchell, *Colonising Egypt*, 44).

108. Said, *Orientalism*, 12.

109. Ibid., 3.

110. Bigo, "Grands Débats dans un Petit Monde," 9.

111. Ibid., 43.

112. al-Azmeh, *Islams and Modernities*, 24.

113. It is consistently noted, for example, that the socioeconomic conditions in the Middle East could have just as easily fueled Marxist insurgency as fundamentalism: but for certain twists of political fate and cultural tendencies, many explanations imply that Marxism and fundamentalism are almost interchangeable because, for example, they draw on similar sociological bases and entail similar utopianist moral visions of the future in response to socioeconomic conditions.

114. Richard John Neuhaus *The Naked Public Square*, 16.

115. The necessity of an ideological enemy suggests not only that Western cultural identity needs an "Other" against which to define itself, but a particular kind of "Other," as evinced by the strikingly similar ways communism and fundamentalism have been constructed.

116. Importantly, the opposition of rationalism is most often to the authority of all religion, not Christianity in particular. For example, in an 1883 journal article, Ernest Renan argues explicitly that although all religions hinder the progress of reason, Islam is even more obscurantist than Christianity ("Science and Islam").

117. In this reference to "brute data" I rely on Taylor's account in "Interpretation and the Sciences of Man," 19.

118. The word "subject" here begs a crucial question, as it does in Foucault's work: if the subject of rationalist analyses is a construction whose correspondence to a concrete reality cannot be assumed, the very use of the word subject presumes that there is, in fact, something "out there" that exists beyond these rationalist representations. However, I have argued that a nonpositivist standard of impartiality makes possible a perspective from which to understand and critique a subject "out there" while remaining attentive to the role of distortion in interpretation.

119. As a reviewer of *Culture and Imperialism* suggested, Said says that he does not believe in any real or true Orient, "[b]ut then there are real people in the imaginary East, and Said's tacit acknowledgment of actualities is louder than he perhaps thought it was at the time, since it embodies a genuine passion for the unrepresented, for those who can't speak, but who flicker in the pages of *Orientalism* whenever Said invokes a neglected human history" (Michael Wood, "Lost Paradises," 47, and *Culture and Imperialism*).

120. Ibrahim, "Anatomy of Egypt's Militant Islamic Groups," 447. Ayubi asks this same question in *Political Islam*, 225.

121. Ayubi, "The Political Revival of Islam," 486. Saad Eddin Ibrahim makes a similar argument in "Anatomy of Egypt's Militant Islamic Groups."

122. Ayubi, "The Political Revival of Islam," 487.

123. Ayubi, *Political Islam*, 225–26.

124. Ayubi, "The Political Revival of Islam," 485.

125. Sami Zubaida, *Islam, the People and the State*, 88.

126. Ayubi, "The Political Revival of Islam," 486.

CHAPTER THREE
A VIEW FROM ANOTHER SIDE

1. As just one example, Bernard Lewis writes: "Islam was . . . associated with the exercise of power from the very beginning. . . . This association between religion and power, between community and polity, can . . . be seen in . . . the religious texts on which Muslims base their beliefs. One consequence is that in Islam religion is not, as it is in Christendom, one sector or segment of life regulating some matters and excluding others; it is concerned with the whole of life, not a limited but a total jurisdiction" (*Islam and the West*, 135–36).

2. See, for example, H.A.R. Gibb, *Modern Trends in Islam*; and G. E. von Grunebaum, *Modern Islam*.

3. Ellis Goldberg, "Smashing Idols and the State," 6.

4. Wolin, *Politics and Vision*, 179.

5. Lapidus, "State and Religion in Islamic Societies," 3.

6. Gibb, *Studies on the Civilization of Islam*, 35.

7. Wilfred Cantwell Smith, *Islam in Modern History*, 36. Indeed, Lapidus argues that the Middle Eastern Islamic heritage provides not one but two paradigms, or "golden ages." The first paradigm is the society in which religion, politics, and morality are all integrated; the second is what Lapidus calls the "imperial Islamic society"

a paradigm that "allows for a differentiated nonreligious concept of political author-ity" ("The Golden Age," 14–15).

8. Smith, *Islam in Modern History*, 37.

9. al-Azmeh, *Islams and Modernities*, 42.

10. All translations of Qutb's work are my own, from the original Arabic. Most of Qutb's major works have been reprinted several times over, and editions often differ from each other. Such differences are, at times, the work of censors: for example, after the 1952 Revolution, a chapter of Qutb's *Islam and Universal Peace* dealing with the hypocrisy of United States policies in the Middle East was deleted by the govern-ment. But some changes represent Qutb's own revisions in light of his later views on politics and Islam. For example, there are at least six editions of Qutb's *Social Justice in Islam*, and comparison of the editions indicates that Qutb revised later editions in accordance with his political radicalization and the more extreme views that charac-terize *Signposts along the Road* (William Shepard, "Gender Relations in the Thought of Sayyid Qutb," and *Sayyid Qutb and Islamic Activism*.

11. At the same time, Qutb insists that Islam is also dynamic and adaptable to changing conditions in history. In the context of Qutb's argument about the "essen-tial Islam," it is interesting to consider Elizabeth Grosz's argument about essential-ism in feminist theory. She argues that essentialism is in many ways unavoidable, particularly in the political struggle for women. But crucial to her argument is that feminists do not and need not use essentialist arguments in the same way that patriar-chy has used them. This suggests that essentialism may be put to radically different purposes; what matters then, is not whether some claim is essentialist, but rather who is making an essentialist claim and why (Grosz, "Sexual Difference and the Problem of Essentialism").

12. This emphasis on epistemology can be found in other works since Qutb: Ziauudin Sardar, for example, explicitly condemns what he terms as Western "epistemological imperialism" (*Islamic Futures*, 85). Indeed, Syed M. N. al-Attas argues that the core of the threat from the West is primarily epistemological, and he argues in response that "the holy Qur'an is the complete and final revelation . . . and there is no other knowledge . . . except based upon it and pointing to it . . . that can guide and save man" (*Islam, Secularism and the Philosophy of the Future*, 127, 138).

13. This is in direct contrast to Olivier Roy's contention that "there is no true Islamist political thought because Islamism rejects political philosophy and the hu-man sciences as such" (*The Failure of Political Islam*, 71). Such an argument makes sense only if "political philosophy" is defined in terms of particular premises and conclusions rather than as a field of inquiry defined by certain questions.

14. Said, *Orientalism*. Anthropologists pointed out the connection between domi-nation and knowledge well before Said's *Orientalism* appeared in 1978, although Said is crucial in bringing the insight to bear on Oriental Studies. See, for example, *Anthropology and the Colonial Encounter*, ed. Talal Asad, 16–19. In this context, it is interesting to note that Said is committed to a secular humanism that drives his admittedly "anticlerical and secular zeal": he acknowledges, for example, his dismay at seeing in the Arab world a "seething cauldron of Islamic revivalism" (*Culture and Imperialism*, 305). Yet Said also tends to downplay the appeal of radical Islamic ideas in favor of a rather patronizing account of the "comfort" of "dressing demurely, going

to prayers, reciting Koranic verses" in the face of economic insecurity (Said, "The Phony Islamic Threat," 64).

15. Enayat, *Modern Islamic Political Thought*, 2.

16. al-Azmeh, *Islams and Modernities*, 80.

17. Qutb, *Khasa'is al-Tasawwur al-Islami wa Muqawwamatihi*, 58–63 (hereafter referred to by its English title, *The Islamic Conception and Its Characteristics*). Qutb did not read many of these texts in their original languages. Such selective awareness of Western political thought takes its inevitable toll: Qutb's grasp of Western political thought remains crude at best. In *The Islamic Conception and Its Characteristics*, the text in which he deals most extensively with Western thinkers, he seems much more comfortable simply lifting lengthy quotations from Arabic writers sympathetic to his own critique of Marx, Plato, the Enlightenment, and so forth, than offering a critique in his own voice.

18. Haddad, "Sayyid Qutb," 79.

19. Ibid., 79.

20. An example of this is the classic modern liberal theorist himself, John Locke, both the author of the "Letter on Toleration" and theorist of natural rights that explicitly presumed, and actively depended on, the existence and authority of God. Moreover, it is important to note that there are ways in which Enlightenment thought was quite continuous with religious tradition, and suffused with religious imagery.

21. Abdallah Benkirane, Morocco, as quoted in *The Islamic Movement in North Africa*, 94.

22. As noted by John Waterbury, "Democracy without Democrats?," 23–47.

23. In this chapter and throughout most of this book, I am expressly referring to Sunni fundamentalism. My use of the phrase "Islamic fundamentalism," for the most part, should be interpreted as referring to the same. An adequate analysis of both Shi'ite and Sunni fundamentalism would require a discussion of theological debates beyond the scope of this work. However, it is worth noting that Qutb's prominence in the movement does not mean that his arguments are absolutely unique; indeed, Qutb shares a number of concerns and commitments with other Islamist thinkers, including Ayatollah Ruhollah Khomeini, whom I will discuss briefly in the following chapter.

24. Of course, Qutb shares that stage with those who influenced him and those leaders of the contemporary Islamist movement such as Sudan's Hassan al-Turabi, Hamas's spiritual guide Sheikh Ahmed Yassin, Pakistani Dar al-I'tisam al-Sadr, and Yusuf al-Qaradawi of the Egyptian Muslim Brotherhood, to name just a few.

25. Haddad, "Sayyid Qutb," 67.

26. Fadl Allah, *Ma'a Sayyid Qutb fi fikrihi al-siyasi wal-dini*.

27. Akhavi, "Qutb, Sayyid," 3:403.

28. Mitchell, *The Society of the Muslim Brothers*, 188.

29. Amin, *Delinking*, 177.

30. Goldberg identifies several commonalities in the ideologies of contemporary Islamic fundamentalist groups, many of which seem clearly influenced by Qutb's thought and the work of those who influenced him (see below) ("Smashing Idols and the State," 26–29). In a writing entitled *Kalimat Haqq*, Sheikh 'Abd al-Rahman follows Qutb in arguing that the right of legislation is God's alone and cannot be located in any institution or body that assumes the right of sovereignty is a function of human

power (pp. 28–29). According to *The New Yorker*, the Sheikh began working with Mawdudi and Qutb's texts during his tenure at the University of Asyut, beginning in 1973 (Mary Anne Weaver, "The Trail of the Sheikh," 77).

31. Haddad, "Sayyid Qutb," Ervand Abrahamian, "'Ali Shari'ati."

32. An even more striking example of early revivalism is Wahhabism, an eighteenth-century fundamentalist movement that fought to build a political community in (Saudi) Arabia under the banner of Islam.

33. Al-Banna, "Nazrat fi islah al-nafs," and *What Is Our Message?*

34. Mitchell, *The Society of the Muslim Brothers*, chaps. 1 and 2.

35. Kepel, *Muslim Extremism in Egypt*, 37.

36. Qutb competed for al-Banna's legacy with Hasan Isma'il Hudhaybi, a judge who was appointed leader of the Muslim Brotherhood following al-Banna's death. Unlike Qutb, Hudhaybi had been associated with the Egyptian monarchy and opposed violence. In *Du'at al-Qudat*, Hudhaybi advocates a gradualist approach to establishing an Islamic state and explicitly insists, against Qutb, that profession of the faith is sufficient to be considered a Muslim. Eric Davis argues that although this split erupted in the 1970s and was exacerbated by a generational divide within the movement, its origins can actually be traced back to the 1940s (Davis, "Ideology, Social Class and Islamic Radicalism in Modern Egypt," 151–52). Influence of both the militant interpretation of Islamic fundamentalism—stressing the power of the sword—and reformist wings of the Muslim Brotherhood—stressing the power of the word—is evident today throughout the Middle East.

37. Also influential on Qutb's thought is Indian thinker Abu al-Hasan al-Nadwi, particularly his *Islam and the World*.

38. Ibn Taymiyya developed a theory of legitimate authority designed at once to challenge the Mongol invaders who had converted to Islam and to underwrite the established power of the Mamluks. Specifically, Taymiyya argued that rulers who neglect or transgress Islamic law or portions thereof can be deemed infidels and therefore are enemies who can be legitimately killed on the battlefield (Emmanuel Sivan, "Ibn Taymiyya"). This criterion itself illustrates a shift in focus in Islamic thought in the wake of the Umayyad's seizure of power in the seventh century. Early debates in Islamic political thought had focused on the sources of legitimacy for authority: was election or affiliation to the Prophet the right criterion for leadership? But the ascension of rulers who had seized power by force turned the focus from sources of legitimacy to criteria by which to judge the quality of de facto rule: actual stewardship was to be evaluated in terms of the extent of a ruler's adherence to Islamic Law.

39. Qutb, *Ma'alim fil-Tariq*, p. 3 (hereafter referred to as *Signposts*). *Signposts* has two distinct parts. The last four chapters—entitled "A Muslim's Nationality Is His Belief," "Far-Reaching Transformations," "The Triumph of Faith," and "This Is the Path"—are Qutb's call to arms. These chapters bring the work to a crescendo of spiritual confidence designed to exhort believers to action and to assure them of victory despite the elusiveness of their reward. This tone is in contrast to the bitter exposition in the eight previous chapters.

40. Muhammad Tawfiq Barakat, *Sayyid Qutb, khulasat hayatihi, manhajuhu fi harakat, al-naqd al-muwajjaha ilayhi*, 11. Hasan Hanafi suggests there are four distinct stages: (1) literary, (2) social, (3) philosophical, and (4) political. (*al-Haraka al-*

Diniyya al-mu'asira, 168). But I tend to agree with Ibrahim Abu-Rabi' that both "periodizations" underplay important continuities in his thought as it evolved (Abu Rabi', *Intellectual Origins of Islamic Resurgence in the Modern Arab World,* 139).

41. Four chapters in *Signposts* are taken from Qutb's Qur'anic commentary, *In the Shade of the Qur'an* (published in the 1950s), and most of the theoretical constructs of this later work were first developed in *Social Justice in Islam* (first published in 1949) (Haim, "Sayyid Qutb"). Given that *Signposts* builds upon and extends arguments advanced in several of his earlier texts, then, I will draw upon them to illuminate the arguments advanced in *Signposts.*

42. It is often suggested that the experience of Nasser's prisons significantly explains Qutb's radicalization, and the radicalization of the Islamic movement in Egypt in general. For example, in 1982 Hasan Hanafi argued the following: "A prison psyche began to develop and impose itself on their minds. Their deep motivation was their hatred of reality, a need to revenge what nationalism, Arabism, secularism, socialism, and all that Nasser and the Ba'th stood for. It was a desire to destroy everything and to build anew, a rejection of the other, a refusal of dialogue, a denial of all compromises, etc. All this had culminated in Sayyid Qutb's *Signs of the Road* [*Signposts along the Road*]." (Hanafi, "The Relevance of an Islamic Alternative in Egypt," 60–61). While such experiences certainly must figure into an account of the radicalization of Islamists in Egypt, its explanatory power is somewhat mitigated, at least in Qutb's case, by the facts that, first, Mawdudi was the first to advance many of the radical ideas Qutb adopted and had never been imprisoned, and, second, Hasan Hudhaybi, the advocate of a gradualist approach to Islamic reform, had himself been Nasser's political prisoner in Egypt in the 1960s. (Ibrahim Abu Rabi', "Sayyid Qutb," 122).

43. Most of these biographical details are found in Yvonne Haddad, "Sayyid Qutb"; A. A. Musallam, "Prelude to Islamic Commitment" and *The Formative Stages of Sayyid Qutb's Intellectual Career;* Ahmad Moussalli, "Sayyid Qutb"; Shepard, *Sayyid Qutb and Islamic Activism;* and Abu Rabi', *Intellectual Origins of Islamic Resurgence in the Modern Arab World.*

44. Indeed, Qutb argues in *The Islamic Conception and Its Characteristics* that there are only two states of being for human beings, belief and unbelief, and that such states exist independent of culture or history (*Khasa'is al Tasawwur al-Islami wa Muqawwamatihi,* 99). In *Fi Zilal al-Qur'an* [In the Shade of the Qur'an], Qutb refers to this modern stage of *jahiliyya* as the "new *jahiliyya*" (p. 16).

45. *Signposts,* 17–18. *Tasawwur* literally means "conception"; Shepard suggests that Qutb intends it to mean "framework" as well, presumably because our concepts frame our understanding of the world ("Islam as a 'System' in the Later Writings of Sayyid Qutb"). In *Islamic Liberalism,* Leonard Binder goes as far as giving it the deconstructionist meaning of "a conceiving, a visioning or an imagining" (p. 189). But I have translated it as "worldview" where appropriate, an interpretation supported by Haddad ("Sayyid Qutb," 85), and by Qutb's own suggestion that the Islamic *tasawwur* is a comprehensive "picture of existence and life," of which a human being's beliefs, intuitions, and creative expressions are a part (*Signposts,* 125). Understanding *tasawwur* as "worldview" helps explain Qutb's insistence on Islam's comprehensiveness, and the impossibility of a compromise between the Islamic and *jahili tasawwur.*

46. Sayyid Qutb, *al-'Adala al-Ijtima'iyya fil-Islam* [Social Justice in Islam], chap. 7. However, as Shepard shows, Qutb moderates his criticism of the Umayyads in later editions of *Social Justice in Islam* (Shepard, *Sayyid Qutb and Islamic Activism*).

47. Again, Mawdudi is credited with generating the twin ideas of *jahiliyya/hakimiyya*. However, unlike *jahiliyya*, *hakimiyya* is not a Qur'anic term, but a contemporary concept that imparts a distinctively political, as opposed to spiritual, meaning to authority. Moreover, this political meaning has been read back into the Qur'anic text: for example, where the Qur'an states that "Those who do not judge by God's revelations are infidels" (5.44), the traditional interpretation is easily transformed, for the verb "to judge" can also mean "to rule, to govern." Hence, the same passage can read: "Those who do not govern by God's revelations are infidels." All translations of the Qur'an are taken from *al-Qur'an*, trans. Ahmed Ali.

48. Qutb, *Signposts*, 88–89.

49. Ibid., 33–10.

50. Following the 1919 Revolution against the British occupation and the mass support mobilized by Wafd ("Delegation") Party leader Sa'd Zaghlul, Britain declared Egypt independent in 1922, reserving some important points of control for itself, including Egyptian foreign policy. Despite Egypt's independence, actual power was split three ways among the conflicting interests of the monarchy, the Wafd Party, and the British. The alliances and animosities among these three poles of power were crucial obstacles to the success of the constitutional experiment. While King Fuad perceived all Wafdist activity as a threat to monarchical prerogatives, Egyptian unity was impossible in the face of British manipulation. And while the Wafd itself was split between popular and elite representatives, the constitutionalists emerged as their own worst enemies, resorting to repression and intrigue while professing the politics of liberal humanism. The constant intervention and manipulation of the British exacerbated the paralysis, and the years that could have presaged the institutionalization of liberalism descended into intra-elite conflict and impotence (Afaf Lufti al-Sayyid-Marsot, *Egypt's Liberal Experiment*). King Fuad's son Faruq ascended to the throne following his father's death in 1936. Described as a mere "playboy masquerading as a king," Faruq perpetuated the paralyzing conflict between the palace and the Wafd that his father had begun during his nineteen-year reign (Afaf Lufti al-Sayyid-Marsot, *A Short History of Modern Egypt*, 96, 98).

51. Qutb studied education at Wilson's Teachers College in Washington, DC (now the University of the District of Columbia), the Teacher's College at the University of Northern Colorado, and Stanford University. He visited several cities, including New York, San Fransisco, and Los Angeles (Ahmad S. Moussalli, "Sayyid Qutb," 45).

52. Quoted by Kepel, in *Muslim Extremism in Egypt*, 41. Upon his return, Qutb wrote a series of critical articles in 1951 entitled "The America I Have Seen." The articles are reprinted in Salah D. al-Khalidi, *Amrika min al-dakhil bi minzar Sayyid Qutb* [America from within as seen by Sayyid Qutb].

53. Sayyid Qutb, *al-'Adala al-Ijtima'iyya fil-Islam* (hereafter referred to as *Social Justice in Islam*), 13, and Shepard, *Sayyid Qutb and Islamic Activism*, 9.

54. Despite the temptation to substitute gender-neutral language for "man," I have deliberately stayed with this gendered term because this is true to Qutb's intention: power and politics are a male preserve, although the moral corruption of which

he speaks is a disease of all humanity. As I will discuss below, women are specifically mentioned when Qutb discusses the family.

55. Qutb, *Signposts*, 90.

56. It is clear here that Qutb's most immediate target is Nasser's socialism. However, in chapter 7 Qutb explicitly describes a regime of tolerance that seems to refer to some kind of modern liberal theory. In this passage, Qutb argues that although the existence of Allah is not denied in these systems, its characteristic tolerance is possible only by restricting his domain to the heavens, denying his sovereignty on earth, and imposing its own kind of intolerance on Islam (ibid., 105–6).

57. This is the coup that deposed Faruq and established an Egyptian Republic under the leadership of Gamal Abd al-Nasser. Led by young officers who were the beneficiaries of an opening of the military academy to the middle and lower bourgeoisie, the coup was initially supported by Islamic forces who had united with the officers in opposing both British control and the Albanian monarchy.

58. Sylvia G. Haim, "Sayyid Qutb."

59. Qutb, *Signposts*, 105.

60. Ibid., 93.

61. From the root meaning mother, source, origin, foundation, the Islamic *umma* originally described Muhammad's community, but its meaning is so varied in the Qur'an that at a minimum, it "always refers to ethnic, linguistic or religious bodies of people who are the objects of the divine plan of salvation" (*First Encyclopædia of Islam*, "*Umma*"). Hence, it is a supranational term, in that the boundaries of such a community are determined primarily by belief and not by geography or political identifications. Over time the *umma* has also come to encompass the more contemporary concepts of nation and people broadly understood, an ideal that now conflicts with the existence of Middle Eastern nation-states.

62. Qutb's challenge to the '*ulama*' (religious scholars) monopoly on interpretation—as well as his attempt at a kind of excommunication of political leaders—was not well received by much of the religious establishment. He was declared a deviant (*munharif*) by al-Azhar, Egypt's preeminent mosque and university (*Muslim Extremism*, 58).

63. *Signposts*, 119.

64. Ibid., 120. My emphasis.

65. It is important to note here that there is a distinction in Islam between '*ibadat* (duties toward God, for example, observance of religious obligations) and *mu'amalat* (duties toward one's fellow men and women). While some scholars have cited this distinction as a possible Islamic foundation for clearly separate spheres of religion and government, still others argue that by virtue of a common divine authorship, the distinction between them is virtually insignificant (Gibb, *Studies*, 198). Qutb, however, leaves no doubt regarding his view on this matter: in *The Islamic Conception and Its Characteristics* (p. 129), he argues that the distinction is a false one, and that, furthermore, the deepening of the distinction has produced manifold "deviations" in Muslim thought and society. Qutb also challenges this distinction in *Fi Zilal al-Qur'an*, vol. 4.

66. The traditions, or *Sunna*, are all the accumulated traditions, practices, and sayings of the Prophet that, along with Qur'anic law, serve as a model for Muslim behavior.

67. Marshall G. Hodgson, *The Venture of Islam*, 1:74; *First Encyclopædia of Islam*, "Shari'a." There is, of course, a complicated relationship between *shari'a* and Islamic jurisprudence that is beyond the scope of this project.

68. It might seem as if there is a tension between insisting that sovereignty is God's alone and that such sovereignty must be expressed in the supremacy of *shari'a*, which includes the practices and sayings of the Prophet. However, the Qur'an exhorts Muslims to follow the example of the Prophet as a "noble paradigm" (*uswa hasana* 33:21), and the *shahada* (confession of faith) in full is, "There is no God but Allah, and Muhammad is his Prophet." Qutb affirms the role of the Prophet Muhammad as the teacher of God's will (*Signposts*, 97).

69. Goldberg, "Smashing Idols and the State," 15.

70. Berlin, "Two Concepts of Liberty."

71. Qutb, *Signposts*, 151.

72. Ibid., 25.

73. Qutb, *Social Justice in Islam*, chap. 2.

74. Ibid., 31.

75. Such a preoccupation with foundations is similarly evident in "The Neglected Duty," or what Johannes J. G. Jansen calls the "creed of Sadat's assassins" (Jansen, *The Neglected Duty*).

76. Qutb, *Signposts*, 107–8.

77. Ibid., 112–13.

78. In *In the Shade of the Qur'an* he argues that women should wear the *hijab*, and in *Islam and Universal Peace* he insists that women should only work outside the home if absolutely necessary (Shepard, "Gender Relations in the Thought of Sayyid Qutb").

79. In *Signposts*, Qutb mentions women briefly, as if in passing. It is worth pointing out that despite the influence of *Signposts*, Qutb's almost incidental discussion of women here has not set the tone for contemporary fundamentalists; on the contrary, it might be fair to say that Islamic fundamentalists have become obsessed with the topic of women's behavior and dress, a concern at least in part driven by the conviction that the moral purity of Muslim women is inextricably tied to the ability of "Islam" to resist Western and modern corruption, sexual, cultural, and otherwise. Such preoccupation with women's clothing and, by extension, with containing women's sexuality, has a parallel in the strict attention paid, for example, to the length of women's skirts by Christian fundamentalists in America.

80. For an illuminating account of the role of women in both traditional and fundamentalist Islam, see Fatima Mernissi, *Beyond the Veil*, and Barbara Stowasser, "Religious Ideology, Women and the Family."

81. Qutb, *Social Justice in Islam*, 13.

82. Ibid., 53–54.

83. Ibid., 55.

84. Haim, "Sayyid Qutb," 152–53, and Shepard, "Gender Relations in the Thought of Sayyid Qutb."

85. For example, even in Qutb's "liberal" phase, he worries that the otherwise laudable book by Egyptian nationalist Taha Husain, entitled *Mustaqbal al-Thaqafa fi Misr* [The Future of Culture In Egypt], is not sufficiently accepting of religion (Qutb, "Naqd Mustaqbal al-Thaqafa fi Misr").

86. Musallam suggests that Qutb's early mystical bent can be explained in terms of his exposure to popular Sufi mysticism during his childhood (*The Formative Stages of Sayyid Qutb's Intellectual Career*, 111). Qutb's later Islamist work seems to reject such influences.

87. I use "modern" here primarily to distinguish between the Islamic schools and those inspired, in part, by Western, secular education. I place the term in quotes to indicate that a "modern" school in Egypt was far from a replica of the English or French educational system at the time. On the contrary, "modern" Egyptian schooling was a compromise between Western, secular disciplines and the disciplines of Islamic culture. This suggests that Egyptian education—like so many other realms subject to the "modernization process" in Egypt and elsewhere—was defined more by tensions among various traditions than by absolute categories such as "modern" and "traditional." All further references to "modern" education in this context will appear without quotation marks, but should be understood this way.

88. Shepard refers to Dar al-'Ulum as more a "halfway house between the traditional education of al-Azhar and the education offered by a modern university" (*Sayyid Qutb and Islamic Activism*, xiv).

89. Again, 'Aqqad's "liberalism"—and, indeed, Egyptian "liberalism" in general—was not a mere blueprint of Western liberalism: it is perhaps best understood as a compromise between Western and Islamic traditions. 'Aqqad, like others, grounded his liberal politics in Qur'anic sources rather than in abstract moral principles. A case in point: 'Aqqad argued for women's equality not on the basis of equal rights for all, but via his own interpretation of the behavior of Zaynab, the Prophet's wife.

90. Abu Rabi', *Intellectual Origins of Islamic Resurgence in the Modern Arab World*, 96.

91. Adnan A. Musallam, "Prelude to Islamic Commitment," 186. At one point, Qutb argues that the truth of existence is embedded in human nature and is thus ascertainable by virtue of being human. Elsewhere he advocates a limited role for religion in the national culture. More than once, Qutb insists along with 'Aqqad that religion must be independent of literature. He portrays the role of religion in the public realm as primarily one of mediation between the individual and the society. Religion must be separate from science as well, he argues, to maintain the integrity of each. Any attempt to bring them together would mean the end of religion, for while religion is grounded upon the convictions of one's conscience, science is based on sensory experience. If forced to choose between them, Qutb warns, people will give credence to experience over faith.

92. Of course, Qutb's conclusions were not the only ones drawn by Egyptian and Arab intellectuals, then and now. While some view the Israeli victory over the Arabs as a function of Israelis' greater religiosity—and hence take it as a sign that Arabs must "return" to Islam—still others interpret the Israeli victory as an indication that, on the contrary, the Arabs have not Westernized enough.

93. Qutb had expressed great anxiety about 'Aqqad's influence on his life. At one point, Qutb is found worrying about the possibility of being "annihilated in the personality" of 'Aqqad (Qutb, "Khawatir mutasawiqa fi l-naqd wa l-adab wa al-fann," *al-Risala* 597 [December 11, 1944], 1087–88; cited by Musallam, *The Formative Stages*, 84).

94. Sivan, *Radical Islam*, 67.

95. Qutb, *Signposts*, 159–60.

96. Qutb, *The Islamic Conception and Its Characteristics*, 152.

97. Ronald Nettler suggests that Qutb's understanding of "vice-regency" (specifically In *Fi Zilal al-Qur'an*) draws on the Qur'anic theme of both "humanity's special status as *khalifa* of God and recipient of the divine breath through Adam, progenitor of the race" ("A Modern Islamic Confession of Faith and Conception of Religion," 106, n. 24).

98. Qutb, *Signposts*, 126.

99. Ibid., 134.

100. Ibid., 127.

101. This is an assumption that has largely remained unquestioned among many contemporary Islamist groups. Modern technology, mass media, and state-of-the-art weaponry are used without hesitation to disseminate fundamentalist ideas, to carry out assassinations, and to organize and control mass movements. In addition, sociological studies have found that Egyptian fundamentalist groups draw much of their membership from universities, and that, furthermore, the backgrounds of student and university members are predominantly in the sciences—engineering, medicine, agricultural science, technology, military science, and pharmacy (Ibrahim, "Anatomy of Egypt's Militant Islamic Groups," 440). Davis attempts to explain this phenomenon by suggesting that the absolutism of Islamist interpretations of the world is fully consistent with, if not parasitic upon, the similarly absolutist approach to knowledge in the natural sciences where something is either simply right or simply wrong ("Ideology, Social Class and Islamic Radicalism In Modern Egypt," 146). However, this explanation does not capture the ways in which a certain kind of indeterminacy is taken as a given in the natural sciences.

102. Qutb, *The Islamic Conception and Its Characteristics*, 17.

103. There was, of course, much discussion of the relationship between *'aql* (reasoning) and *naql* (transmission) in the formative years of Islamic scholarship. Yet, as Hodgson points out, when the Ash'ari school (associated with the Shafi'i legal tradition) discussed *'aql* and *naql*, for example, they were "contrasting, properly speaking, not natural evidence to supernatural authority, but subjective conjecture ('reasoning') to (one kind of) objective evidence (transmitted reports)," the latter of which "referred to any evidence of past events or usages, including reports or revelatory events, among others." As opposed to the division of religion from philosophy that came later, then, the Ash'aris illustrate the argument that reason and faith together sustain the Islamic system. "Reliance on transmitted reports, as such, does not exclude or even set special limits to the use of reason; rather, it seems tacitly to imply a choice of the sort of evidence one is to reason about—a choice on the basis of what it is one puts one's faith in" (Hodgson, *The Venture of Islam*, 2:321–22).

104. Qutb, *The Islamic Conception and Its Characteristics*, 52.

105. Ibid., 63–64.

106. Ibid., 20–21.

107. Ibid., 14. This is, of course, Qutb's reading of *modern* Western philosophy. From Plato's forms to Augustine's City of God, premodern Western political philosophy has often been preoccupied with the "transcendent."

108. Ibid.

109. Ahmad Moussalli, "Sayyid Qutb's View of Knowledge," 332.

110. Qutb, *The Islamic Conception and Its Characteristics*, 188–89.

111. Qutb, *Signposts*, pps. 47–48.

112. In *Social Justice in Islam*, this dichotomy is between Islam and what Qutb calls "the Crusader Spirit," a spirit perhaps best characterized as a kind of globalizing materialism. Indeed, Qutb concludes *Social Justice* with the argument that a shared materialism makes the distinction between communism and the West meaningless.

113. Haddad, "The Quranic Justification for an Islamic Revolution," 21.

114. Although, as Shepard notes, Qutb eventually attempts to purge even this vestige of Western influence from his work by articulating a view of history without direction most explicitly in *The Islamic Conception and Its Characteristics*. Yet even Shepard acknowledges that Qutb by no means embraces a narrative of decline: "In his last stage Sayyid Qutb retains a motive for change perhaps functionally equivalent to that supplied by the myth of progress" ("The Myth of Progress in the Writings of Sayyid Qutb," 262.

115. Qutb, *Signposts*, 184.

116. Ibid., 75–76.

117. Given the connotation of *jihad* in the West, it is important to note that in the Islamic tradition, the "greater *jihad*" (*jihad al-akbar*) is actually the inner struggle of the Muslim against Satan. The battle against the infidels is often termed the "lesser" *jihad*, although Rudolph Peters points out that, without qualification, *jihad* usually connotes holy war (*Islam and Colonialism*, 10).

118. Goldberg, "Smashing Idols and the State."

119. Qutb, *Signposts*, 60–61.

120. Ibid., 74.

121. Ibid., 82.

122. Quoted in ibid, 94.

123. While Qutb challenges the Sunni orthodoxy that early in Islamic history there was a "closing of the gates of *ijtihad*," he reserves for his own interpretation the status of truth despite a long and rich history of contested Qur'anic interpretations.

124. Ibid., 100–101.

125. Haddad, "The Qur'anic Justification for an Islamic Revolution," 24.

126. *Signposts*, 31–32.

127. Ibid., 34.

128. Roy, *The Failure of Political Islam*, 61.

129. Avineri, *The Social and Political Thought of Karl Marx*, 138.

130. Binder, *Islamic Liberalism*, 203.

131. Qutb, *Signposts*, 40.

132. Although in *Fi Zilal al-Qur'an* (4:2006), Qutb distinguishes between two different kinds of *fiqh*, the static and irrelevant *fiqh* of the 'Ulama' [*fiqh awraq*] and a dynamic *fiqh* [*fiqh haraki*] in tune with the conditions of the modern world. However, as Shepard rightly points out, the contrast between *shari'a* and *fiqh* becomes less important to Qutb in his later writings, where the contrast between Islam and *jahiliyya* becomes central, and as Qutb becomes less critical of traditional Islam (Shepard, Personal communication).

133. On a cautionary note, in this earlier book Qutb often evaluates Islam in terms of Western categories, and, as Leonard Binder suggests, it at times pressages the apologies he would later revile in *Signposts* (*Islamic Liberalism*, 186).

134. *Shura*—along with the concepts of *bay'a* (contract of allegiance to the Caliph), *ijma'* (consensus—in theory, the unanimous agreement of all believers in general, and in particular, the consensus of those most qualified to make decisions on juridical matters), and *ahl al-hall wal-'aqd* (those that loose and bind)—has received a fair amount of attention in the context of debates about the potential for Islamic democracy.

135. Qutb, *Social Justice in Islam*, 95.

136. Qutb, *Islamic Liberalism*, 205.

137. Wolin, *Politics and Vision*, 53–55.

138. Qutb, *Social Justice in Islam*, 103, 143.

139. Qutb, *al-Salam al-'Alami wal-Islam*, 63.

140. Musallam, *The Formative Stages*, 205.

141. Aristotle, *The Politics of Aristotle*, book 1.

142. Here Qutb quotes from "Possession and Religious Theory in Islamic Law" by Muhammad Abu Zuhra: "That possession is not established unless confirmed and ratified by the law is a matter agreed upon by Islamic jurists. All rights, among them the right of possession, are not established unless ratified by their lawgivers. Right of possession is not an intrinsic quality of things but rather arises from the sanction of the law." Qutb goes on to say that all property belongs to the community. However, much like John Locke, he also argues that the right of acquisition is achieved through work—although such work includes not only hunting, irrigating, wage-labor, and mining, but also raiding the possessions of unbelievers killed by a Muslim (*Social Justice in Islam*, 111).

143. A 1982 work in German reviews many of the publications and conferences undertaken by research institutes, banks, and government agencies to develop principles of an Islamic political economy. Although there are many different versions of what an Islamic economy should look like, much of the literature seems to cohere around some key principles, most of which are fully in line with Qutb's arguments (Volker Nienhaus, *Islam und moderne Wirtschaft*). Reviewed by Ira M. Lapidus, *Middle East Journal*, 773–74.

144. Qutb, *Social Justice in Islam*, 256.

145. Ibid., 67.

146. Shepard notes that Qutb's socialism, like that of many other Egyptian intellectuals, was more Fabian than anything else (Shepard, personal communication).

147. The five pillars of Islam are *zakat*, *salat* (prayer), *shahada* (the profession of faith), the *hajj* (pilgrimage to Mecca), and *saum* (fasting).

148. In 1951 Qutb devoted an entire book to an assault on capitalism: *Ma'rakat al-Islam wal-Ra'smaliyya* [*The Battle of Islam and Capitalism*].

149. 2:215, 2:263–68, 3:91, 3:133–34, 4:37–38, 14:31, 24:22, 35:29–30, 57:18, 63:10–11, 64:15–16, 68:17–33, 74:43–48, 90:12–16.

150. Shahrough Akhavi, "The Dialectic in Contemporary Egyptian Social Thought." Olivier Carré also argues that the concept of "social justice" became a feature of Sunni Islamic political thought in the years 1949–1951 in part through Sayyid Qutb as well as through Muhammad al-Ghazzali and 'Abd al-Qadir (Olivier Carré and Gerard Michaud, *Les Freres musulmans*, 84, 223). Indeed, social justice was a topic common to many educated circles in Egypt in the 1940s.

151. Haddad, "The Qur'anic Justification for an Islamic Revolution."

152. As Bernard Lewis notes, the anti-imperialist tone of Muslim discontent during this century, coupled with an ever-widening gap between rich and poor, generated a set of concerns often associated with Marxist or socialist movements ("Communism and Islam," 313–317.

153. Roy, *The Failure of Political Islam*, 133.

154. Such suspicion of minorities varies from region to region. As Sivan notes, in Upper Egypt where Coptic Christians constitute a sizable minority, there was much talk about the "Coptic danger," an anxiety rarely heard in Lower Egypt, for example (*Radical Islam*, 79).

155. Qutb, *Signposts*, 56–62.

156. Qutb, *Social Justice in Islam*, 25.

157. Bernard Lewis, CH. Pellat, and J. Schacht, eds, *The Encyclopædia of Islam*, "Fitna."

158. Qutb, *Signposts*, 90.

159. Qutb, *Social Justice in Islam*, 175, 195.

160. Quoted by Sivan, *Radical Islam*, 73.

161. Ayubi, *Political Islam*, 218.

162. Qutb, *Social Justice in Islam*, 156, 202, 256. Qutb's reference to "preferential treatment" here is a critique of aristocratic privilege and patronage, not affirmative action as it is understood in the United States.

163. In his dissertation, John Calvert similarly situates Qutb's work and radicalization in the context of the modern Egyptian state and the hegemony of its elites. ("Discourse, Community and Power").

164. Kepel, *Muslim Extremism*, 52.

165. Sivan, *Radical Islam*, 77.

166. Ibid., 38. Qutb's argument here is not unlike that of some subaltern studies scholars of India who contend that nationalism is an "ideological humanism engendered from colonialist discourse" (*Cosmopolitics*, 21, n. 2). Indeed, Qutb's critique of nationalism in favor of a supranational political entity— the Muslim *umma*—lends support to recent books, such as *Cosmopolitics*, that emphasize the relevance of transnational and subnational allegiances in a postcolonial, increasingly globalized world. However, Qutb's critique here need not be in the service of postnationalist arguments in contemporary cultural studies that there is something like a "global/ national duality" such that "what one wins, the other loses" (Saskia Sassen, *Globalization and Its Discontents*, xxvii). Indeed, many argue that such a zero-sum opposition between globalization and nation makes little sense because first, the "shift towards the idea of the homogeneous unitary nation-state was itself one aspect of the [globalization] process and should not be misunderstood as an impediment, for it was itself an idea which became rapidly globalized" (Featherstone, "Global Culture," 6), and, second, while economic globalization "does indeed extend the economy beyond the boundaries of the nation-state" a key component of this transformation is the "formation of new claims on national states to guarantee the domestic and global rights of capital" (Sassen, *Globalization and Its Discontents*, xxvii; see also *Cosmopolitics*, 30–38). Moreover, while Qutb defines the *umma* in opposition to the nation-state, the very conception of membership in a Muslim *umma* emerged in Islam's formative period; it is "produced" neither in opposition to the nation-state nor by globalization, although such developments might arguably intensify its appeal.

167. This observation does not negate the ways in which Qutb's radicalism can be seen as a modern version of the Khawarij (plural of *Khariji*, meaning outsider or seceder), a revolutionary break-off sect that came into being twenty-five years after the Prophet's death. Enayat argues that the Khawarij were characterized by "strict adherence to the letter of the Book . . . [the] exaltation of action as a criterion of faith," the use of violence against enemies, and an insistence on the right of all Muslims to rule or to determine the ruler (*Modern Islamic Political Thought*, 6–7). It is also compatible with John Voll's effort to place Qutb and other modern Islamists within a long tradition of *tajdid* (renewal) and *islah* (reform), one that Voll argues has been ongoing from the ninth century to the present ("Renewal and Reform in Islamic History"). Moreover, Qutb was a Hanbalite, and al-Azmeh points out that the Hanbali school was originally "characterized by a moralistic rigour which homogenizes public life on the one hand, and an economic liberalism on the other, much like some early Protestant politics." The Islamism inspired by Qutb and Mawdudi is thus indebted to such medieval Hanbalite moralism as well as Wahhabite literalism along with a marked tendency to absorb "much of the social and economic programmes of left-wing movements" (*Islams and Modernities*, 78, 99, 101).

168. Another case in point is Qutb's emphasis on Islam as a "system," rather than as a faith. As Shepard argues, this emphasis is part of a gradual trend of Muslims over the centuries to reify Islam. Such "reification" is itself a product of the tendency to view Islam from the outsider's point of view. Furthermore, despite Qutb's emphasis on Islamic purity, his view of Islam as a "system" recalls the neo-Platonic view of a cosmos as a "system of conceptions coordinated to work for some useful end" (Philo, *Works*, vol. 6). "Perhaps it is fair to say that in Sayyid Qutb's concept of Islam as a 'system' Greece has entered the Muslim tradition—partly via the classical Muslim philosophers and partly via its offspring, the West, and altered the measuring rods of the Muslim mind, but without conquering Islam" (Shepard, "Islam as a 'System' in the Later Writings of Sayyid Qutb," 45.

169. Of course, the distinctively pragmatist turn in *Signposts* is in the service of an absolute truth. This is in stark contrast to the philosophical pragmatism he rejects in *Social Justice in Islam*. In this earlier work he virtually condemns pragmatism as dangerous, insisting that its logic leads to the negation of God's existence and the reduction of humans to the status of mere instrument, although Qutb removes this discussion of pragmatism in the last edition of *Social Justice in Islam*, perhaps because, as Shepard suggests, Qutb no longer considered it worthwhile to engage with *jahili* thought in this way (Shepard, *Sayyid Qutb and Islamic Activism*, xliv).

170. Indeed, scholars such as Richard Falk have pointed out that both liberal and Marxist states are expressions of the same modern, Western project ("Religion and Politics," 381–82).

171. The "rationalism" to which I am referring is generally associated with the European Enlightenment and must be distinguished from the variety of "rationalisms" in Western thought, most notably in its Greek, and specifically Aristotelian, variety. In contrast to modern rationalism, Greek rationalism viewed reason as the means by which to discover and appreciate the order of nature underlying all things. Concomitantly, as Arendt argues, "modern science is based on a philosophy of doubt, as distinguished from ancient science, which was based on a philosophy of *thaumadzein*, or wonder at that which is as it is" ("Religion and Politics," 370). Greek

rationalism influenced Islamic philosophy, and, as will become clear in the following chapter, Qutb objects to the project of the Islamic philosophers as well. Yet in that context, Qutb's complaints have more to do with the way Islamic philosophers incorporated what was foreign to, and therefore corrupting of, Islam than with the intentional and explicit negation of divine authority.

172. Dallmayr, *Alternative Visions*, 2. Foucault argues that we must "refuse everything that might present itself in the form of a simplistic and authoritarian alternative: you either accept the Enlightenment and remain within the tradition of rationalism . . . or else you criticize the Enlightenment and try to escape from its principles of rationality" (Foucault, "What Is Enlightenment?," *The Foucault Reader*, 42–43).

173. The obvious example of this is his treatment of the principle of *shura* (consultation), where he argues both that *shura* is an absolute principle but that it will be realized in different ways at different historical moments. This is an important point given Qutb's argument that *ijtihad* (personal or human interpretation) can come into play, but only when the Qur'an and Sunna do not dictate a specific practice, and even then is strictly delimited by Islamic principles (*Signposts*, 94–95). Shepard's discussion of the relationship between "fixity" and "flexibility" in Qutb's Islam is illuminating here ("Islam as a 'System,' " 36–37).

174. He is, however, open about, for example, the details of the Islamic state, and Shepard further suggests that in his earlier Islamist writing Qutb reveals more uncertainty about his own approach than in later Islamist works (Shepard, personal communication).

175. Ira M. Lapidus, "Islamic Revival and Modernity," 448.

176. Hammoudi, *Master and Disciple*, xx.

177. This is evident in Bassam Tibi's excellent discussion of contemporary Sunni Islamist attitudes toward science and technology ("The Worldview of Sunni Arab Fundamentalists," 73–78).

178. Hannah Arendt, "What Is Authority?," 103.

179. Gellner argues that the "shrill 'post-modernist' pan relativism" is a dogmatism that legitimates what he calls "cognitive egalitarianism." According to Gellner, this view entails the assumptions that all interpretations are equally viable since no one interpretation is objectively true. Gellner parodies this position at length in *Postmodernism, Reason and Religion*.

180. Isaiah Berlin, "Joseph de Maistre and the Origins of Fascism," 130.

181. The parallels between de Maistre and Qutb only strengthen Berlin's point in regard to this analysis. For example, Qutb and de Maistre share what can only be called a nonrationalist argument: for both, the world has at its center a deep mystery that eludes human reason. Religion is thus superior to reason "not because it returns more convincing answers to reason, but because it returns no answer at all. . . . It does not persuade or argue, it commands" (ibid., 130). Revealingly, the European thinker to whom Qutb refers repeatedly and favorably is Alexis Carrel, a French Nobel Prize winner in science who later served in the Vichy government. Carrel's book, *Man the Unknown*, is quoted at length by Qutb in *The Islamic Concept and Its Characteristics*, and Qutb's *al-Islam wa Mushkilat al-Hadara* [Islam and the Problems of Civilization] is full of references to Carrel. The connections between Qutb and fascist thought are discussed by al-Azmeh; Said Amir Arjomand also explores the fascinating parallels between the Iranian Revolution and European fascism in "The Iranian Revolution in

Comparative Perspective." Carrel's book was also widely read by Shi'ite modernists (H. E. Chehabi, *Iranian Politics and Religious Modernism*, 46–50).

182. Sheldon S. Wolin, *Hobbes and the Epic Tradition of Political Theory*, 4.

183. Berlin, "Joseph de Maistre and the Origins of Fascism," 161–62.

184. Ernest Gellner, "Letter to the Editor." The initial review by Gellner is "The Mightier Pen?: Edward Said and the Double Standards of Inside-out Colonialism." A series of exchanges among Gellner, Said, and their supporters followed this initial review from February to April 1993 in *The Times Literary Supplement* (Said's response, "Letter to the Editor.") The exchanges between Said and Gellner eventually deteriorate into mutual denunciations and wars over which books are important and which are not. This exchange can be regarded as the latest installment in the "Orientalism" debate between Said and Middle Eastern scholars about what counts as valid scholarship, which criteria can be legitimately employed in scholarship on the Middle East, and whose credentials confer the greater authority to judge its quality. The two most prominent antagonists in this debate are Said and the historian Bernard Lewis. For Said's discussion of Lewis's work, see *Orientalism*, 314–21. For Lewis's most recent response, see his chapter entitled "The Question of Orientalism," in *Islam and the West*.

CHAPTER FOUR
A VIEW ACROSS TIME

1. Geertz, "Thick Description," 14.

2. I place "modernism" within quotation marks here to signal the ways in which what is called Islamic "modernism" is not an uncomplicated embrace of the ideas and processes constitutive of what we in the West identify as modernity, but rather reflects a complex and eclectic amalgamation of Western ideas and reinterpreted Islamic traditions. For all future references, then, modernism is meant to signal this syncretism.

3. Qutb, *The Islamic Conception and Its Characteristics*, 17–21.

4. Qutb, *Signposts*, 159–60.

5. Qutb, *The Islamic Conception and Its Characteristics*, 20.

6. There is some terminological confusion, however. For example, Muhammad 'Abduh's student, Muhammad Rashid Rida (1865–1935) is more often referred to as the leader of the *salafiyya* movement in contradistinction to the modernist school. By contrast, Sylvia Haim argues that Afghani and 'Abduh "inaugurated" the *salafiyya* movement, but that Rashid Rida was its "undoubted intellectual leader" (*Arab Nationalism: An Anthology*, 20). Other scholars have described Afghani or 'Abduh as the "founders" or the center of Islamic modernism or revival; still others have argued that the *salafiyya* project unites the work of 'Abduh and Rida. Moreover, Lapidus persuasively argues that there is a difference between Islamic modernism and Islamic reformism: Islamic reformism should be identified with the *'ulama'*, Islamic modernism should be associated with Muslim elites and intelligentsias (*A History of Islamic Societies*, 560–70). What is clear is that Afghani, 'Abduh, and Rida are all central to nineteenth-century Islamic revival, a conclusion echoed by M. A. Said Badawi's *The Reformers of Egypt*, and in keeping with al-Azmeh's suggestion that

salafiyya can be regarded as a generic term that captures the call to "return to the Koran and the salutary example of pious epigones (the *salaf*)" (*Islams and Modernities*, 87, n. 1). Yet adding to the confusion are the ways in which Afghani's and 'Abduh's ideas subsequently influenced a diverse array of movements and people: as Anouar Abdel Malek argues, 'Abduh's ideas, for example, simultaneously influenced Mustafa Kamel's (Atatürk) National Party, the renovation of al-Azhar, and Rashid Rida's "fundamentalism" (Abdel Malek, *Egypt*, 202).

7. Such a Golden Age of Islam is generally identified as the time from the Prophet Muhammad through the period of the "Rightly Guided Caliphs" (621–661).

8. Hisham Sharabi, *Arab Intellectuals and the West*, 27.

9. Albert Hourani, *Arabic Thought in the Liberal Age*, 103.

10. Ibid., 104.

11. Sharabi, *Arab Intellectuals and the West*, 31.

12. The modernist school has also encompassed, among others, the more conservative political thought of Muhammad Rashid Rida. Yet while Afghani, 'Abduh, and Rida all strove for a revitalization of Islam, only Rida interpreted such revival as, in Haim's words, a "puritanical revival of strict Islamic practices and religious fervor; it was for this reason that [like Qutb] he was a Hanbalite, following the strictest of the four schools of Islamic law, and that he later cast his lot with the Saudi and the Wahhabi revival" (Haim, *Arab Nationalism*, 21). Indeed, it is Rida who is often credited with initiating the Ibn Taymiyya (d. 1328) renaissance in Egypt (although Qutb still complains that Rida tended to stretch the Qur'anic text inappropriately in an attempt to bring it into conformity with reason (*The Islamic Conception and Its Characteristics*, 20). Thus I focus on Afghani and 'Abduh in the interests of exploring the diversity of views grouped under the umbrella of "Islamic revival."

13. Hourani, *Arabic Thought in the Liberal Age*, 130; B. Michel et le Cheikh Moustapha 'Abdel Razik, *Cheikh Mohammed 'Abdou: Rissalat al-Tawhid* (Paris, 1925), p. xlii, cited by C. C. Adams, *Islam and Modernism in Egypt*, 2.

14. W. C. Smith, *Islam in Modern History*, 47–51.

15. Sharabi, in his *Arab Intellectuals and the West*, and Hasan Rida exemplify the literature extremely skeptical both of the intellectual powers of Afghani and 'Abduh, and of the substantive merit of their work (Rida, "Les discussions sur le système social prennent l'aspect de controverses grammaticales," *L'Égypte nassèrienne* [Paris, 1964], cited by Sharabi, 35). Among the texts that challenge their sincerity are Elie Kedourie, *Afghani and 'Abduh*; and Nikki Keddie, *An Islamic Response to Imperialism* and *The Roots of Revolution*.

16. Keddie, *An Islamic Response to Imperialism*, 96, 3.

17. Haim, *Arab Nationalism*, 6, 10, 15.

18. Abdallah Laroui outlines the Enlightenment spirit of Afghani's reformism in *Islam et modernité*. al-Azmeh notes the irony in the ways contemporary Islamic fundamentalism has "resurrected the Romanticism of Afghani and re-established him as the fount of authenticity and its main proponent and, indeed, its idol" (*Islams and Modernities*, 54).

19. Afghani, "Lecture on Teaching and Learning," *An Islamic Response to Imperialism*, 107. I have relied on Keddie's excellent translation of this and Afghani's other works from the original Persian.

20. Most of these biographical details are drawn from Hourani's *Arabic Thought in the Liberal Age* and Keddie's two seminal works on Afghani: *An Islamic Response to Imperialism*, and *Sayyid Jamal al-Din "al-Afghani."* Much of what Keddie calls the "standard biography" of Afghani has been based either on what Afghani said about himself during his lifetime or on the work of "admiring biographers" such as Muhammad 'Abduh or Jurjī Zaidān, both of whom tended to take Afghani's own account of his life as definitive.

21. Badawi, *The Reformers of Egypt*, 7.

22. Keddie, *Sayyid Jamal al-Din "al-Afghani,"* and *An Islamic Response to Imperialism*. A similar argument is also made by Haim in *Arab Nationalism*.

23. Kedourie, *Afghani and 'Abduh*. By contrast, Keddie avoids the charge of "unbelief," preferring to refer to Afghani, for example, as an "Islamic deist." But in a later book she attributes a "secret secularism" to him (*The Roots of Revolution*, 188).

24. Although the term "pan-Islamism" was originally coined by Turkish Young Ottomans, Afghani is credited with spreading its call for superseding sectarian, class, and territorial divisions to unify all Muslims in a single community capable of recapturing the greatness and strength of Islamic civilization in its heyday.

25. Although there is no surviving text of the talk, Keddie infers its content from various responses and commentaries (*An Islamic Response to Imperialism*, 17).

26. "Lecture on Teaching and Learning," 104–5.

27. Ibid., 102.

28. The argument that Islam had contributed substantially to what is now European knowledge was made by earlier writers such as Tahtawi and Khayr al-Din, who argued that the adoption of "Western knowledge" constituted not imitation but reclamation.

29. Ibid., 107.

30. Ibid., 104.

31. Gibb, *Modern Trends in Islam*, 65.

32. Afghani, "Refutation," *An Islamic Response to Imperialism*, 140.

33. Afghani, "Commentary on the Commentator," *An Islamic Response to Imperialism*, 126–27.

34. Hourani, *Arabic Thought in the Liberal Age*, 109.

35. Keddie, *Roots of Revolution*, 66.

36. Muhammad al-Makhzumi, *Khatirat Jamal al-Din al-Afghani al-Husayni* [Thoughts of Jamal al-Din al-Afghani al-Husayni] (Beirut, 1931), 88, cited by Sharabi, *Arab Intellectuals and the West*, 26.

37. Afghani, "The Benefits of Philosophy," *An Islamic Response to Imperialism*, 110, 113–14.

38. Afghani, "Refutation," *An Islamic Response to Imperialism*, 142.

39. Here Afghani posits a dubious contrast between the inherent rationality of Islam and the irrationality of Christianity, which has at its core the worship of the Trinity.

40. Ibid., 171.

41. Keddie, *An Islamic Response to Imperialism*, 38. As with Afghani's dim view of most people's capacity to reason, and his linkage of virtue and knowledge, Keddie (p. 48) suggests that this de facto primacy of reason is an extension of Islamic philosophy, and moreover an attempt to rewrite the outcome of the ancient debate between

philosophers who argued that reason was the path to truth, and (victorious) theologians who argued that truth was given by authority.

42. Qutb, *The Islamic Conception and Its Characteristics*, 20.

43. Afghani, "Answer of Jamal ad-Din to Renan," *An Islamic Response to Imperialism*, 183.

44. Badawi, *The Reformers of Egypt*, 25.

45. The apparent inconsistency in Afghani's writings surely betrays the complexity of the relationship between political activism and theories of reform, oppositional politics and the conservatizing force of actual power. Yet his writings do not, it seems to me, clearly sustain the contention advanced by Kedourie that as "what is done has no necessary connection with what is said, and that what is said in public, may be quite different from what is believed in private," Afghani was actually an unbeliever (Kedourie, *Afghani and 'Abduh*, 2). Kedourie's thesis rests upon his assertion, for example, that he can determine which of Afghani's commitments are "authentic" and which are acts of deception: "How much of what Afghani says can be believed? For him speech more frequently serves to persuade and deceive, but it is clear that on occasion we may take him to be speaking the truth." But Kedourie provides no criteria by which to judge which inconsistencies indicate Afghani's insincerity and which statements express "convictions which lay close to his heart" (p. 52). The difficulty of retrospectively distinguishing between what is "authentic" and what is merely duplicitous, and the questions begged by assuming a single definition of what it means to be a "real Muslim" mean that, in the end, I am inclined to agree with Hourani that Kedourie's thesis regarding Afghani is far from obvious (Hourani, "Preface to the 1983 Reissue," *Arabic Thought in the Liberal Age*, viii).

46. Keddie, *Islamic Response to Imperialism*, 38.

47. See Keddie's discussion, *An Islamic Response to Imperialism*, 84–95.

48. Ernest Renan, *Journal des Debats*, May 19, 1883; H. E. Chehabi, *Iranian Politics and Religious Modernism*, 51.

49. Hourani, *Arabic Thought in the Liberal Age*, 122–23.

50. This argument appears in Sharif al-Mujahid's "Sayyid Jamal al-Din al-Afghani," 79–89, and Keddie endorses it in *An Islamic Response to Imperialism*.

51. *Mu'tazila* refers to a school of speculative theology founded in Basra in the first half of the eighth century, and which continued to flourish in Baghdad and Basra in the eighth to tenth centuries. It was made the official theology of the *umma* in the caliphate of al-Ma'mun (827–849) but became marginal over the course of the centuries. However, Akhavi argues that *Mu'tazili* doctrines continue to be important for Shi'i thought: *Mu'tazili* emphases upon reason (*'aql*) and independent judgment (*ijtihad*) are evident not only in Afghani's work, but also in the writings of such Shi'i *mujtahids* as Ansari (d. 1864), Na'ini (d. 1936), and Khomeini and Taliqani (d. 1979), and lay intellectuals such as 'Ali Shari'ati (d. 1977) and Abd al-Karim Surush (Akhavi, personal communication, May 11, 1998; and "Mu'tazila," *Encyclopedia of Islam: New Edition*, vol. 7 (Leiden: E. J. Brill, 1992).

52. "Mu'tazila," *Encyclopedia of Islam*, 791.

53. Hourani, *Arabic Thought in the Liberal Age*, 108; Keddie, *The Roots of Revolution*.

54. Watt, *An Islamic Philosophy and Theology*, 47. According to Watt, the most influential of the Islamic neoplatonists following in al-Kindi's footsteps were Abu 'Ali

ibn Sina (Avicenna) and al-Farabi, the latter of whom became known as the "second teacher"—Aristotle having been the first. Al-Farabi's neoplatonism also incorporated the work of Aristotle: Watt aptly describes his philosophy as "having a foundation in Aristotelianism, and a superstructure of Neoplatonic metaphysics" (pp. 54–55).

55. Keddie, *An Islamic Response to Imperialism*, 46.

56. al-Afghani, "The Benefits of Philosophy," 116. It is interesting to note that this very argument about the indebtedness of Greek culture to non-Western cultures has been advanced by Martin Bernal's *Black Athena*, sparking an extraordinary amount of controversy in classical studies. Contrary to Afghani's suggestion, however, the Greeks themselves were more than willing to acknowledge their debt to other cultures: as many scholars have noted, Herodotus believed that the founder of Thebes, Cadmus, was a Semite, and that some of the names of the Greek gods were Egyptian. Diodorus of Sicily acknowledged a tremendous debt to Egyptian culture, and some Greek philosophers even suggested a connection between Plato's philosophy and the teachings of Moses (Glen Bowersock, "Rescuing the Greeks," 6).

57. 'Abduh, *al-Islam wa al-Nasraniyya* [Islam and Christianity], 149.

58. 'Abduh, *Risalat al-Tawhid* (hereafter referred to as *The Theology of Unity*), 176. All translations from this work are my own, from the original Arabic.

59. These biographical details are drawn from C. C. Adams's *Islam and Modernism in Egypt*; Hourani's *Arabic Thought in the Liberal Age*; Kedourie's *Afghani and 'Abduh*; and Badawi's *The Reformers of Egypt*.

60. 'Abduh's first book, in 1874, was a reflection on mysticism entitled *Risalat al-Waridat* (Mystic Inspirations).

61. 'Abduh, *Theology of Unity*, 143.

62. Ibid., 83–84.

63. Muhammad 'Abduh, *Al-Manar*, vii, 292, cited in C. C. Adams, *Islam and Modernism in Egypt*, 136.

64. 'Abduh, *Theology of Unity*, 18–32.

65. Ibid., 122.

66. Ibid., 143–52.

67. Ibid., 26–32.

68. Ibid., 147.

69. Adams, *Islam and Modernism in Egypt*, 95, 167.

70. Hourani, *Arabic Thought in the Liberal Age*, 143–44.

71. This particular balance between reason and revealed truth recalls not only the eighteenth- and nineteenth-century European debates over reason and religion, but also the theological arguments about the place of rationalism in a divinely ordered cosmos engaged in by such thinkers as St. Augustine and St. Thomas Aquinas.

72. 'Abduh was particularly attuned to the growing gulf in an educational system increasingly split between traditional Islamic education and a parallel system of schooling based on the European model.

73. 'Abduh, *Theology of Unity*, 55.

74. Ibid., 108.

75. Ibid., 64.

76. Sharabi argues that while 'Abduh's (and Afghani's) emphasis on the rationality of Islam opened the door for radical critiques of religious dogma, in fact neither

thinker seriously challenged much of Islamic doctrine; the emphasis on reaffirming the "true" Islam was tantamount to an affirmation of fairly traditional orthodoxies of Islamic faith (*Arab Intellectuals and the West*). Malcolm Kerr similarly suggests that 'Abduh avoided many radical departures from traditional doctrine, yet he was a "conservative by language and manner and a radical by the implication of many of his teachings" (*Islamic Reform*, 105).

77. 'Abduh, *Theology of Unity*, 120.

78. Ibid., 118.

79. Ibid., 19.

80. Kerr, *Islamic Reform*, 125.

81. Ibid., 127.

82. Nadav Safran, *Egypt in Search of Political Community*, 69.

83. 'Abduh, *Theology of Unity*, 122.

84. Ibid., 181.

85. Kerr, *Islamic Reform*, 110.

86. 'Abduh, *Theology of Unity*, 112; Kerr, *Islamic Reform*, 129.

87. Rida, *Tarikh al-Ustadh al-Imam al-Shaikh Muhammad 'Abduh*, 1:11–12, cited in Kerr, *Islamic Reform*, 109.

88. Adams, *Islam and Modernism in Egypt*, 69, n. 4.

89. Ibid., 79.

90. Kedourie, *Afghani and 'Abduh*, 38–39.

91. Kerr, *Islamic Reform*, 151.

92. Adams, *Islam and Modernism in Egypt*, 80. Osman Amin echoes this estimation: 'Abduh, Amin says, "did not limit his office to the mere function of answering whatever questions were put to him, as his predecessors had done, but saw it as something higher than that: he broadened its special powers and filled it with a prestige and influence hitherto unknown" (*Muhammad 'Abduh*, 79). Hourani's estimate of 'Abduh's activities as Mufti is more restrained but generally in keeping with the conclusion that 'Abduh helped reinterpret religious law "in accordance with the needs of the age" (*Arabic Thought in the Liberal Age*, 134).

93. Kerr, *Islamic Reform*, 150. For example, he endorses the view that Qur'anic teachings differ in matters political from matters religious. Some Muslim intellectuals who followed him concluded that there is an Islamic equivalent to the Western separation between church and state. Yet 'Abduh did not support this conclusion. For 'Abduh as for Qutb, the legitimacy of political authority is always determined by the adherence of the ruler to Islamic law, not to the terms of a political contract between ruler and ruled.

94. Ibid., 147.

95. Hourani, *Arabic Thought in the Liberal Age*, 144.

96. See Hourani's chapter on "'Abduh's Disciples: Islam and Modern Civilization" in *Arabic Thought in the Liberal Age*, 161–92; and Detlev Khalid, "Ahmad Amin and the Legacy of Muhammad 'Abduh," for discussions of the successors to 'Abduh's reformism.

97. Hourani, *Arabic Thought in the Liberal Age*, 162. In a different take, al-Azmeh suggests that little of Afghani's "irrationalist vitalism" remained in 'Abduh's naturalistic and ultilitarian interpretation of Islam (*Islams and Modernities*, 53).

98. Gibb, *Modern Trends in Islam*, 69–70.

99. al-Azmeh underscores both Western Enlightenment and "anti-Enlightenment" influences on Islamic modernism. For example, he suggests that 'Abduh's Islamic reformism is "much in keeping with the laudatory ideas, some Enlightenment thinkers held about Islam as a natural religion, superior to Christianity on this score, and in keeping with the natural course of life." And while Laroui demonstrates the ways in which Afghani's reformism was in the spirit of the Enlightenment, al-Azmeh also argues that Afghani's notion of authenticity owes something to Herder and the German historical school of law associated with Savigny (Abdallah Laroui, *Islam et modernité*; al-Azmeh, *Islams and Modernities*, 44, 52–53).

100. Şerif Mardin points to a similar paradox in the work of the Turkish Islamist Bediüzzaman Said Nursi (1876–1960) (Mardin, *Religion and Social Change in Modern Turkey*); and Sami Zubaida suggests that "even a doctrine as apparently immune to the influence of Western models as Khomeini's *wilayat al-faqih* (guardianship of the jurist) relies upon presuppositions about politics that are the product of Western practices since the late 18th century" (Shahrough Akhavi, "Review," 355; Zubaida, *Islam, the People and the State*).

101. For an excellent overview, see Hamid Enayat's "Shi'ism and Sunnism: Conflict and Concord," in his *Modern Islamic Political Thought*.

102. Khomeini, "Veils of Darkness, Veils of Light," in *Islam and Revolution*, 394.

103. Khomeini, "He Is the Outward and the Inward," in *Islam and Revolution*, 410. Paradoxically, however, Khomeini's work is characterized by a tension similar to that which haunts Qutb. Khomeini's insistence on the primacy of human intuition over reason is undercut by the extraordinarily *rationalist* form and content of his arguments. For example, he repeatedly tells us of the ways in which reason makes the need for Islamic government both urgent and obvious. Although Khomeini invokes the authority of reason along with that of revealed law and the example of Muhammad (pp. 42, 51), Akhavi concludes that Khomeini "is a mystic who rejects logic in the search for truth . . . but he uses reason above all other classical Islamic methods in his formal arguments on behalf of clerical rule" ("Islam, Politics and Society," 428).

104. Alexander Knysh, "*Irfan* Revisited," 651.

105. Akhavi, "Islam, Politics and Society," 406.

106. It is possible that for both Afghani and 'Abduh, the issue of sovereignty was less central because the Islamic *umma* still nominally existed with its head in Istanbul. With the abolition of the Sultanate in 1922, and of the Caliphate in 1924 by Turkey's Mustafa Kemal (Atatürk), questions about the nature and viability of Islamic government assumed a new importance. Furthermore, the range of political possibilities at that time was sharply constrained by the actualities of colonialist occupation: as Rashid Rida notes, 'Abduh's occasional political proposals must be seen as representing 'Abduh's sense of what was possible under British occupation, rather than a theory of ideal politics (Rashid Rida *Tarikh al-Ustadh al-Imam al-Shaikh Muhammad 'Abduh* [Cairo: Al-Manar Manar Press, 1931], 1:903–7, cited in Kerr, *Islamic Reform*, 148).

107. Khomeini, "Islamic Government," in *Islam and Revolution*, 66.

108. Ibid., 55.

109. Ibid., 37.

110. Ibid., 67–68.

111. Knysh notes that Khomeini was at one time interested in neoplatonism and in particular in neoplatonist emanational theories that were fairly consistent with aspects of Muslim esotericism ("*Irfan* Revisited," 639).

112. Robinson, "Modern Islam and the Green Menace."

113. Khomeini, "Islamic Government," 44.

114. Ibid., 36. Emphasis in the original.

115. Sivan, however, suggests that Qutb's influence was limited, and the work that made the most impact came before his radicalization. He argues that, by contrast, Qutb's later, more radical thought was highly influential in Turkey. This account is in some tension with Said Amir Arjomand's interpretation, set out in the quote below ("Sunni Radicalism in the Middle East and the Iranian Revolution," 1).

116. Haddad, "Sayyid Qutb," 68; Algar, *Islam and Revolution*, 426, n. 5.

117. Enayat, *Modern Islamic Political Thought*, 93–95.

118. It is interesting to note that Khomeini actually refers to Qutb in a vaguely critical way in his series of lectures on the opening chapter of the Qur'an following the Islamic Revolution in 1979. Specifically, in the lecture entitled "Everything is a Name of God," Khomeini refers to Qutb's *Fi Zilal al-Qur'an* [In the Shade of the Qur'an] as one among several examples of Qur'anic commentaries that focus upon a "single aspect" of the Qur'an rather than a "complete interpretation of the Qur'an with respect to all of its meanings" (Algar, *Islam and Revolution*, 365).

119. Arjomand, "Iran's Islamic Revolution in Comparative Perspective," 407.

120. Mamoun Fandy makes the case that Egyptian Islamism, for example, must be understood in terms of regional differences between north and south ("Egypt's Islamic Group").

121. Arjomand, "Iran's Islamic Revolution in Comparative Perspective," 407–8.

122. See, for example, Sivan's "Sunni Radicalism in the Middle East and the Iranian Revolution," and Arjomand's "Iran's Islamic Revolution in Comparative Perspective."

123. Hammoudi, *Master and Disciple*, xx.

124. Although for Khomeini, training in rationalism and logic is useful as one albeit limited path to knowledge.

125. Indeed, Enayat points out numerous points of convergence between Sunni and Shi'a in recent years, including Khomeini's 1979 *fatwa* exhorting Shi'a to put aside their reluctance to pray behind Sunni leaders during the pilgrimage to Mecca. Enayat, *Modern Islamic Political Thought*, 51.

CHAPTER FIVE
INSIDE THE LOOKING GLASS

1. Bendix suggests that even such champions of the bourgeois individual as Goethe and Proudhon shared with their conservative counterparts the anxiety that these processes were stultifying and inimical to human development ("Tradition and Modernity Reconsidered," 298–300).

2. For example, this perspective is expressed in Leo Strauss's *Natural Right and History*. A radically different Western critique of modernity is advanced in Max Horkheimer and Theodor W. Adorno's *Dialectic of Enlightenment*. Horkheimer and

Adorno argue that enlightenment is not characterized either by a teleological ascent to freedom nor decay, but rather by a dialectical process whereby enlightenment returns to myth and back again.

3. In focusing the following discussion in relation to Qutb's critique of modernity and the sense of degeneration that unites Qutb with others, I am necessarily excluding those whom Charles Taylor would call the "boosters" or supporters of modern culture (*The Ethics of Authenticity*, 22).

4. Wolin, *Hobbes and the Epic Tradition of Political Theory*, 5.

5. Hannah Arendt's critique of modernity is more complicated than this immediately suggests. Her ultimate assessment of modernity continues to be the subject of lively debates among liberals, communitarians, participatory democrats, Habermasians, and others. I will return to this point in my discussion of Arendt's critique of authority.

6. For useful critiques and/or analyses of some of these positions and those of their opponents, see Amy Gutmann, "Communitarian Critics of Liberalism"; and Charles Taylor, "Cross Purposes."

7. Of course, the Western voices represented here do not influence political activists in the way, for example, that *Signposts* influences the contemporary Islamist movement. But while MacIntyre's *After Virtue* may not inspire Jerry Falwell (no doubt to MacIntyre's great relief), there are perhaps looser connections between Western theoretical critiques of rationalism and the strength of "antirationalist" cultural and political tendencies that are worth exploring. At any one moment the *New York Times Book Review* list of nonfiction best-sellers reflects the political purchase of texts addressing the questions of existential meaninglessness and the inadequacy of our rationalist resources to cope with it. These books are a far cry from *After Virtue* or Richard John Neuhaus's *Naked Public Square*, but they are perhaps the counterpart in popular culture of the more abstract critique of rationalism in the academy.

8. Hannah Arendt, "What Was Authority?"

9. Arendt, "What Is Authority?," in *Between Past and Future*, 109.

10. Aristotle *The Politics*, 1328b35; Arendt, "What Is Authority?," 119–20. Arendt's translation of this passage differs substantially from those of Barker and Jowett. Barker's translation is the following: "the best constitution is that under which the state can attain the greatest felicity; and that, as we have already stated, cannot exist without goodness. Upon these principles it clearly follows that a state with an ideal constitution—a state which has for its members men who are absolutely just, and not men who are merely just in relation to some particular standard—cannot have its citizens living the life of mechanics or shopkeepers, which is ignoble and inimical to goodness" (*The Politics*, trans. Ernest Barker).

11. In "On Violence," Arendt argues that coercion exists in the space where legitimate politics ends (*Crises of the Republic*).

12. Arendt, "What Is Authority?," 123.

13. Ibid., 122.

14. Ibid., 124.

15. Arendt, "Religion and Politics," 383.

16. Arendt, "What Is Authority?," 95.

17. John H. Schaar, *Legitimacy in the Modern State*, 33.

18. Ibid., 39.

19. Ibid., 43.
20. Ibid., 36.
21. Arendt, "The Concept of History," in *Between Past and Future*, 89–90.
22. Arendt, *The Human Condition*.
23. Arendt, "The Concept of History," 63–64.
24. Arendt, "The Crisis in Education," in *Between Past and Future*, 195.
25. "The Concept of History," 63; "What Is Authority?," 140. Yet in "What Is Authority?" Arendt concludes that even the French and American Revolutions, those grand attempts to repair these foundations by "renewing the broken thread of tradition," have so far failed to remedy the degradation of meaning in human affairs.
26. Dana Villa, *Arendt and Heidegger*, 270. The debate over Arendt's assessment of modernism is beyond the scope of this chapter. For two alternative readings of Arendt in this regard, see George Kateb, *Hannah Arendt*; and Seyla Benhabib, *The Reluctant Modernism of Hannah Arendt*.
27. Hannah Arendt, "What Is Freedom?," in *Between Past and Future*, 146.
28. Kateb, *Hannah Arendt*, 1.
29. Villa, *Arendt and Heidegger*, 269.
30. Wolin, *Politics and Vision*, 53–55.
31. This is not to deny the extent to which Arendt, for example, viewed material processes such as capitalism and imperialism as a source of human degradation.
32. "Emotivism" was first articulated by Hobbes, who argued that the judgments we make refer not to the thing judged but to our own prejudices, and then rearticulated by logical positivism. See, for example, the work of C. L. Sevenson.
33. MacIntyre, *After Virtue*, 11, 19.
34. Ibid., 22.
35. Ibid., 52.
36. Ibid., 82.
37. Ibid., 59.
38. Ibid., 119.
39. The theme that our moral and community life is littered with remnants of older traditions that can no longer retain their coherence in such fragmented form will return in the discussion of Robert N. Bellah et al., *Habits of the Heart*.
40. MacIntyre, *After Virtue*, 111.
41. Ibid., 250.
42. Ibid., 117–18.
43. Ibid., 109.
44. Ibid.
45. Ibid., 263.
46. Ibid., 259.
47. Ibid., 258.
48. Ibid., 23–24.
49. Taylor, *The Ethics of Authenticity*, 26.
50. Ibid., 29.
51. Daniel Bell, Allan Bloom, and Christopher Lasch are among his targets here.
52. Ibid., 72.
53. Taylor, "Atomism," 57.
54. Taylor, *The Ethics of Authenticity*, 82.

55. Taylor, "Atomism," 60.

56. Thus Neuhaus regards "transcendence" as an integral part of political life, but distinguishes between "good" and "bad" transcendence: he invokes "transcendence" here in the name of democracy and opposes it to the false transcendence manipulated by a despotic state.

57. Neuhaus, *The Naked Public Square*, 80.

58. Ibid., 37.

59. Ibid., 221.

60. Ibid., 82.

61. Ibid., 28; Michael Sandel, *Liberalism and the Limits of Justice*, 182.

62. Neuhaus, *The Naked Public Square*, 126.

63. Ibid., 93.

64. The question, of course, remains: what is the meaning of democracy presupposed here? Neuhaus, for example, at times takes it to mean rule that reflects the majority of people in a given community. But even the more nuanced accounts in these texts do not resolve the question as to the extent to which democracy is fully compatible with, for example, a theologically informed vision of shared ends. This is where Arendt's emphasis on *politics* rather than *community* distinguishes her project from those of MacIntyre, Neuhaus, Taylor, and Qutb.

65. MacIntyre, *After Virtue*, 31.

66. Ibid., 21.

67. Taylor, *The Ethics of Authenticity*, 17.

68. Max Horkheimer and Theodor W. Adorno, *Dialectic of Enlightenment*, xvii.

69. Spragens, *The Irony of Liberal Reason*. In Spragens's narrative, like that of MacIntyre, Kant is portrayed as both the central culprit and the grand theorist.

70. Taylor, *The Ethics of Authenticity*, 4.

71. Ibid., 89.

72. Robert N. Bellah et al., *Habits of the Heart*, vii.

73. Ibid., 335.

74. Ibid., 50, 51, 81, 277.

75. Tocqueville, *Democracy in America*, 692.

76. Bellah et al., *Habits of the Heart*, 296.

77. Ibid., 284.

78. Ibid., 277. The opening passage of Qutb's *Signposts* runs: "Humanity is standing today at the brink of an abyss, not because of the threat of annihilation hanging over its head . . . but because humanity is bankrupt in the realm of 'values,' those values which foster true human progress and development" (p. 3).

79. Bellah, 143.

80. Ibid., 284.

81. Although the historical linkage between capitalism and democracy has been justified by philosophical liberalism, Bell acknowledges a tension between a social structure that is bureaucratic and hierarchical, and a polity that is animated by the belief in equality and participation. This particular tension, however, is not at the heart of the contradictions of capitalism (*The Cultural Contradictions of Capitalism*, 14).

82. Ibid., 19.

83. Ibid., 28.
84. Ibid.
85. Bell, "The Return of the Sacred?," 333.
86. Bell, *The Cultural Contradictions of Capitalism*, 168.
87. Ibid., 155.
88. Ibid., 169.
89. Octavio Paz, *One Earth, Four or Five Worlds*, 7–8.
90. Falk, "Religion and Politics," 382.
91. Bellah's book in particular illustrates what has become a veritable industry of tomes on America's spiritual, moral, and political alienation often entitled "The culture of this-that-and-the-other-thing." A case in point: in *The Culture of Narcissism*, Christopher Lasch argues that contemporary American culture is the product of forces of rationalization that have at once undermined the permanence and continuity of tradition and created a gap between our dependence on technology and the dream of mastery it embodies and the powerlessness and victimization such dependence generates. Like Bellah, Neuhaus, and Bell, Lasch argues that an inherent need for meaning has fed a growing number of escapist solutions to modern alienation; rationalization has thus generated the paradoxical resurgence of the occult, ancient superstitions, and archaic myths in modern "rationalist" culture.
92. Vincent Harding analyzes the implications of excluding middle-class people who are not white from *Habits of the Heart* ("Toward a Darkly Radiant Vision of America's Truth").
93. Bell, "The Return of the Sacred?," 331, n. 7.
94. Stephen Holmes also argues persuasively that there is a common structure to this perspective, although his analysis is ultimately overshadowed by a polemical condemnation of it as essentially "antiliberal" ("The Permanent Structure of Antiliberal Thought").
95. Schaar, *Legitimacy in the Modern State*, 37.
96. Weber, *The Protestant Ethic and the Spirit of Capitalism*, 182.
97. Spragens, *The Irony of Liberal Reason*.
98. Despite Qutb's emphasis on absolute truth, there is also an anti-elitist, anticlerical bias in his understanding of who can "know" the truth. Indeed, Qutb's challenge not only to received interpretation but also to Islamic jurists' monopoly on scriptural interpretation has been likened to Calvinists' refusal to accept received interpretations of revelation and the insistence on encountering the example of Jesus directly (Goldberg, "Smashing Idols and the State"). Yet despite the spirit of radical egalitarianism in such a project, Qutb's attempt to democratize access to Qur'anic meanings does not entail an endorsement of democracy. Rather it functions to legitimate a populist absolutism not incompatible with totalitarianism.
99. Chattergee, *The Nation and Its Fragments*, 5.
100. Featherstone, *Global Cultures*, 12.
101. Despite radical differences, fundamentalism may in this way be continuous with the Romantic Reaction to the Enlightenment, which was also intent on such "reenchantment" of the world (Gay, "The Re-enchantment of the World").
102. Arendt, *The Human Condition*, 11.
103. Ibid.

104. Ibid., 10–11.

105. Friedrich Nietzsche, *The Birth of Tragedy*, 139.

106. Taylor, *The Ethics of Authenticity*, 33.

107. It is a paradox noted by many critics of modernity. Indeed, in *Dialectic of Enlightenment*, Horkheimer and Adorno suggest that modern bureaucracy in particular has given birth to its own peculiar forms of "irrationality" in a dialectical process they describe as a barbarous combination of myth and enlightenment. Having set out to discover "why mankind, instead of entering into a truly human condition, is sinking into a new kind of barbarism," they conclude that the Holocaust was not an isolated descent into barbarism but rather an expression of the organizing principle of modern civilization: the "irrationalism" of anti-Semitism is "deduced from the nature of the dominant *ratio* itself, and the world which corresponds to its image" (pp. xi, xvii).

CHAPTER SIX
CONCLUSION

1. Geertz, "Thick Description," 25.

2. Leonard Binder, *Islamic Liberalism*, 22.

3. By contrast, Leonard Binder looks to Qutb's "presumably most radical" text not only to examine it on its own terms but also to show that it is less intransigent than it appears, and thus that "[t]here is considerable room for a rhetorical convergence between fundamentalism and Islamic liberalism" (ibid.). Binder sees the possibility of such convergence because Islamic liberalism here means the rejection of a secular state in favor of an Islamic state that can nevertheless accommodate liberal political practices. For "Islamic liberals" such accommodation is possible either because the Qur'an does not forbid it or because there are passages that explicitly support something like it. Binder concludes that Qutb's similar rejection of the secular state and emphasis on practice rather than theory opens up the possibility of accommodation despite rhetoric to the contrary. While a provocative suggestion and worthwhile endeavor, such a reading sets aside Qutb's explicit antipathy to liberal practices, institutions, and the methodological individualism upon which it rests, an antipathy reflected in contemporary Islamist political practice. While Binder is surely right to show the multiplicity of ways Islamists might have interpreted, and indeed might still interpret, Qutb's work or resolve his contradictions, I submit that both Qutb and the fundamentalist political actors influenced by his work would find this account unfamiliar, and even pernicious. Yet Binder's analysis of Qutb stands in stark contrast to, for example, rational actor explanations where accounts of fundamentalist ideas become methodologically irrelevant to the task of explaining political behavior.

4. Robert Segal, "Joachim Wach and the History of Religions," 200.

5. Salkever and Nylan, "Teaching Comparative Political Philosophy," 24–25. MacIntyre also argues for a "conversation between traditions," each rooted in particular histories and experiences. Yet the argument here is that in a postcolonial world, the boundaries between such histories and experiences are permeable, and thus the traditions may be more culturally syncretic than such formulations suggest. MacIntyre, *Whose Justice? Which Rationality?*, 398.

6. Kepel, *The Revenge of God*, 11.

7. In considering the implications of these arguments for education, the thorny question about power remains: what are the conditions that render some texts, and thus certain kinds of cross-cultural conversations, relevant and others irrelevant in, for example, a course on politics and on political theory in particular? Why, for example, is Thomas Aquinas included in the canon of political theory but Averroes is not? One implication of the arguments here is that many of our disciplinary methods overdetermine not only the focus of the comparative analysis but also which comparisons, which texts, which conversations appear central, others peripheral. As Salkever and Nylan argue, when *The Encyclopedia of Philosophy* distinguishes poetry from a philosophic discourse that should be as "systematic and as free from ambiguity as possible," it not only excludes Chinese philosophy from consideration—and, I would venture to add, much of modern Islamic thought—but also premodern Western thinkers such as Plato and Aristotle, "who were anything but systematic and who rejected the idea that the system and precision of mathematics or symbolic logic provide appropriate models for philosophic reasoning and philosophic discourse" (John Passmore, "Philosophy," and Salkever and Nylan "Comparative Political Philosophy and Liberal Education," 239–40). Conversely, by insisting upon an essential difference between Islamic and Western thought, Orientalist literature has at once underwritten its own authority on Islam and discouraged interdisciplinary engagement. By contrast, Salkever and Nylan suggest that in the context of liberal education, books on a political theory syllabus are already "chosen on the basis of several not always harmonious criteria: their historical importance (since part of liberal education is coming to terms with a particular historical past or tradition), the extent to which they are open to a variety of conflicting interpretations (since critical interpretation and argument about the meaning of words and things is the practice that defines the liberal classroom), and the extent to which they can be read with an eye to questions and problems of the present (since liberal education is justified largely by its capacity to encourage deliberation and informed action in the future). In deciding what books to teach, we worry less about adhering to conventional genre distinctions than about finding books that demand active and critical response, ones that incline us to re-consider the past and to imagine ourselves as participants in a continuing 'conversation' about the shape of life in the future. Such an education is not about the transmission of either facts or values in any simple way, though it is indeed a kind of moral education insofar as we try to develop the preferences, skills, and habits of mind that support lives of persistent curiosity and self-reflection" (Salkever and Nylan, "Teaching Comparative Philosophy," 1–2).

8. Pat Robertson, *The New Millennium*, in *The Collected Works of Pat Robertson*, 50, 67.

9. Kepel, *The Revenge of God*, 192.

10. Lawrence, *Defenders of God*, 2.

11. Marshall Berman, *All That Is Solid Melts into Air*, 345–46.

12. Marsden, *Fundamentalism and American Culture*, 148, 160, 166. See also Roberston, *The New Millennium*, for example, 19.

13. Lawrence, *Defenders of God*, 3.

14. Kepel, *The Revenge of God*, 192.

15. Ibid., 137–38.

16. Like Islamic fundamentalism, both early and recent Christian fundamentalism tends to incorporate and, at times, mimic scientific rhetoric and standards while rejecting the very idea of scientific authority unshackled from revealed truths, and in the way its advocates use modern technologies in, for example, mass communication, to lambast the scientific worldview. See, for example, Marsden, *Fundamentalism and American Culture*, 169; and Robertson, *The New Millennium*, 16.

17. Shepard, "'Fundamentalism' Christian and Islamic"; Emmanuel Sivan, "The Mythologies of Religious Radicalism"; Hava Lazarus-Yafeh, "Contemporary Fundamentalism—Judaism, Christianity and Islam"; Kepel, *The Revenge of God*.

18. Kepel, *The Revenge of God*, 192.

19. Such sociological comparisons are invaluable, of course. They show, for example, that Islamic, Christian, and Jewish fundamentalists all tend to be children of urban immigrants, educated, and disproportionately in the natural and applied sciences. Indeed, Malise Ruthven suggests that the linkage between fundamentalists and applied science may be due to the fact that "[t]he applied, unlike the 'pure,' scientist can use reason without having to adopt a posture of epistemological doubt" ("Was Weber Wrong?," 19).

20. Kepel, *The Revenge of God*, 4.

21. Several scholars have rightly pointed out the ways in which the attempt to control women's bodies is not just one among many but a central feature of fundamentalism (see, for example, Gita Sahgal and Nira Yuval-Davis, eds., *Refusing Holy Orders*). Yet it is also important to note that the attempt to control women's bodies in general, and the attempt to control them in this particular way, is not unique to fundamentalist movements and ideas nor religiously inspired politics. A particularly germane case in point: Sondra Hale shows that in the years 1961–1988, despite radically different ideologies, both the Sudanese Communist Party (SCP) and the National Islamic Front (NIF) sought to position women as the repositories of cultural authenticity and the carriers of morality, subjects to be acted upon, to be "guided and guarded" (Hale, *Gender Politics in Sudan: Islamism, Socialism and the State*).

22. Lawrence, *Defenders of God*, 232.

23. Kishore Mahbubani, "The West and the Rest."

24. Lawrence, *Defenders of God*, 2.

25. Félix Guattari, *Chaosophy*, 87. Of course, for Guattari and Gilles Deleuze, schizophrenia is not a pathology to be overcome as it is for Qutb. On the contrary, "The schizophrenic has a lightening-like access to you. . . . He's in the position of a 'seer' . . . whereas individuals who are frozen in their logic, in their syntax, in their interests, are totally blind" (ibid., 92; and Deleuze and Guattari, *Anti-Oedipus*).

26. Bull, "Who Was the First to Make a Pact with the Devil?," 22–23.

27. Ahmed, *Postmodernism and Islam*, 13.

28. Falk, "Religion and Politics," 380.

29. Jean-François Lyotard, "Lessons in Paganism."

30. Philippa Berry and Andrew Wernick, eds., *Shadow of Spirit*.

31. Tibi, "Culture and Knowledge," 13.

32. Ibid., 20.

33. W. Montgomery Watt, *Islamic Fundamentalism and Modernity*, 13–14. Tibi uses this quote to begin his essay. See Jan Nederveen Pieterse for a critique of both

Tibi's and Watt's arguments regarding the dichotomy between "Western modern" and "Islamic knowledge" ("A Severe Case of Dichotomic Thinking").

34. Although William Connolly points out "momentary points of convergence" between communitarians such as Taylor and "antiteleologists" such as Foucault ("Beyond Good and Evil," 370).

35. Personal communication, July 25, 1995. I am grateful to Shlomo Avineri for this point.

36. Taylor, *The Ethics of Authenticity*, 89.

Bibliography

Abdel-Malek, Anouar. *Egypt: Military Society*. New York: Random House, 1968.

'Abd al-Rahman, 'Umar. *Kalimat Haqq*. Egypt: Dar al-I'tisam, n.d.

'Abduh, Muhammad. *Al-Islam wal-Nasraniyya* [Islam and Christianity]. Cairo: Al-Manar, 1905–1906.

———. *Risalat al-Tawhid* [The Theology of Unity]. Cairo: Dar al-Ma'arif, 1966.

Abu Rabi', Ibrahim. *Intellectual Origins of Islamic Resurgence in the Modern Arab World*. Albany: State University of New York Press, 1996.

———. "Sayyid Qutb: From Religious Realism to Radical Social Criticism." *Islamic Quarterly* 78 (1984): 103–26.

Adams, Charles C. *Islam and Modernism in Egypt*. New York: Russell & Russell, 1933.

Adorno, Theodor. *In Search of Wagner*. Translated by Rodney Livingstone. London: Verso, 1981.

Ahmed, Akbar. *Postmodernism and Islam: Predicament and Promise*. London: Routledge, 1992.

———. "Review of *Islams and Modernities*, by Aziz al-Azmeh." *The Middle East Journal* 48 (1994): 735–37.

Ajami, Fouad. *The Arab Predicament*. Cambridge: Cambridge University Press, 1981.

———. "The Summoning," *Foreign Affairs* 72 (September/October 1993): 2–9.

Akhavi, Shahrough. "The Dialectic in Contemporary Egyptian Social Thought: The Scripturalist and Modernist Discourses of Sayyid Qutb and Hasan Hanafi." *The International Journal of Middle East Studies* 29 (1997): 377–401.

———. "Islam, Politics and Society in the Thought of Ayatullah Khomeini, Ayatullah Taliqani and Ali Shariati." *Middle Eastern Studies* 24 (1988): 404–31.

———. "Qutb, Sayyid." *The Oxford Encyclopedia of the Modern Islamic World*. Vol. 3. New York: Oxford University Press, 1995.

———. "Review of *Islam, the People and the State*, by Sami Zubaida." *International Journal of Middle East Studies* 27 (August 1995): 355–56.

Almond, Gabriel. *The Appeals of Communism*. Princeton: Princeton University Press, 1954.

Amin, Osman. *Muhammad 'Abduh*. Washington, D.C.: American Council of Learned Societies, 1953.

Amin, Samir. *Delinking: Towards a Polycentric World*. Trans. Michael Wolfers. London: Zed Books, 1990.

Anchor, Robert. *The Enlightenment Tradition*. New York: Harper & Row, 1967.

Ansari, Hamied N. "The Islamic Militants in Egyptian Politics." *The International Journal of Middle East Studies* 16 (1984): 123–44.

Arendt, Hannah. *Between Past and Future*. New York: Penguin Books, 1968.

———. *Crises of the Republic*. New York: Harcourt Brace Jovanovich, 1972.

———. *The Human Condition*. Chicago: University of Chicago Press, 1958.

———. *The Origins of Totalitarianism*. New York: Harcourt Brace Jovanovich, 1968.

218 · Bibliography

Arendt, Hannah. "Religion and Politics." In *Essays in Understanding: 1930–1954.* New York: Harcourt Brace & Company, 1994.

———. "What Was Authority?" In *Nomos.* Vol. 1, *Authority,* edited by Carl J. Friedrich. Cambridge: Harvard University Press, 1958.

Aristotle. *The Politics of Aristotle.* Translated by Ernest Barker. Oxford: Oxford University Press, 1958.

Arjomand, Said Amir. "Iran's Islamic Revolution in Comparative Perspective." *World Politics* 38 (1986): 383–414.

Asad, Talal. *Anthropology and the Colonial Encounter.* Atlantic Highlands, N.J.: Humanities Press, 1973.

Associated Press. "Polls Fall Victim to Lifestyles." *Boston Globe,* August 17, 1988, A3.

al-Attas, Syed M. N. *Islam, Secularism and the Philosophy of the Future.* London: Mansell Publishers, 1985.

Avineri, Shlomo. *The Social and Political Thought of Karl Marx.* Cambridge: Cambridge University Press, 1968.

Ayubi, Nazih, N. M. *Political Islam: Religion and Politics in the Arab World.* New York: Routledge, 1991.

———. "The Political Revival of Islam: The Case of Egypt." *The International Journal of Middle East Studies* 12 (1980): 481–99.

al-Azmeh, Aziz. *Islams and Modernities.* London: Verso, 1993.

Azzi, Corry, and Ronald Ehrenberg. "Household Allocation of Time and Church Attendance." *The Journal of Political Economy* 83 (February 1975): 27–56.

Badawi, M. A. Said. *The Reformers of Egypt.* London: Croom Helm, 1978.

Ball, Terence. "The Ontological Presuppositions and Political Consequences of a Social Science." In *Changing Social Science,* edited by Daniel R. Sabia and Jerald Wallulis. Albany: State University of New York Press, 1983.

Ball, Terence, and James Farr, eds. *After Marx.* New York: Cambridge University Press, 1984.

al-Banna, Hasan. "Nazrat fi islah al-nafs." Cairo: Dar al-I'tisam, 1944.

———. *What Is Our Message?* Translated by Aziz Ahmad Bilyameeni. Pakistan: Islamic Publications, 1978.

Barakat, Muhammad Tawfiq. *Sayyid Qutb: khulasat hayatihi, manhajuhu fi harakat al-naqd al-muwajjaha ilayhi.* Beirut: Dar al-Da'wa, 1970.

Barnouw, Erik. *The Magician and the Cinema.* Oxford: Oxford University Press, 1981.

Becker, Carl. *The Heavenly City of the Eighteenth Century Philosophers.* New Haven: Yale University Press, 1932.

Becker, Gary. *The Economic Approach to Human Behavior.* Chicago: Chicago University Press, 1976.

———. "The Economic Approach to Human Behavior." In *Rational Choice,* edited by Jon Elster. New York: New York University Press, 1986.

Becker, Gary, and Kevin M. Murphy. "A Theory of Rational Addiction." *Journal of Political Economy* 96 (1988): 675–700.

Bell, Daniel. *The Cultural Contradictions of Capitalism.* New York: Basic Books, 1976.

———. *The Winding Passage: Essays and Sociological Journeys, 1960–1980.* Cambridge, Mass.: ABT Books, 1980.

Bellah, Robert. "The Ethical Aims of Social Inquiry." In *Social Science as Moral Inquiry*, edited by Normann Haan, Robert Bellah, Paul Rabinow, and William M. Sullivan. New York: Columbia University Press, 1983.

Bellah, Robert N., Richard Madsen, William M. Sullivan, Ann Swidler, and Steven M. Tipton. *Habits of the Heart: Individualism and Commitment in American Life*. New York: Harper & Row, 1985.

Bendix, Reinhard. "Tradition and Modernity Reconsidered." *Comparative Studies in Society and History* 9 (April 1967): 292–346.

Benhabib, Seyla. *The Reluctant Modernism of Hannah Arendt*. Albany: Sage Publications, 1996.

Bennoune, Karima. "Algerian Women Confront Fundamentalism." *Monthly Review* (September 1994): 26–39.

Berlin, Isaiah. *Four Essays on Liberty*. Oxford: Oxford University Press, 1986.

———. "Joseph de Maistre and the Origins of Fascism." In *The Crooked Timber of Humanity: Chapters in the History of Ideas*, edited by Henry Hardy. London: John Murray, 1990.

Berman, Marshall. *All that Is Solid Melts into Air: The Experience of Modernity*. New York: Simon and Schuster, 1982.

Bernal, Martin. *Black Athena: The Afroasiatic Roots of Classical Culture*. New Brunswick: Rutgers University Press, 1987.

Bernstein, Richard. "The Rage against Reason." *Philosophy and Literature* 10 (1986): 186–210.

Berry, Philippa, and Andrew Wernick, eds. *Shadow of Spirit: Postmodernism and Religion*. New York: Routledge, 1992.

Bigo, Didier. "Grands Débats dans un Petit Monde: Les débats en relations internationales et leur lien avec le monde de la sécurité." *Cultures & Conflits* (Automne/Hiver 1995): 7–48.

Binder, Leonard. *Islamic Liberalism*. Chicago: University of Chicago Press, 1988.

Binmore, Ken. *Playing Fair*. Cambridge: MIT Press, 1994.

Black, Cyril Edwin. *The Dynamics of Modernization*. New York: Harper & Row, 1966.

Blumenthal, Sidney. "Christian Soldiers." *The New Yorker*, July 18, 1994.

Bosworth, C., E. van Donzel, W. P. Heinrichs, and CH. Pellat, et al. *Encyclopaedia of Islam: New Edition*. Leiden: E. J. Brill, 1992.

Bosworth, C. E., E. van Donzel, B. Lewis, and CH. Pellat. *The Encyclopaedia of Islam: New Edition*. Leiden: E. J. Brill, 1986.

Bourdieu, Pierre. "The Disenchantment of the World." In *Algeria 1960*. Translated by Richard Nice. New York: Cambridge University Press, 1979.

Bowersock, Glen. "Rescuing the Greeks." *The New York Times Book Review*, February 25, 1996.

Bruce, Steve. "Religion and Rational Choice: A Critique of Economic Explanations of Religious Behavior." *Sociology of Religion* 54 (1993):193–205.

Bull, Malcolm. "Who Was the First to Make a Pact with the Devil?" *London Review of Books*, May 14, 1992.

Burgat, François, and William Dowell. *The Islamic Movement in North Africa*. Austin: Center for Middle Eastern Studies, 1993.

Burke, Edmund, III, and Ira M. Lapidus, eds. *Islam, Politics and Social Movements.* Berkeley: University of California Press, 1988.

Calvert, John. "Discourse, Community and Power: Sayyid Qutb and the Islamic Movement in Egypt." Ph.D. dissertation, Institute of Islamic Studies, McGill University, 1993.

Carré, Olivier, and Gerard Michaud. *Les Freres musulmans: Egypt et Syrie.* Paris: Editions Gallimard/Juillard, 1983.

Carrel, Alexis. *Man the Unknown.* New York: Halcyon House, 1935.

Chattergee, Partha. *The Nation and Its Fragments: Colonial and Postcolonial Histories.* Princeton: Princeton University Press, 1993.

Cheah, Pheng, and Bruce Robbins, eds. *Cosmopolitics: Thinking and Feeling Beyond the Nation.* Minneapolis: University of Minnesota Press, 1998.

Chehabi, H. E. *Iranian Politics and Religious Modernism: The Liberation Movement of Iran under the Shah and Khomeini.* London: I. B. Tauris & Co., 1990.

Condorcet, Antoine-Nicolas de. *Sketch for a Historical Picture of the Progress of the Human Mind.* Translated by June Barraclough. Westport, Conn.: Hyperion Press, 1955.

Connolly, William. "Beyond Good and Evil: The Ethical Sensibility of Michel Foucault." *Political Theory* 21, 3: 365–89.

Crary, Jonathan. *Techniques of the Observer: On Vision and Modernity in the Nineteenth Century.* Cambridge: MIT Press, 1996.

Crossette, Barbara. "U.S. Official Calls Muslim Militants a Threat to Africa." *The New York Times*, January 1, 1992.

Cunningham, Karla J. "Islamic Fundamentalism and the Domino Theory." Paper presented at the American Political Science Association Convention, New York, September 1994.

Dallmayr, Fred. *Alternative Visions: Paths in the Global Village.* New York: Rowman & Littlefield, 1998.

———. *Beyond Orientalism: Essays on Cross-Cultural Encounter.* Albany: State University of New York Press, 1996.

Davis, Eric. "Ideology, Social Class and Islamic Radicalism in Modern Egypt." In *From Nationalism to Revolutionary Islam*, edited by Said Amir Arjomand. Albany: State University of New York Press, 1984.

Deleuze, Gilles, and Félix Guattari. *Anti-Oedipus: Capitalism and Schizophrenia.* New York: The Viking Press, 1972.

Derrida, Jacques. *The Other Heading: Reflections on Today's Europe.* Translated by Pascale-Anne Brault and Michael B. Naas. Bloomington: Indiana University Press, 1992.

Diderot, Denis. *Oeuvres Completes.* Vol. 1, *Pensees Philosophiques.* France: le Club français du livre, 1969.

Diesing, Paul. *Reason in Society.* Westport, Conn.: Greenwood Press, 1973.

Dirks, Nicholas B., ed. *Colonialism and Culture.* Ann Arbor: University of Michigan Press, 1992.

Djerejian, Edward. *Statement to the House Foreign Affairs Committee*, July 27, 1993.

Donohue, John J., and John L. Esposito, eds. *Islam in Transition: Muslim Perspectives.* New York: Oxford University Press, 1982.

Enayat, Hamid. *Modern Islamic Political Thought*. Austin: University of Texas Press, 1982.

Esposito, John L. *The Islamic Threat: Myth or Reality?* New York: Oxford University Press, 1992.

————. ed. *Voices of Resurgent Islam*. New York: Oxford University Press, 1983.

Euben, J. Peter. "Creatures of a Day: Thought and Action in Thucydides." In *Political Theory and Praxis: New Perspectives*, edited by Terence Ball. Minneapolis: University of Minnesota Press, 1977.

Euben, Roxanne L. "Comparative Political Theory: An Islamic Fundamentalist Critique of Rationalism." *The Journal of Politics* 59 (February 1997): 28–55.

————. "Islamic and Western Critiques of Modernity." *The Review of Politics* 59 (Summer 1997): 429–59.

————. "When Worldviews Collide: Conflicting Assumptions about Human Behavior Held by Rational Actor Theory and Islamic Fundamentalism." *Political Psychology* 16 (March 1995): 157–78.

Falk, Richard. "Religion and Politics: Verging on the Postmodern." *Alternatives* 8 (1988): 379–94.

Fandy, Mamoun. "Egypt's Islamic Group: Regional Revenge?" *Middle East Journal* 48 (Autumn 1994): 607–25.

Featherstone, Mike, ed. *Global Culture: Nationalism, Globalization and Modernity*. London: Sage, 1990.

Fischer, Michael. "Becoming Mollah: Reflections on Iranian Clerics in a Revolutionary Age." *Iranian Studies* 13 (1980): 83–117.

————. *Iran: From Religious Dispute to Revolution*. Cambridge: Harvard University Press, 1980.

————. "Islam and the Revolt of the Petit Bourgeoisie." *Daedalus* 3 (Winter 1982): 101–122.

Foucault, Michel. "Is It Useless to Revolt?" *Le Monde*, 11–12 Mai 1979.

————. *Language, Counter-memory, Practice*, edited by Donald F. Bouchard. Ithaca: Cornell University Press, 1977.

————. *Power/Knowledge*. New York: Pantheon Books, 1980.

————. "What Is Enlightenment?" In *The Foucault Reader*, edited by Paul Rabinow. New York: Pantheon Books, 1984.

Fukuyama, Francis. "The End of History?" *National Interest* 16 (Summer 1989): 3–18.

————. *The End of History and the Last Man*. New York: The Free Press, 1992.

————. "The New World Disorder: Review of *Civil Wars: From L.A. to Bosnia*, by Hans Magnus Enzenberger." *The New York Times Book Review*, October 9, 1994.

Gadamer, Hans-Georg. *Philosophical Hermeneutics*. Translated by David E. Linge. Berkeley: University of California Press, 1976.

————. *Truth and Method*. Translated by Joel Weinsheimer and Donald G. Marshall. New York: Crossroad Publishing Co., 1992.

————. *Wer bin Ich und Wer bist Du? Ein Kommentar zu Paul Celans Gedichtfolge "Atemkristall."* Frankfurt-Main: Surhkamp, 1973.

Gay, Peter. *The Enlightenment: An Interpretation*. Vol. 2. New York: Alfred A. Knopf, 1969.

Gay, Peter. "The Re-enchantment of the World." Paper presented at the Political Philosophy Colloquium, Princeton University, March 1995.

Geertz, Clifford. "Ideology as a Cultural System." In *Ideology and Discontent*, edited by David Apter. New York: Macmillan, 1964.

———. "Thick Description: Toward an Interpretive Theory of Culture." In *The Interpretation of Cultures*. New York: Basic Books, 1973.

Gellner, Ernest. "Letter to the Editor." *The Times Literary Supplement*, April 9, 1993.

———. "The Mightier Pen?: Edward Said and the Double Standards of Inside-out Colonialism." *The Times Literary Supplement*, February 19, 1993.

———. *Muslim Society*. Cambridge: Cambridge University Press, 1981.

———. *Postmodernism, Reason and Religion*. New York: Routledge, 1992.

Gerth, H. H., and C. Wright Mills, eds. *From Max Weber: Essays in Sociology*. New York: Oxford University Press, 1958.

Gibb, H.A.R. *Modern Trends in Islam*. Chicago: University of Chicago Press, 1947.

———. *Studies on the Civilization of Islam*. Boston: Beacon Press, 1962.

Giddens, Anthony. *Capitalism and Modern Social Theory*. Cambridge: Cambridge University Press, 1971.

———. *Sociology*. Cambridge: Polity Press, 1989.

Gilsenan, Michael. *Recognizing Islam*. New York: Pantheon Books, 1982.

Goldberg, Ellis. "Smashing Idols and the State: The Protestant Ethic and Egyptian Sunni Radicalism." *Comparative Studies in Society and History* 33 (1991): 3–35.

Grosz, Elizabeth. "Sexual Difference and the Problem of Essentialism." In *Space, Time and Perversion*. New York: Routledge, 1995.

Grunebaum, Gustave Edmund von. *Modern Islam: The Search for Cultural Identity*. Berkeley: University of California Press, 1962.

———. *Unity and Variety in Muslim Civilization*. Chicago: University of Chicago Press, 1955.

Guattari, Félix. *Chaosophy*, edited by Sylvère Lotringer. New York: Semiotext[e], 1995.

Gutmann, Amy. "Communitarian Critics of Liberalism." *Philosophy & Public Affairs* 14 (Summer 1985): 308–22.

Habermas, Jürgen. *Knowledge and Human Interests*. Translated by Jeremy Shapiro. Boston: Beacon Press, 1971.

———. *Legitimation Crisis*. Translated by Thomas A. McCarthy. Boston: Beacon Press, 1975.

———. "A Review of Gadamer's *Truth and Method*." In *Understanding and Social Inquiry*, edited by Fred R. Dallmayr and Thomas A. McCarthy. Notre Dame: University of Notre Dame Press, 1977.

———. *Theory and Practice*. Translated by John Viertel. Boston: Beacon Press, 1973.

———. *Theory of Communicative Action*. Translated by Thomas A. McCarthy. Boston: Beacon Press, 1984.

———. "What Is Universal Pragmatics?" *Communication and the Evolution of Society*. Translated by Thomas A. McCarthy. Boston: Beacon Press, 1979.

Hacking, Ian. "The Archaeology of Foucault." In *Foucault: A Critical Reader*, edited by David C. Hoy. Oxford: Basil Blackwell, 1986.

Haddad, Yvonne. "The Qur'anic Justification for an Islamic Revolution: The View of Sayyid Qutb." *The Middle East Journal* 37 (Winter 1983): 14–29.

————. "Sayyid Qutb: Ideologue of Islamic Revival." In *Voices of Resurgent Islam*, edited by John Esposito. New York: Oxford University Press, 1983.

Haim, Sylvia G. *Arab Nationalism: An Anthology*. Berkeley: University of California Press, 1962.

————. "Sayyid Qutb." *Asian and African Studies* 16 (1982): 147–56.

Hale, Sondra. *Gender Politics in Sudan: Islamism, Socialism and the State*. Boulder: Westview Press, 1996.

Halliday, Fred. *Islam and the Myth of Confrontation*. London: I. B. Tauris, 1996.

Hammoudi, Abdellah. *Master and Disciple: The Cultural Foundations of Moroccan Authoritarianism*. Chicago: University of Chicago Press, 1997.

Hanafi, Hasan. *al-Harakah al-Diniyya al-mu'asira*. Cairo: Maktaba Madbuli, 1988

————. "The Relevance of an Islamic Alternative in Egypt." *Arab Studies Quarterly* 4 (Spring 1982): 54–74.

Harding, Vincent. "Toward a Darkly Radiant vision of America's Truth: A Letter of Concern, an Invitation to Re-Creation." In *Community in America: The Challenge of Habits of the Heart*, edited by Charles H. Reynolds and Ralph V. Norman. Berkelely: University of California Press, 1988.

Harris, Marvin. *Cows, Pigs, Wars and Witches: The Riddles of Culture*. New York: Vintage Books, 1974.

Hassan, Riffat. "The Burgeoning of Islamic Fundamentalism: Toward an Understanding of the Phenomenon." In *The Fundamentalist Phenomenon*, edited by Norman J. Cohen. Michigan: William B. Eerdmans, 1991.

Havel, Vaclav. Speech delivered at Independence Hall. Philadelphia, July 4, 1994. Reprinted in *The New York Times*, July 8, 1994.

Hawthorn, Geoffrey. *Enlightenment and Despair*. Cambridge: Cambridge University Press, 1987.

Hechter, Michael. *Principles of Group Solidarity*. Berkeley: University of California Press, 1987.

Heidegger, Martin. *Being and Time*. Translated by John Macquarrie and Edward Robinson. New York: Harper & Row, 1962.

Henningsen, Manfred. "The New Politics of History." In *The Philosophy of Order: Essays on History, Consciousness and Politics*, edited by Peter J. Opitz and Gregor Sebba. Stuttgart: Ernst Klett, 1981.

Hermassi, Elbaki. *Leadership and National Development in North Africa*. Berkeley: University of California Press, 1972.

Herodotus, *The History*. New York: Harper's New Classical Library, 1887.

Hodgson, Marshall G. *The Venture of Islam: Conscience and History in a World Civilization*. Chicago: University of Chicago Press, 1974.

Holmes, Stephen. "The Gatekeeper: John Rawls and the Limits of Tolerance." *The New Republic*, October 11, 1993.

————. "The Permanent Structure of Antiliberal Thought." In *Liberalism and the Moral Life*, edited by Nancy L. Rosenblum. Cambridge: Harvard University Press, 1989.

Horkheimer, Max, and Theodor W. Adorno. *Dialectic of Enlightenment*. Translated by John Cumming. New York: Herder and Herder, 1972.

Hourani, Albert. *Arabic Thought in the Liberal Age: 1798–1939*. Cambridge: Cambridge University Press, 1983.

Houtsma, M. Th., A. J. Wensick, H.A.R. Gibb, W. Heffening, and E. Levi-Provencal, eds. *E. J. Brill's First Encyclopædia of Islam: 1913–1936*. New York: E. J. Brill, 1987.

Hoy, David C. *The Critical Circle*. Berkeley: University of California Press, 1978.

Hudhaybi, Hasan Isma'il. *Du'at al-Qudat*. Cairo: Dar al-Tabi'a wa al-Nashr al-Islamiyya, 1977.

Hume, David. *A Treatise on Human Nature*. Oxford: Clarendon Press, 1968.

Huntington, Samuel. *The Clash of Civilizations and the Remaking of World Order.* New York: Simon and Schuster, 1996.

———. "The Clash of Civilizations?," *Foreign Affairs* 72 (Summer 1993): 22–49.

———. "If Not Civilizations, What?" *Foreign Affairs* 72 (November/December 1993): 186–94.

———. *Political Order in Changing Societies*. New Haven: Yale University Press, 1968.

Husain, Taha. *Mustaqbal al-Thaqafa fi Misr* [The Future of Culture in Egypt]. Cairo: Matba'at al-Ma'arif, 1938.

Iannaccone, Laurance R. "A Formal Model of Church and Sect." *American Journal of Sociology* 94, supplement (1988): S241–68.

———. "Heirs to the Protestant Ethic? The Economics of American Fundamentalists." In *Fundamentalisms and the State: Remaking Polities, Economies and Militance*, edited by Martin E. Marty and R. Scott Appleby. Chicago: University of Chicago Press, 1993.

———. "Risk, Rationality, and Religious Portfolios." *Economic Inquiry* 33 (1995): 285–95.

Ibrahim, Saad Eddin. "Anatomy of Egypt's Militant Islamic Groups." *The International Journal of Middle East Studies* 12 (1980): 423–53.

Ibrahim, Youssef. "Palestinian Religious Militants: Why Their Ranks Are Growing." *New York Times*, November 8, 1994.

Jansen, Johannes J. G. *The Neglected Duty: The Creed of Sadat's Assassins and Islamic Resurgence in the Middle East*. New York: Macmillan, 1986.

Juergensmeyer, Mark. *The New Cold War?: Religious Nationalism Confronts the Secular State*. Berkeley: University of California Press, 1993.

Kalberg, Stephen. "Max Weber's Types of Rationality: Cornerstones for the Analysis of Rationalization Processes in History." *American Journal of Sociology* 85 (March 1980): 1145–79.

Kateb, George. *Hannah Arendt: Politics, Conscience, Evil*. Totowa, N.J.: Rowman and Allanheld, 1984.

Keddie, Nikki. "Comparative Method in the Study of 'Fundamentalism.'" Paper presented at the Middle East Studies Association Meeting, Washington, DC, December 1995.

———. *An Islamic Response to Imperialism*. Berkeley: University of California Press, 1968.

———. *The Roots of Revolution*. New Haven: Yale University Press, 1981.

———. *Sayyid Jamal al-Din "al-Afghani": A Political Biography*. Berkeley: University of California Press, 1972.

Kedourie, Elie. *Afghani and 'Abduh: An Essay on Religious Unbelief and Political Activism in Modern Islam.* London: Frank Cass, 1966.

Kennedy, Paul. *The Rise and Fall of Great Powers.* New York: Random House, 1987.

Kepel, Gilles. *Muslim Extremism in Egypt: The Prophet and Pharaoh.* Berkeley: University of California Press, 1985.

———. *The Revenge of God: The Resurgence of Islam, Christianity and Judaism in the Modern World.* Translated by Alan Braley. University Park: Pennsylvania State University Press, 1994.

Kerr, Malcolm H. *Islamic Reform: The Political and Legal Theories of Muhammad 'Abduh and Rashid Rida.* Berkeley: University of California Press, 1966.

Khalid, Detlev. "Ahmad Amin and the Legacy of Muhammad 'Abduh." *Islamic Studies* 9 (March 1970): 1–31.

al-Khalidi, Salah D. *Amrika min al-dakhil bi minzar Sayyid Qutb* [America from within as Seen by Sayyid Qutb]. Jedda: Dar al-Manara, 1986.

Khomeini, Ayatollah Ruhollah. *Islam and Revolution: Writings and Declarations of Imam Khomeini.* Translated by Hamid Algar. Berkeley: Mizan Press, 1981.

Khoury, Philip. "Islamic Revivalism and the Crisis of the Secular State." In *Arab Resources*, edited by Ibrahim Ibrahim. Washington, D.C.: Center for Contemporary Arab Studies, 1983.

Knysh, Alexander. "*Irfan* Revisited: Khomeini and the Legacy of Islamic Mystical Philosophy." *Middle East Journal* 46 (Autumn 1992): 631–53.

Krauthammer, Charles. "The Unipolar Moment." *Foreign Affairs* 70 (1991): 23–33.

Lapidus, Ira M. "The Golden Age: The Political Concepts of Islam." *The Annals of the American Academy of Political and Social Science* 524 (1992): 13–25.

———. *A History of Islamic Societies.* Cambridge: Cambridge University Press, 1988.

———. "Islamic Revival and Modernity: The Contemporary Movements and the Historical Paradigms." *Journal of the Economic and Social History of the Orient* 40 (1997): 444–60.

———. "Review of *Islam und moderne Wirtschaft: Einführung in Positionen, Probleme und Perspecktiven*, by Volker Nienhaus." *Middle East Journal* 38 (1984): 773–74.

———. "State and Religion in Islamic Societies." *Past & Present* 150 (1996): 3–27.

Laroui, Abdallah. *Islam et modernité.* Paris: La Découverte, 1987.

Lasch, Christopher. *The Culture of Narcissism: American Life in an Age of Diminishing Expectations.* New York: W. W. Norton, 1991.

Lawrence, Bruce B. *Defenders of God.* San Fransisco: Harper & Row, 1989.

———. *Shattering the Myth: Islam beyond Violence.* Princeton: Princeton University Press, 1998.

Lazarus-Yafeh, Hava. "Contemporary Fundamentalism: Judaism, Christianity and Islam." *The Jerusalem Quarterly* 47 (Summer 1988): 27–39.

Lerner, Daniel. *The Passing of Traditional Society.* London: Collier-Macmillan, 1958.

Lester, Toby. "What Is the Koran?" *The Atlantic Monthly* (January 1999): 43–56.

Lewis, Bernard. "Communism and Islam." In *The Middle East in Transition*, edited by Walter Z. Laqueur. New York: Frederick A. Praeger, 1958.

Lewis, Bernard. *Islam and the West*. Oxford: Oxford University Press, 1993.

———. "The Roots of Muslim Rage." *The Atlantic Monthly* 266 (September 1990): 47–57.

Lewis, Bernard, CH. Pellat, and J. Schacht, eds. *The Encyclopædia of Islam: New Edition*. London: Luzac, 1965.

Lind, William. "Defending Western Culture." *Foreign Policy* 84 (Fall 1991): 40–50.

Lyotard, Jean-François. *The Lyotard Reader*, edited by Andrew Benjamin. Oxford: Blackwell, 1989.

McCarthy, Thomas A. *The Critical Theory of Jürgen Habermas*. Cambridge: MIT Press, 1978.

———. *Ideals and Illusions: On Reconstruction and Deconstruction in Contemporary Critical Theory*. Cambridge: MIT Press, 1991.

———. "Rationality and Relativism: Habermas's 'Overcoming' of Hermeneutics." In *Habermas: Critical Debates*, edited by John B. Thompson and David Held. London: MacMillan, 1982.

McGuinn, Bradford. "Why the Fundamentalists Are Winning," *New York Times*, March 22, 1993.

MacIntyre, Alasdair. *After Virtue*. Notre Dame: University of Notre Dame Press, 1984.

———. *Whose Justice? Which Rationality?* Notre Dame: University of Notre Dame Press, 1988.

Mahbubani, Kishore. "The West and the Rest." *The National Interest* (Summer 1992): 3–13.

Mahdi, Fadl Allah. *Ma'a Sayyid Qutb fi fikrihi al-siyasi wal-dini*. Beirut: Mu'assasat al-Risala, 1979.

Mardin, Şerif. *Religion and Social Change in Modern Turkey*. New York: State University of New York Press, 1989.

Marsden, George. *Fundamentalism and American Culture: The Shaping of Twentieth-Century Evangelicalism, 1870–1928*. Oxford: Oxford University Press, 1980.

Martin, Kingsley. *French Liberal Thought in the Eighteenth Century*. London: Turnstile Press, 1954.

Marty, Martin E., "Explaining the Rise of Fundamentalism," *The Chronicle of Higher Education*, October 28, 1992.

Marty, Martin E., and R. Scott Appleby, eds. *Fundamentalisms Observed*. Chicago: University of Chicago Press, 1991.

Marx, Karl. *Capital*. New York: The Modern Library, 1906.

———. "The Eighteenth Brumaire of Louis Bonaparte." In *Karl Marx: Selected Writings*, edited by David McLellan. Oxford: Oxford University Press, 1987.

———. *The Marx-Engels Reader*, edited by Robert C. Tucker. New York: W. W. Norton, 1978.

Mearsheimer, John J. "Back to the Future." *International Security* 15 (Summer 1990): 5–56.

A Mere Phantom. *The Magic Lantern: How to Buy and How to Use It* also *How to Raise a Ghost*. London: Houlston and Wright, 1870.

Mernissi, Fatima. *Beyond the Veil*. Bloomington: Indiana University Press, 1987.

Miller, Judith. "The Islamic Wave." *The New York Times Magazine*, May 31, 1992.

Mitchell, Richard P. *The Society of the Muslim Brothers*. London: Oxford University Press, 1969.

Mitchell, Timothy. *Colonising Egypt*. Berkeley: University of California Press, 1988.

Monroe, Kristen R. "Rational Actor Theory and Fundamentalism." Department of Politics and Society, University of California at Irvine.

———. "The Theory of Rational Action: What Is It? How Useful Is It for Political Science?" In *The Theory and Practice of Political Science*. Vol. 1, edited by William Crotty. Evanston: Northwestern University Press, 1991.

Montagne, Robert. *The Berbers*. Translated by David Seddon. London: Frank Cass, 1973.

Montesquieu, *Persian Letters*. Translated by John Davidson. London: George Routledge & Sons, 1891.

Moon, J. Donald. *Constructing Community: Moral Pluralism and Tragic Conflicts*. Princeton: Princeton University Press, 1993.

Moore, Barrington, Jr. *Social Origins of Dictatorship and Democracy*. Boston: Beacon Press, 1966.

Moussalli, Ahmad S. *Radical Islamic Fundamentalism: The Ideological and Political Discourse of Sayyid Qutb*. Beirut: American University of Beirut, 1992.

———. "Sayyid Qutb: The Ideologist of Islamic Fundamentalism." *al-Abhath* 38 (1990): 42–75.

———. "Sayyid Qutb's View of Knowledge." *The American Journal of Islamic Social Sciences* 7(1990):315–33.

al-Mujahid, Sharif. "Sayyid Jamal al-Din al-Afghani: His Role in the Nineteenth Century Muslim Awakening." M.A. thesis, McGill University, 1954.

Musallam, Adnan A. "The Formative Stages of Sayyid Qutb's Intellectual Career and His Emergence as an Islamic Da'iya: 1906–1952." Ph.D. dissertation, University of Michigan, 1983.

———. "Prelude to Islamic Commitment: Sayyid Qutb's Literary and Spiritual Orientation, 1932–1938." *Muslim World* 80 (1990): 176–89.

Myers, Milton L. *The Soul of Economic Man*. Chicago: University of Chicago Press, 1983.

al-Nadwi, Abu al-Hasan. *Islam and the World*. Translated by Muhammad Kidawi. Kuwait: IIFSO, 1977.

Nederveen Pieterse, Jan." Globalization as Hybridization." In *Global Modernities*, edited by Mike Featherstone, Scott Lash, and Roland Robertson. London: Sage Publications, 1995.

———. "A Severe Case of Dichotomic Thinking: Bassam Tibi on Islamic Fundamentalism." *Theory, Culture & Society* 13 (1996): 123–26.

Nettler, Ronald. "A Modern Islamic Confession of Faith and Conception of Religion: Sayyid Qutb's Introduction to the *Tafsir, Fi Zilal al-Qur'an*." *The British Journal of Middle Eastern Studies* 21 (1994): 102–14.

Neuhaus, Richard John. *The Naked Public Square: Religion and Democracy in America*. Grand Rapids: William B. Eerdmans, 1984.

Nienhaus, Volker. *Islam und moderne Wirtschaft: Einführung in Positionen, Probleme und Perspecktiven*. Graz and Cologne: Verlag Styria, 1982.

Nietzsche, Friedrich. *The Birth of Tragedy*. Translated by Francis Golffing. New York: Anchor Press, 1956.

Parsons, Talcott. *The Social System*. England: Routledge & Kegan Paul, 1991.

Passmore, John. "Philosophy." In *Encyclopedia of Philosophy*, Vol. VI, edited by Paul Edwards. New York: MacMillan, 1967.

Paz, Octavio. *One Earth, Four or Five Worlds: Reflections on Contemporary History*. Translated by Helen R. Lane. San Diego: Harcourt Brace Jovanovich, 1985.

Peters, Rudolph. *Islam and Colonialism: The Doctrine of Jihad in Modern History*. The Hague: Mouton Publishers, 1979.

Philo. *Works*. Translated by Francis H. Colson and George H. Whitaker. Cambridge: Harvard University Press, Loeb Classical Library, 1929.

Pipes, Daniel. "Fundamental Questions about Islam." *Wall Street Journal*, October 30, 1992.

Plato. *The Republic*. Translated by Francis M. Cornford. Oxford: Oxford University Press, 1945.

al-Qur'an. Translated by Ahmed Ali. Princeton: Princeton University Press, 1984.

Qutb, Sayyid. *al-'Adala al-Ijtima'iyya fil-Islam* [Social Justice in Islam]. Cairo: Lajnat al-Nashr li al-Jami'iyyin, 1949.

————. *Fi Zilal al-Qur'an* [In the Shade of the Qur'an]. Beirut: Dar al-Shuruq, 1982. [Eight volumes published, the first originally in 1952.]

————. *al-Islam wa Mushkilat al-Hadara* [Islam and the Problems of Civilization]. Beirut: Dar al-Shuruq, 1980 [originally published 1962].

————. *Khasa'is al-Tasawwur al-Islami wa Muqawwamatihi* [The Islamic Conception and Its Characteristics]. Cairo: Dar Ihya al-Kutub al-'Arabiyya, 1962.

————. *Ma'alim fil-Tariq* [Signposts along the Road]. Beirut: Dar al-Shuruq, 1991 [originally published in 1964].

————. *Ma'rakat al-Islam wal-Ra'smaliyyah* [The Battle of Islam and Capitalism]. Beirut: Dar al-Shuruq, 1980 [originally published in 1950].

————. *al-Mustaqbal li-hadha al-Din* [The Future of this Religion]. Cairo: Dar al-Shuruq, 1988 [originally published in 1962].

————. *Naqd Kitab Mustaqbal al-Thaqafa fi Misr* [A Critique of the Book The Future of Culture in Egypt]. Jedda: Al-Dar al-Su'udiyya lil-Nashr wal-Tawzi', 1969 [originally published 1939].

————. *al-Salam al-'Alami wal-Islam* [Islam and Universal Peace]. Beirut: Dar al-Shuruq, 1974 [originally published in 1951].

Rawls, John. "Justice as Fairness: Political Not Metaphysical," *Philosophy and Public Affairs* 14 (Summer 1985): 223–51.

————. *Political Liberalism*. New York: Columbia University Press, 1993.

Renan, Ernest. "Science and Islam." *Journal des Debats*, May 19, 1883.

Richards, Alan, and John Waterbury. *A Political Economy of the Middle East: State, Class and Economic Development*. Boulder: Westview Press, Inc., 1990.

Robertson, Pat. *The Collected Works of Pat Robertson*. New York: Inspirational Press, 1994.

Robinson, Francis. "Modern Islam and the Green Menace." *The Times Literary Supplement*, January 21, 1994.

Rousseau, Jean-Jacques. *Discourse on the Origin and the Foundations of Inequality among Men*. Translated by Victor Gourevitch. New York: Harper & Row, 1986.

Roy, Olivier. *The Failure of Political Islam*. Cambridge: Harvard University Press, 1994.

Ruthven, Malise. "Was Weber Wrong?" *The London Review of Books*, August 18, 1994.

Sabia, Daniel R., Jr., and Jerald Wallulis, eds. *Changing Social Science*. Albany: State University of New York Press, 1983.

Sachedina, Abdulaziz. "Activist Shi'ism in Iran, Iraq and Lebanon." In *Fundamentalisms Observed*, edited by Marty E. Marty and R. Scott Appleby. Chicago: Chicago University Press, 1991.

Safran, Nadav. *Egypt in Search of Political Community*. Cambridge: Harvard University Press, 1961.

Sahgal, Gita, and Nira Yuval-Davis, eds. *Refusing Holy Orders: Women and Fundamentalism in Britain*. London: Virago Press, 1992.

Said, Edward. *Culture and Imperialism*. New York: Alfred A. Knopf, 1993.

————. "Letter to the Editor." *The Times Literary Supplement*. March 19, 1993.

————. *Orientalism*. New York: Vintage Books, 1978.

————. "The Phony Islamic Threat." *The New York Times Magazine*, November 20, 1993.

Salkever, Stephen, and Michael Nylan. "Comparative Political Philosophy and Liberal Education: 'Looking for Friends in History.'" *Political Science and Politics* 26 (June 1994): 238–47.

————. "Teaching Comparative Political Philosophy: Rationale, Problems, Strategies or On Trying to Avoid the Anthropologist/Economist/Missionary Trilemma." Paper presented at the American Political Science Association Meeting, Washington D.C., August/September 1991.

Sandel, Michael. *Liberalism and the Limits of Justice*. Cambridge: Cambridge University Press, 1986.

Sardar, Ziauudin. *Islamic Futures: The Shape of Ideas to Come*. London: Mansell Publishers, 1985.

Sassen, Saskia. *Globalization and Its Discontents*. New York: The New Press, 1998.

al-Sayyid Marsot, Afaf Lufti. *Egypt's Liberal Experiment*. Berkeley: University of California Press, 1977.

————. *A Short History of Modern Egypt*. Cambridge: Cambridge University Press, 1985.

Schaar, John H. *Legitimacy in the Modern State*. New Brunswick: Transaction Books, 1981.

Schluchter, Wolfgang. *The Rise of Western Rationalism: Max Weber's Developmental History*. Berkeley: University of California Press, 1981.

Schutz, Alfred. "The Problem of Rationality in the Social World." In *Collected Papers*. Vol. 2, edited by Arvid Brodersen. The Hague: Mouton, 1964.

Segal, Robert. "Joachim Wach and the History of Religions." *Religious Studies Review* 20,3 (July 1994): 197.

Seligman, Edwin R. A. *Encyclopædia of the Social Sciences*. New York: Macmillan, 1931.

Sen, Amartya. "Rational Fools: A Critique of the Behavioral Foundations of Economic Theory." *Philosophy & Public Affairs* 6 (1977): 317–44.

Sharabi, Hisham. *Arab Intellectuals and the West: The Formative Years, 1875–1914*. Baltimore: Johns Hopkins University Press, 1970.

Sharabi, Hisham. In "The Scholarly Point of View: Politics, Perspective, Pardigm." In *Theory, Politics and the Arab World: Critical Responses*, edited by H. Sharabi. New York: Routledge, 1990.

Shepard, William. "'Fundamentalism' Christian and Islamic." *Religion* 17 (1987): 355–78.

———. "Gender Relations in the Thought of Sayyid Qutb." Paper presented at the Middle East Studies Association Meeting, Washington, D.C., 1995.

———. "Islam as a 'System' in the Later Writings of Sayyid Qutb." *Middle Eastern Studies* 25 (1989): 31–50.

———. "The Myth of Progress in the Writings of Sayyid Qutb." *Religion* 27 (1997): 255–66.

———. *Sayyid Qutb and Islamic Activism: A Translation and Critical Analysis of Social Justice in Islam*. New York: E. J. Brill, 1996.

Simon, Herbert. "Human Nature in Politics: The Dialogue of Psychology with Political Science." *The American Political Science Review* 79 (1984): 293–304.

Sivan, Emmanuel. "Ibn Taymiyya: Father of the Islamic Revolution." *Encounter* 60 (1983): 41–50.

———. Lecture in the Department of Near Eastern Studies. Princeton University, October 21, 1992.

———. "The Mythologies of Religious Radicalism: Judaism and Islam." *Terrorism and Political Violence* 3 (Autumn 1991): 71–82.

———. *Radical Islam: Medieval Theology and Modern Politics*. New Haven: Yale University Press, 1985.

———. "Sunni Radicalism in the Middle East and the Iranian Revolution." *The International Journal of Middle East Studies* 21 (1989): 1–29.

Smith, Adam. *An Inquiry into the Nature and Causes of the Wealth of Nations*. London: A. Strahan, Printers-Street, 1802.

Smith, Wilfred Cantwell. *Islam in Modern History*. Princeton: Princeton University Press, 1957.

Spiegal, Henry William. *The Growth of Economic Thought*. Durham: Duke University Press, 1983.

Spragens, Thomas A. *The Irony of Liberal Reason*. Chicago: University of Chicago Press, 1981.

Stowasser, Barbara. "Religious Ideology, Women and the Family." In *The Islamic Impulse*. Washington, D.C.: Center for Contemporary Arab Studies, 1987.

Strauss, Leo. *Natural Right and History*. Chicago: University of Chicago Press, 1953.

Taylor, Charles. "Atomism." In *Powers Possessions and Freedom*, edited by Alkis Kontos. Toronto: University of Toronto Press, 1979.

———. "Cross Purposes: The Liberal-Communitarian Debate." In *Liberalism and the Moral Life*, edited by Nancy L. Rosenblum. Cambridge: Harvard University Press, 1989.

———. *The Ethics of Authenticity*. Cambridge: Harvard University Press, 1992.

———. "Interpretation and the Sciences of Man." In *Philosophy and the Human Sciences*, Vol. 2. Cambridge: Cambridge University Press, 1985.

Tessler, Mark. "The Origins of Popular Support for Islamist Movements: A Political Economy Analysis." Center for International Studies, University of Wisconsin-Milwaukee, 1993.

Tibi, Bassam. *The Challenge of Fundamentalism: Political Islam and the New World Disorder.* Berkeley: University of California Press, 1998.

———. "Culture and Knowledge: The Politics of Islamization of Knowledge as a Postmodern Project? The Fundamentalist Claim to De-Westernization." *Theory, Culture and Society* 12 (February 1995): 1–24.

———. *Islam and the Cultural Accommodation of Social Change.* Transl. Clare Krojzl. Boulder: Westview Press, 1991.

———. "The Worldview of Sunni Arab Fundamentalists: Attitudes toward Modern Science and Technology." In *Fundamentalisms and Society,* edited by Martin E. Marty and R. Scott Appleby. Chicago: University of Chicago Press, 1993.

Tocqueville, Alexis de. *Democracy in America.* Translated by George Lawrence. New York: Anchor Books, 1969.

Villa, Dana. *Arendt and Heidegger: The Fate of the Political.* Princeton: Princeton University Press, 1996.

Voll, John O. "Fundamentalism in the Sunni Arab World: Egypt and the Sudan." In *Fundamentalisms Observed,* edited by Martin E. Marty and R. Scott Appleby. Chicago: University of Chicago Press, 1991.

———. *Islam: Continuity and Change in the Modern World.* Boulder: Westview Press, 1982.

———. "Renewal and Reform in Islamic History: *Tajdid* and *Islah.*" In *Voices of Resurgent Islam,* edited by John L. Esposito. New York: Oxford University Press, 1983.

Waterbury, John. "Democracy without Democrats?: The Potential for Political Liberalization in the Middle East." In *Democracy Without Democrats? The Renewal of Politics in the Muslim World,* edited by Ghassan Salame. London: I. B. Tauris, 1994.

Watt, W. Montgomery. *Islamic Fundamentalism and Modernity.* London: Routledge, 1988.

———. *Islamic Philosophy and Theology.* Edinburgh: Edinburgh University Press, 1962.

Weaver, Mary Anne. "Revolution by Stealth." *The New Yorker,* June 8, 1998.

———. "The Trail of the Sheikh." *The New Yorker,* April 12, 1993.

Weber, Max. *The Protestant Ethic and the Spirit of Capitalism.* Translated by Talcott Parsons. New York: Charles Scribner's Sons, 1958.

———. *The Sociology of Religion.* Translated by Ephraim Fischoff. Boston: Beacon Press, 1964.

Whitehead, Jaan W. "The Forgotten Limits: Reason and Regulation in Economic Theory." In *The Economic Approach to Politics,* edited by Kristen R. Monroe. New York: Harper Collins, 1991.

Wilcox, Clyde. *God's Warriors: The Christian Right in Twentieth-Century America.* Baltimore: Johns Hopkins University Press, 1992.

Wolin, Sheldon S. *Hobbes and the Epic Tradition of Political Theory.* Los Angeles: William Andrews Clark Memorial Library, University of California, Los Angeles, 1970.

———. "Political Theory: Trends and Goals." *The International Encyclopedia of the Social Sciences,* Vol. 12. Macmillan and The Free Press, 1968.

———. *Politics and Vision.* Boston: Little, Brown and Company, 1960.

Wolin, Sheldon S. "The Politics of the Study of Revolution." *Comparative Politics* 5 (April 1973): 343–58.

Wong, David. "Three Kinds of Incommensurability." In *Relativism: Interpretation and Confrontation*, edited by Michael Krausz. Notre Dame: University of Notre Dame Press, 1989.

Wood, Michael. "Lost Paradises." *The New York Review of Books*, March 3, 1994.

Wright, Georg Henrik von. *Explanation and Understanding*. Ithaca: Cornell University Press, 1971.

Zubaida, Sami. "Is There a Muslim Society? Ernest Gellner's Sociology of Islam." *Economy and Society* 24 (May 1995): 151–88.

———. *Islam, the People and the State: Essays on Political Ideas and Movements in the Middle East*. London: Routledge, 1989.

Zuckerman, Morton B. "Beware of Religious Stalinism." *U.S. News & World Report*, March 22, 1993.

Index

'Abduh, Muhammad: association with Afghani, 106–7; as Grand Mufti of Egypt,
113; influence of Sufi mysticism on, 118;
influences on thinking of, 109; role in Islamic modernism, 95–96
Adams, Charles C., 95, 114
Adorno, Theodor, 140, 150, 212n107
al-Afghani, Jamal al-Din: response to Renan's
article "Science and Islam," 102–3; role in
Islamic modernism, 95–96
Ahmed, Akbar, 171n28
Ajami, Fouad, 170n12, 179n42
Akhavi, Shahrough, 54, 81, 118
al-'Aqqad, 'Abbas, 67–68
al-Attas, Syed M. N., 186n12
al-Azmeh, Aziz, 9, 43, 51, 52
Algar, Hamid, 120
Allah's sovereignty (hakimiyya), 57–58,
190n47
Amin, Samir, 54, 175n69
Ansari, Hamied, 29, 30
antifoundationalism, 3
Appleby, R. Scott, 174n65
'aql. See reasoning ('aql)
Arendt, Hannah, 34–35, 40–41, 127–33, 148,
151, 152
Aristotle, 80
Arjomand, Said Amir, 120
authenticity, 48; Afghani's notion of, 206n99;
claims to Islamic, 48, 116–17, 165, 179;
moral ideal of, 136–38, 140; women and
cultural, 214n21
authority: Arendt's conception of political,
127–33; in Greek political thought, 128;
Khomeini's interpretation of, 119; Qutb's
interpretation of divine, 116, 131;
Taymiyya's legitimate, 188n38
Ayubi, Nazih, 29, 47–48
Azzi, Corry, 32

Badawi, M. A., 111
al-Banna, Hasan, 54–55
Barakat, Muhammad Tawfiq, 56
Becker, Gary S., 30–31
Bell, Daniel, 144–47, 149
Bellah, Robert, 142–49

Bendix, Reinhard, 21
"The Benefits of Philosophy" (Afghani), 105
Berlin, Isaiah, 62, 90
Bernstein, Richard, 11
Bigo, Didier, 4, 43
Binder, Leonard, 79, 212n3
body of believers (jama'a), 56, 77
Bourdieu, Pierre, 28
Bruce, Steve, 33
Bull, Malcolm, 163

call (da'wa), 73
capitalism: Bell on, 144–46; Qutb's vilification
of, 81
Carrel, Alexis, 52
chaos (fitna), 82
Chattergee, Partha, 10
Cheah, Pheng, 41
collective obligation (fard al-kifayah), 69
colonialism: Dirks's view, 9, 12; in Egypt, 54;
influence on Qutb's thought, 93; in Islamic
thought, 85; postcolonial world (Chattergee), 10; Qutb's experience, 8–9
community: decline of, 142–50; Islamic community as tree (Qutb), 77
community, Islamic (umma), 60–61, 63, 73,
83, 97
Condorcet, Antoine-Nicolas de, 34
consensus (ijma'), 114
consultation principle (shura), 79, 114,
199n173
"The Crisis in Education" (Arendt), 130
The Cultural Contradictions of Capitalism
(Bell), 144
culture: contemporary American, 211n91;
emotivist (MacIntyre), 133–37; filtered
through Western thought, 23; important
symbols of (Bell), 145; influence on Qutb's
thought of Western, 93; semiotic approach
to, 13
Cunningham, Karla, 171n19

Dallmayr, Fred, 37
Dar al-'Ulum, 107
da'wa. See call (da'wa)
de Bonald, M., 124